R2009

MAYA ANG~~~~~~~ ~~~~~, Missouri.
After the brea~~~~~~~~~~~~~~~~~~ ~nd her
beloved brothe~~~~~~~~~~~~~~~~~~ ndmother,
whose general store was the centre of life for the Black
co~~~~~~~~~~ Stamps, Arkansas. At eight Maya was raped by

Also by Maya Angelou

I Know Why the Caged Bird Sings
Gather Together In My Name
Singin' and Swingin' and Gettin' Merry Like Christmas
The Heart of a Woman
All God's Children Need Travelling Shoes
And Still I Rise
Just Give Me a Cool Drink of Water 'Fore I Diiie
Now Sheba Sings the Song

CONVERSATIONS
WITH
MAYA ANGELOU

Edited by Jeffrey M. Elliot

VIRAGO

Published by VIRAGO PRESS Limited 1989
20–23 Mandela Street, Camden Town, London NW1 0HQ

First published in USA by the University Press of Mississippi 1989

Copyright © 1989 by the University Press of Mississippi

*A CIP catalogue record for this book
is available from the British Library*

Printed and bound in Great Britain
by Cox & Wyman Ltd, Reading, Berkshire

Contents

Introduction

Authoress, poet, playwright, editor, songwriter, singer, teacher, dancer. In the words of one critic, Maya Angelou has touched more bases in her career than Hank Aaron. Yet, all these categories fail to reflect the scope of her life and the magnitude of her achievements. Self-described as "six foot, black, and female," Angelou is, in sundry ways, larger than life. Blessed with a mellifluous southern accent, a voice caressingly seductive yet strong, this artful conversationalist has come a long way from Stamps, Arkansas, where she was raised by her grandmother, and from the years she spent in silence, between the ages of eight and thirteen, traumatized by the murder of the man who raped her. Of pain and disappointment, Maya Angelou has known more than most, but she remains a well-spring of strength and integrity. More than a mere survivor, she has defeated the demons of her past and her personal insecurities to produce a body of work that is both intensely personal and embracingly universal.

According to her long-time editor, Robert Loomis, "Maya *is* her books." In the same interview, she herself observed, "I am a writer. Every writer is his or her books. Just as every singer is the song, while you're doing it. The dancer *is* the dance. . . ."[1] Angelou calls herself an autobiographer, but insists that what she really is about is being human. "I use the first person singular and I'm talking about the third person plural all the time; what it's like to be a human being. So the person who reads my work and suspects that he or she knows me, hasn't gotten the half of the book, because he or she should know himself or herself better after reading my work. That's my prayer."[2]

Because Maya Angelou writes what she knows, she writes of race and racism. Her work is not limited, however, to the black-white issue. Instead, it is expansive in its focus on such universal issues as romantic love lost, friendship, betrayal, and loyalty. Ultimately her work is about survival, the survival of Afro-Americans, but also the

[1] Sandi Russell, "Maya Angelou," *Women's Review* (December 1985), pp. 8-9.
[2] Ibid.

survival of the human race. In her words, "I am talking about *all* people—that's what I know, but I'm always talking about the human condition. So, if it's possible for me, Maya Angelou, me, myself to feel thirst then I know it's possible for you to feel thirst. And if my tongue dries up with thirst, then I know how your tongue must feel when there's no liquid. . . . I accept that we human beings are more alike than unalike and it is that *similarity* that I talk about all the time. Yes, not just surviving . . . but thriving with passion and compassion, and humor and style, and excitement and glory, and generosity and kindness."[3]

As a writer Angelou seeks not only to portray but to change the way people think about life. In that sense, her work is revolutionary. She writes to inform, to entertain, to express, and to elevate. She freely confesses her literary likes and dislikes and influences, standing with other writers on the shoulders of James Weldon Johnson, Paul Laurence Dunbar, William Shakespeare, and Edgar Allan Poe. She has high praise for James Baldwin, Toni Cade Bambara, and Toni Morrison, as well as Calvin Hernton, Paule Marshall, Ralph Ellison, John Killens, and Richard Wright. Angelou's style, her expression, and her tone, she admits, were, to a large extent, shaped by the lyricism of the black American preacher.

Angelou's success as a writer is, in no small measure, attributable to her discipline and drive. She usually awakes at 5:30 A.M. By 6:30 she is sitting down to work in the hotel room she keeps in whatever city she is living in. Six hours later, she packs up her book, her Bible, her yellow pads, her cigarettes, and her sherry, only to return the next morning. Even during her "periodic nervous breakdowns" she continues to function, but at half-speed. She explains: "I've trained myself to keep operating in the familiar. I keep functioning. I get up. I take baths. I pay my credit cards. I sustain myself on the love of friends." It is the "painful actions of my fellow human beings" that causes Angelou such suffering. "My mind is blown when I read about somebody beating a child. I read about a little girl in the Bay Area, a three-and-a-half-year-old child named Susan. And she'd been hideously burned and beaten. My God, how that tears me up!"[4]

Maya Angelou's success as an individual of force and character is

[3] Dawn Ellen Nubell, "Maya Angelou: Phenomenal Woman," *Coraddi* (1987), p. 4.
[4] Richard Ballad, "VIVA Interview: Maya Angelou," *VIVA* (September 1977), p. 88.

built on a steely strength that she, like many black women of her generation, has developed. That strength has enabled her "to stand up and talk back."[5] In the long tradition of her ancestors, she has spent a lifetime fighting against defeat and denigration, against the dying of the light that is life itself. While critics have called her a "tower of strength," she disagrees. Rather, life offers her circumstances where she is obliged "to stand up and be counted," so she does. Also, she notes, "Black women are party to, creators of, and victims of their press. So, we're told we're strong and sometimes we have to live up to that propaganda!"[6]

It seems natural that Angela has frequently been described as a "liberated woman," but she is reluctant to accept that accolade. "I'm not really. And I'll tell you why. It goes way back. After slavery, the black woman was the one who could get work. She didn't represent an economic threat to the white man—neither did the white woman, for that matter. But the black man was a potential threat, so he was blocked out. The black woman got the jobs. Most of the work was menial, but at least it was work. And the black woman began to believe her own publicity. She was the breadwinner. She *did* keep families together. She *did* clean and cook and raise her own children. She became bigger than life. And she was not immune to the whisperings of her own ego. The black man found his position impossible. No human being could take the humiliation that was inflicted upon jobless black men. When the black men couldn't feed their families, their self-respect was destroyed. So they left. . . . In most areas of endeavor the black woman has forged ahead of her man while the white woman has been held back. The weird fact is that within the black community, the self-reliant black woman was created by the white man more than a century ago. Think about that."[7] Still, Angelou expresses profound admiration for the work of the women's movement, and is quick to acknowledge the far-reaching contributions of such women as Gloria Steinem, Germaine Greer, and Betty Friedan, as well as those of such black pioneers as attorney Florence Kennedy.

As for herself, Maya Angelou is a dreamer—a woman who believes

---

[5]Sonya Pascall, "Africa Woman," *Africa* (November 1985), p. 75.
[6]Ibid., p. 75.
[7]*VIVA*, p. 88.

that to live life is to dream it first. The dream is the mother of fact.
Yet, one must not only dream, Angelou reminds her readers, but
must actively pursue love, and courage, and wisdom. It is in this
quest that literature has its role. It can both teach and inspire; it is
essential, she insists, that young people, especially young black men
and women, read Afro-American literature. "It is for your security. It
tells you, implicitly and explicitly: someone was here before you, and
survived it. . . . The minute you start to inject this literature,
something happens to the spirit. It lifts. . . . You pick yourself up, dust
yourself off, and prepare yourself to love somebody. I don't mean
sentimentality. I mean the condition of the human spirit so profound
that it encourages us to build bridges."[8]

Angelou has dreams, yes, but few illusions anymore. She recalls
her mother's words: "You may not get what you paid for, but you will
pay for what you get."[9] This realism, too, is part of what she has to
say, whether to students or fellow worshippers in church. As a
speaker, she combines the skills of entertainer, teacher, and preacher,
her voice rollercoasting from a roar to a rumble, then to a sudden
soft whisper. She exalts the mysterious power of creativity: "Creativity
or talent, like electricity, is something I don't understand," she
confesses, "but something I'm able to harness and use. While
electricity remains a mystery, I know I can plug into it and light up a
cathedral or a synagogue or an operating room and use it to help
save a life. Or I can use it to electrocute someone. Like electricity,
creativity makes no judgment. I can use it productively or destruc-
tively." The important thing is to use it, she affirms. "You can't use up
creativity," she stresses. "The more you use, the more you have.
Sadly, too often creativity is smothered rather than nurtured. There
has to be a climate in which new ways of thinking, perceiving,
questioning are encouraged. People also have to feel needed.
Frequently, we just offer a job and 'perks.' We don't always offer
people a purpose, a need for being there to use their skills and
creativity. When people feel there is a purpose and that they're
needed, there's not much else to do except let them do the work."[10]

Maya Angelou has been called "a giant among people," "a

---

[8]"Keeping the Message Alive," Whitney M. Young, Jr. Distinguished Lectureship, Wake-
Forest University, Winston-Salem, NC (1987).

[9]Mary Ardito, "It's the Thought that Counts," *Bell Telephone Magazine*, 1 (1982), p. 32.

[10]Ibid., p. 33.

protean woman" with "a spine of iron," but her own preference is simpler: "I'd just like to be thought of as someone who tried to be a blessing rather than a curse to the human race."[11] In the interviews that follow, this is the writer, the woman, the person revealed.

The interviews are arranged chronologically. As with other collections in the Literary Conversations series, the interviews are reprinted as originally published, except where reprint rights could only be secured if a minor cut was made (that instance is indicated in the headnote). In newspaper interviews, paragraph breaks have been omitted. In all texts, titles of plays have been regularized into italics. Where transcriptions of interviews have been provided, they have not been edited. A certain amount of repetition has necessarily resulted, for inevitably questions were repeated in several interviews, and the same stories told and retold. Even so, no two interviews are exactly alike; each one adds to the portrait of this remarkable and intriguing artist.

A project of this scope involves many people. I would like to acknowledge those whose inspirations, comments, and assistance throughout the production of this book enabled it to appear in its final form. It was Seetha Srinivasan, associate director of the University Press of Mississippi, who convinced me of the worthiness of compiling this volume and provided often-needed moral support. Assistant editor Ginger Tucker, responsible for the day-to-day management of the undertaking, offered unfailing good humor and tolerance. Also invaluable was the support and assistance of Sharon Snow, manuscript librarian of the Rare Books Department, Z. Smith Reynolds Library, Wake Forest University. Without the assistance of these three, the volume might never have seen completion. I am grateful as well to the various interviewers, editors, publishers, and agents who granted permission to reprint material.

This book is for my friend, Maya Angelou, with whom I have spent countless hours and whose support and encouragement allowed me

---

[11]Ibid., p. 33.

the opportunity to share her wit and wisdom with you, the reader.
For that I will always be grateful.

JME
October 1988

Chronology

1928	Maya Angelou (Marguerite Johnson) born in St. Louis on 4 April to Bailey and Vivian (Baxter) Johnson. Her brother, Bailey, gives her the name Maya.
1930	MA's divorced parents send her and her brother to Stamps, Arkansas, to live with their paternal grandmother, Anne Henderson.
1940	Graduating with honors from Lafayette County Training School, MA and Bailey move to San Francisco to rejoin their mother, who has recently remarried.
1944	At age 16, MA, who is unmarried, gives birth to a son, Guy Johnson.
1945	MA graduates from Mission High School, in San Francisco.
1952	MA marries Tosh Angelos, an ex-sailor of Greek origin.
1954-55	Appearing in *Porgy and Bess,* MA departs on a 22-nation tour sponsored by the U. S. Department of State.
1957	MA appears in the Off-Broadway play, *Calypso Heatwave,* and records "Miss Calypso," for Liberty Records.
1959-1960	At the urging of civil rights leader Bayard Rustin, MA is appointed Northern Coordinator for the Southern Christian Leadership Conference.
1960	MA appears in Jean Genet's *The Blacks,* an Off-Broadway production, and writes and performs in *Cabaret for Freedom,* with Godfrey Cambridge, Off-Broadway.
1961-62	MA serves as associate editor of the *Arab Observer,* an English-language news weekly in Cairo, Egypt.
1963-66	While living in Africa, MA serves as assistant administrator of the School of Music and Drama, at the University of Ghana, Institute of African Studies, in Legon-Accra, Ghana. She also works for the Ghanian

Broadcasting Corporation and as a free-lance writer for the *Ghanian Times.*

1964-66   MA appears in *Mother Courage* at the University of Ghana and in Jean Anouilh's, *Medea,* in Hollywood. During this period, she also serves as feature editor of the *African Review,* in Ghana, and as a lecturer at the University of California, Los Angeles. She writes a two-act drama, *The Least of These,* which is first produced in Los Angeles.

1966-67   Anxious to stretch her talents, MA pens a two-act drama, "The Clawing Within," and a two-act musical, "Adjoa Amissah," both as yet unproduced.

1968   MA narrates "Black! Blues! Black!," a ten-part television series on African traditions in American life, for National Educational Television.

1969   MA records "The Poetry of Maya Angelou," on GWP Records.

1970   Appointed Writer-in-Residence at the University of Kansas, and a Yale University fellow, MA publishes the first of her five-volume autobiographical series, *I Know Why the Caged Bird Sings.* The idea for writing her autobiography came during a dinner conversation with several friends, among them James Baldwin and Jules Feiffer. The book is nominated for a National Book Award.

1971   MA publishes *Just Give Me a Cool Drink of Water 'Fore I Diiie,* a volume of poetry, which includes many of the lyrics from her 1969 recording of "The Poetry of Maya Angelou," for GWP Records.

1972   Writing the screenplay, *Georgia, Georgia,* for Independent-Cinerama, MA becomes the first black woman to have an original script produced. She receives a Pulitzer Prize nomination for *Just Give Me a Cool Drink of Water 'Fore I Diiie.* MA also serves as a television narrator, interviewer, and host of several Afro-American specials and theatre series.

1973   Making her Broadway debut in *Look Away,* she receives a Tony nomination. She marries Paul Du Feu, whom she divorces several years later.

1974   MA writes the screenplay, *All Day Long,* and serves as Distinguished Visiting Professor at Wake Forest University, Wichita State University, and California State University, Sacramento. She also adapts Sophocles' *Ajax,* a two-act drama, which is first produced in Los Angeles at the Mark Taper Forum. MA writes her second autobiographical work, *Gather Together in My Name.*

1975   President Gerald R. Ford appoints MA to the American Revolution Bicentennial Council. *Oh Pray My Wings Are Gonna Fit Me Well,* a collection of poems, is published. MA is selected as a Rockefeller Foundation scholar in Italy, and is awarded honorary degrees from Smith College and Mills College. MA records "An Evening with Maya Angelou," for the Pacific Tape Library, and is appointed to the board of trustees of the American Film Institute.

1976   *Singin' and Swingin' and Gettin' Merry Like Christmas,* her third autobiographical volume, is published. MA also writes two Afro-American television specials, "The Legacy" and "The Inheritors." MA is named Woman of the Year in Communications by the *Ladies' Home Journal,* and is awarded an honorary doctorate from Lawrence University. She writes the play, *And Still I Rise,* which is performed at the Ensemble Theatre, in Oakland, California.

1977   Named by President Jimmy Carter to the National Commission on the Observance of International Women's Year, MA receives a Tony nomination for her best supporting actress role of Nyo Boto's grandmother in "Roots." For her documentary series, "Afro-American in The Arts," she receives the coveted Golden Eagle award from the Public Broadcasting System.

1978   MA publishes her third volume of poetry, *And Still I Rise.*

1981   *The Heart of a Woman,* the fourth work in her

autobiographical series, is published. She also records
"Women in Business" for the University of Wisconsin.

1982   MA receives a lifetime appointment as Reynolds Professor of American Studies at Wake Forest University, in
Winston-Salem, NC.

1983   MA publishes *Shaker, Why Don't You Sing,* a collection
of song-like poems.

1984-1985 MA is named by Governor James B. Hunt to the Board
of the North Carolina Arts Council.

1986   *All God's Children Need Traveling Shoes,* MA's fifth
autobiographical work, chronicles her four-year sojourn
in Ghana.

1987   MA publishes *Now Sheba Sings the Song* with Tom
Feelings, a distinguished artist and illustrator.

Conversations with Maya Angelou

Involvement in Black and White: Interviewing Author, Actress Results in Fascinating Afternoon

Susan Berman/1971

The Oregonian, 17 February 1971, sec. 2. Copyright © 1971 by
The Oregonian, Portland, Oregon. Reprinted by permission.

The interview was arranged with Jessica Mitford, an author who is
sometimes referred to as the "Queen of the Muckrakers."

Then Maya Angelou, dancer, actress, and author of *I Know Why
the Caged Bird Sings,* came to visit. The result: an afternoon with
two fascinating women.

Miss Mitford, a small slender person with short brown hair and
piercing blue eyes, is the wife of Robert Truehaft, a lawyer. They live
in a rambling brown house close to the city line of Berkeley, Calif.

The house is filled with furniture of the past and mementoes of
Miss Mitford's literary efforts. For instance, pages torn from a
mortuary magazine, remembrances of her best-selling expose on the
high cost of dying, *The American Way of Death,* hang in one
bathroom.

"I still get all those magazines and gloat over them," she said with
an impish grin.

The thing that strikes you first about Miss Mitford is her voice. She
started to talk about Maya. The words were soft, the accent English
and the sentences ended in a lilt.

"Maya Angelou rang up a few days ago when she got to town and
is staying here," she said. "She's much more interesting than I am."

The two women met more than a year ago when they both were in
London at the home of Sonia Orwell, widow of the late writer,
George Orwell.

"Maya kind of floated in one day with the manuscript for her
book," Miss Mitford said. "We started reading it at the breakfast table
and it was so fascinating that we kept reading it all night."

Maya Angelou, a tall graceful woman in African dress, laughed. "At
the same time, I started reading Jessica's *Trial of Dr. Spock* and
couldn't put it down," she said.

The two friends are now involved in the social issues of the day, as they always have been.

"I was organizing and raising money for the California Labor School when Maya was a teenager living in the area," Miss Mitford noted. "And later on, I went there for two years," added Miss Angelou.

Both women have other things in common. For one, colorful and eccentric families. Miss Mitford chronicled the adventures of hers in a book entitled, *Daughters and Rebels,* published in 1960. She lived in London until she was 19, when she eloped with Esmond Romilly, Winston Churchill's nephew. He was later killed in World War II.

"My family was almost as unique in their way as yours," insisted Miss Angelou.

"I was born in Stamps, Ark., a town almost that size. My grandmother owned her own grocery store and was a real Puritan. She raised us until we were about ten. She never bought anything she could make and my little brother and I looked like walking wallpaper—all our clothes were made out of the same material."

"When I was about ten, my grandmother brought us out to live with my mother's family in San Francisco. They were a real change— always popping their fingers, laughing and dancing and talking about pool halls.

"It was about then that I became conscious of my height. I was tall but my grandmother had always said, 'You can't reach that shelf Maya.' Now everyone asked help to reach or move anything—even a piano—I felt like a horse."

"After high school, I took odd jobs. I guess I left home about the age of 16. I had a day and night restaurant in Stockton, Calif. After I lost that I used to peel paint off cars with my hands. I had a son to support and I had to find work to support him.

"Finally, I started dancing. I danced for Elks and Eastern Star dances. In the black community, other women don't look down at you at all for dancing. In fact, they used to say, 'Boy, honey, you sure can dance, can you come to my club next week and entertain?'"

Miss Angelou had many small dancing and singing engagements before she got her first big dramatic break. It was a part in *The Blacks* by Jean Genet.

"After that, I lived in Cairo for a couple of years and was editor of the newspaper, *The Arab Observer,* she said. "Then I moved to Ghana and I consider that home. Whenever I'm away from Ghana, I feel that I am travelling. While the rest of the world has been developing technology, Ghana has been improving the quality of man's humanity to man."

Before she left the United States, she had been one of Martin Luther King's assistants and had done work with Malcolm X.

"I remember when I used to stand on soap boxes in New York with Malcolm and say that the worst thing about being sold into slavery was that the blacks had lost their African heritage. But in Africa, I saw many customs that were the same as here, so that wasn't wholly true."

Miss Mitford, concerned with civil rights also, helped to organize the Oakland Civil Rights Congress.

According to Miss Mitford, she is still doing her bit for people. She cites her attack on The Famous Writers School of Westport, Conn. She stated in an article in the *Atlantic Monthly* a few months back that the mail order school takes the customers for $850 plus and does little more than proceed to count it.

Not only do computers partially grade the essays and aptitude tests, she charged, but the Fifteen Famous writers who besiege you to sign up—Faith Baldwin, Phyllis McGinley, Clifton Fadiman and Random House's Bennett Cerf among them—never even see the students' work.

Did it scare her to step on such prominent people's toes?

"Oh, no," she said. "I was delighted. It all started when my husband had a case which involved a woman who had signed up for the course and wanted to get out of her contract. I decided to investigate."

So far, her probing has been worthwhile, she thinks. The Federal Trade Commission has decided to investigate the school, and Attorney General Richard Turner of Iowa has filed a suit asking that the school be enjoined from selling its courses in the state until he has a chance to look into it.

Recently Bennett Cerf said that after the hoopla dies down, he may retire from the school. Jessica's husband, Robert, said, "If he thinks it's going to die down, he doesn't know Jessica."

Next, Jessica wants to debate Cerf publicly on the issue.

"I get letters from people who say they haven't learned anything and don't want to pay their contract," she said. Her answer: "Don't. And tell them I told you not to."

Miss Mitford is now examining the prison system and has just finished another article for the *Atlantic* entitled "Kind and Usual Punishment" dealing with the civil rights of prisoners.

"I've tried to get into several prisons and am refused. They say it would embarrass the prisoners. No one ever asks the prisoners, of course," she said.

Maya Angelou's Lonely, Black Outlook

George Goodman, Jr./1972

The *New York Times*, 24 March 1972, 28. Copyright © 1972 by The New York Times Company. Reprinted by permission.

An autobiography in 1970. A volume of poems in 1971. And a quarter of the way into 1972, one controversial film script—*Georgia, Georgia*—and another in the works. This has been the course of 43-year-old Maya Angelou's writing career over the last three years. This success has whetted the appetite for more.

"I have the energy, and more importantly, I have lots of time," Miss Angelou said recently. "My looks don't fit the current fashion in terms of feminine beauty. I am a woman who is black and lonely."

Miss Angelou, who lives in Berkeley, Calif., was in New York on the way to Stockholm for work on her latest film, an adaptation of her autobiography, *I Know Why the Caged Bird Sings*, in which she will also make her debut as a director. As if that weren't enough to keep her occupied for a stay of less than two months, she is also taking along the final draft of a novel scheduled for delivery to Random House this spring.

There is, Miss Angelou said in an interview, a common thread running through all her work, a theme derived from the lessons of her life and the lives of the black women for whom she speaks.

"It is universal in application perhaps," she said, seductively soft-spoken with full lips that are quick to smile. "But when I see, it is through the eyes of black women."

For black women, Miss Angelou said, the sickness of racism is doubly hard, not only because they must bear up under conflicting internal impulses but also because they must shoulder such troubles without their men.

This is the dilemma that is explored in *Georgia, Georgia*.

One of the characters in the film, Mrs. Anderson, is a racial zealot, played by Minnie Gentry, who strangles Georgia, played by Diana Sands, a young singer who has just become a celebrity in Sweden.

Work in Progress: Maya Angelou

Sheila Weller/1973

Intellectual Digest, June 1973, 11-12, 14. Copyright © 1973 by
Ziff-Davis Publishing Company. Reprinted by permission.

Maya Angelou is an artist for whom the term "Renaissance
Woman" seems apt. At 43, she is a singer, songwriter,
dancer, actress, journalist, playwright, poet, fiction- and
screenwriter. When she begins work on the film version of
her autobiography, *I Know Why the Caged Bird Sings,* she
will also become America's first black female film director.

Maya considers herself primarily a writer. I visited her
one morning while she was in New York (her home is in
Berkeley, California) trying to clear time from two commit-
ments—a role in a Broadway play and the planning of a
lecture tour—in order to work on a new book, *Gather
Together in My Name.*

In a black sweater, floor-length print skirt and matching
kerchief, Maya opens the door to her sparsely furnished
suite in the Chelsea Hotel. She is a commandingly elegant
woman: six feet tall, graceful of movement, spare with
words. The influence of five years spent in Africa is apparent, but her roots are here—a childhood in the South,
adolescence in San Francisco and work as Martin Luther
King, Jr.'s Northern Coordinator for the Southern Christian Leadership Conference.

Maya brings out coffee and danish pastry. Then she
slumps sideways in an easy chair, dangles her bare feet
over its arm and speaks in a deep, deliberate voice at once
oratorical and melodic, punctuated, here and again, with
hearty laughter . . .

Q: Do you find it possible to work on several projects simultaneously?

Angelou: No, I've never been able to work that way. I have to put
all my equipment—all my stuff—into one thing at a time. I know
there are some writers who contend they are working on two or three

different projects at the same time. [She laughs.] I'm amazed.
Because when I'm working on a book, when I'm writing, I work
about 16 hours a day. I just lock myself up. I walk, bathe and work.

Q: You live each writing project, then.

Angelou: *It* lives me. It's as if I've been created by my characters
just to draw them. I'm not fit company for man o beast. [She
laughs.] For me to do any writing involves the blowing out of
everything else in the world. So first there's that cutting off that one
has to do. The closing of the blinds, the ripping out of the telephone,
the forgetting of one's own name. Severing relationships that weren't
very secure and securing those that are important.

I become very ruthless when I work. I have to warn my friends:
"I'm going to work now. Don't phone. Because I'll say something I'll
be sorry about in three months." So, to maintain relationships, I have
to do all that preparation.

Q: You lead a very solitary life when you're working, then.

Angelou: Yes. I have to. There are so many appurtenances to
everything—so many little stringers and streamers and side effects—
that one has to trim a lot of energy in keeping those things off,
backing them away from you. When I'm writing at home in Berkeley,
I keep the drapes in the living room drawn. I can't even have the
intrusion of sunlight. I take breaks to tend my garden, to go for walks,
to clean the house. While I'm at work, I don't let anybody in to help
me with the housework. I use that energy to keep my thoughts
together.

Q: And when you're writing here in New York?

Angelou: I just stay in my hotel room. There are about four or five
friends that I see, but that's all. I don't do anything. Once when I was
working here, a very dear friend of mine came and knocked on the
door. I wouldn't answer it. She kept knocking. Then I opened the
door, and she was standing there with a big casserole in her hands.
She just handed it to me and went away. I took it, and then I realized
that for the past four or five days I'd just been drinking Scotch and
eating cheese and bread—that's all there was in the fridge.

Q: Do you ever feel you're sacrificing something by living this
way?

Angelou: Oh, no, I would sacrifice something if I didn't live this
way, if I let people leech onto me. You know, the minute you believe

the publicity, the groupie cults, you may as well forget it. I appreciate the popularity of my work, but I don't believe it. I *dare* not. I say, "Thank you, that's very nice of you, but where's my next work? What am I supposed to be doing now?"

I get a lot of work done. And I work very hard. But I always feel that I've just started. The work to be, the work that's yet to come: that's the one loyalty I can count on. Loyalty—not mine to the work, but of the work to me. That is to say, it will remain there, to be done, no matter what happens. If the reviews of a play of mine are the best in the world, my work remains to be done. If a book of mine wins all the prizes in the world, the work remains to be done. I've just skimmed a little of the surface. Those yellow pages are still empty.

Q: This unending work to be done—does it flow from the need to communicate, into an indeterminate end product? Or do you start each project with a specific idea and then try to translate it?

Angelou: It starts with a definite subject, but it might end with something entirely different. When I start any project, the first thing I do is write down, in longhand, everything I know about the subject, every thought I've ever had on the subject. This may be 12 or 14 pages. Then I read it back through, for quite a few days, and find— given that subject—what its rhythm is. 'Cause everything in the universe has a rhythm. So if it's free form, it still has a rhythm. And once I hear the rhythm of the piece, then I try to find out what are the salient points that I must make in the piece. And then it begins to take shape.

I try to set myself up in each chapter by saying: "This is what I want to go from—say B to, say, G-sharp. Or from D to L." And then I find the hook. It's like knitting, where, after you knit a certain amount, there's one thread that begins to pull. You know, you can see it right along the cloth. Well, in writing, I think: "Now where is that one hook, that one little thread?" It may be a sentence. If I can catch that, then I'm home free. It's the one that tells me where I'm going. It may not even turn out to be in the final chapter. I may throw it out later or change it. But if I follow it through, it leads me right out.

Q: How is your writing affected by the mood you're in?

Angelou: Energy is like electricity to me, so when I work, I try to put myself in a mood that creates a friction. If I'm writing a short story that's really quite funny, I try to put myself almost in a mood of tragedy—certainly drama, melodrama—so that I have to *fight* against it. If I'm writing something that's heavy, then I try to get as light as possible. I call on the energy to get me to the opposite place.

Q: Having written two screenplays, how do you find that form as opposed to your narrative writing?

Angelou: Well, I haven't found any form of writing *easy,* ever. But in a screenplay, the dialogue doesn't have the crutch of narrative. So that makes it challenging. Because narrative, exposition, is what I'm all about. In a screenplay, all the exposition, all the explanation has to be there: in a line, in an exchange between two characters. It can't preach. It can't have asides. It has to stand by itself until the actors come along to bring their own understanding to it. It has to be poetry. What I'm trying to be is a poet. Not just with my work, but with my life. I think it's possible to lead a poetic life.

Q: Film direction is a craft that calls on a knowledge of the different arts you've engaged in—playwriting, screenwriting, poetry, fiction, music, acting and dance. Were you drawn to it as a sort of summation of your various energies?

Angelou: No. I was drawn to it as a way to translate my work accurately onto the screen. Last year, when I wrote *Georgia, Georgia,* I thought that I just liked to write. I wrote the screenplay and the music for the movie, and I thought that would be just fine. Then I went to Sweden for the production. The producers asked me to make myself available to the director, Stig Bjorkman. But he was male, white and European, so he was quite removed from my screenplay. No amount of my talking could relay certain things to him. I decided then that if I write any screenplays in the future, I'll also direct them.

So I went to Sweden this year and took an eight-month course in cinematography. I crammed it in in a little less than two months. Since I'll be directing, I want to know what the camera will do. I don't have to know how to handle a camera, but I have to be able to know how to ask a man who's been successful in keeping blacks out of his union to do something for me.

Q: What are your plans for the filming of *Caged Bird*?

Angelou: I'm trying for something, and I don't want to use any gimmicks. No slow motion or ultraviolet or anything like that. The story line is very delicate. I don't want to mar it. But it is a Hollywood film, so one is kind of poking the devil in the ribs, double-dog daring him.

Q: Who is doing the film?

Angelou: Cinerama will probably be the studio. I hope to get Cicely Tyson and Roscoe Lee Browne. And Bobby Hooks. Those are the actors I want for it.

Q: Do you have any interest in directing a screenplay that somebody else has written?

Angelou: Yes. Alex Haley has a new piece, a small piece, and I hope to direct it in the fall.

Q: Can you tell me something about the book you've been working on?

Angelou: It's called *Gather Together in My Name.* It's really a continuation of *Caged Bird.* But what I'm really trying to do is something new. *Caged Bird* is autobiography. This will be something else.

You see, I'm often asked: "How did you *escape* it all: the poverty, the rape at an early age, a broken home, growing up black in the South?" My natural response is to say: "How the hell do you know I *did* escape? You don't know what demons I wrestle with." But I *know* what people mean when they ask that loaded question. So, what I'm doing with *Gather Together* is writing the autobiography but carrying a fictional character along—the woman who *didn't* escape. So that each time I reached a crossroads, and because somebody loved me, I went [she hooks her two index fingers, then twists them] this way, and she goes that way. And then another crisis came along, and, because I was lucky, I went that way, but she goes the other way. So the book will deal with my life from the birth of my son—which is where *Caged Bird* leaves off. At that point, I made a choice. And she makes a different choice.

Q: What are these choices dependent upon? Strength? Luck?

Angelou: Luck, exactly. What I want to examine is: Who along this woman's path didn't discharge their human duties? Who saw her about to fall and trip into a pit of snakes and didn't even bother to stick his foot out to hold her back?

Sometimes, of course, it depends on the strength that one has accumulated. You know, the dares one has dared, the risks one has taken. In that case, a denigration might be an impetus to movement.

Of course, it's much more painful than if there were help along the way.

Q: Can you tell me a little about this fictional character, this alter ego?

Angelou: She's a character that's never been written. And I've been trying to get her for about ten years. I've got pieces of her in my short stories, my poems, my plays. In *Getting Up Stayed on My Mind,* a play a while back, she's a junkie who kicked and then went onto cheap red wine. But I haven't got her yet. When I talk about her, I begin to sound very strange, but she's demanding as a character. She wakes me up. She's just a vicious bitch. [She laughs in exasperation.] I want to grab her and say: "Tell the story! Tell the truth!" She's the worst of all to write.

Q: It seems to me that the basic theme of your work is the refusal of the human spirit to be hardened.

Angelou: You're the first person I haven't had to tell that to. I mean, really, that's what it is. You know, my book of poetry is called *Just Give Me a Cool Drink of Water 'Fore I Diiie.* And by that—the title—I mean: I believe we are still so innocent. The species is still so innocent that a person who is apt to be murdered believes that the murderer, just before he puts the final wrench on his throat, will have enough compassion to give him one sweet cup of water. If I didn't believe that, I wouldn't get up in the morning.

Q: So you're dealing with the persistence of innocence against overwhelming obstacles.

Angelou: Exactly. And an *unconscious* innocence, which is even lovelier than trying to remain innocent, trying to keep oneself pure.

What I'm interested in is *survival.* But not just bare, awful, plodding survival. Survival with some *style,* with faith.

Q: Is that fictional character of yours still surviving?

Angelou: Well, that's one of the difficulties in writing her. She's *barely* surviving. I was reading in the paper this morning the case of a young boy who died from a shot of methadone at Bellevue. And the two assistant principals at his school said not only was he bright and had a great future, but his sister—who could have become a great singer—had, at 18, committed herself to some hospital for drug addiction. It's an interesting story. You know, why didn't they survive?

Well, immediately I think of my character. My character is a composite of all these things.

I love stories about survival, I'm thrilled by them, enchanted. I have no compunction about using other people's achievements to spur me on, to fill me, inspire me. I take these stories as my own. I read everybody indiscriminately who talks about this . . . survival. Like the story of those South Americans who survived the plane crash in the Andes last winter. It thrills me! They immediately got into a helicopter and went back up in that awful weather. They survived, but they weren't crippled by it. They risked again.

Q: What role does this risk taking have for you as an artist?

Angelou: Well, let me say this: I believe that probably the most important single thing, beyond discipline, in any artistic work is to *dare*. To write, I have to feel as if I am in some uninhabitable place with some people, and everybody else has to come out but they're afraid. And I dare to go out and test the ledge. Then, after that, I can dare a little bit more. I can dare to just sort of get over and hang on. The person who dares to go out there and test that ledge, that shaky place: that's the artist.

Q: As a writer who depends largely on autobiography, the dare must be painful.

Angelou: Yes. It's a question of probing yourself so deeply and then admitting what you find. You reexamine all the trusts betrayed. Writing this sort of thing is painful, but . . . I *do* like myself. I like the fact that I take responsibility for being human—which is, to me, a grave responsibility. It means that I cannot deny any human act, however inhumane. If a human being runs mad and kills 18 babies, then I cannot deny that *I* have that possibility.

I like the fact that I don't indulge anybody's prejudices, not even my own. I like the person I'm becoming.

Q: You say "becoming." Do you see your work as processional, too?

Angelou: Yes. The last song I write is, to me, the best song I've written. The last play is the best play. The piece of work I'm about to start is always the most important. Maybe in 15 or 20 years—or maybe even sooner—I'll get to write a piece that I think is the most important. But in the meantime, everything is preparation for the next. I'm interested in the process, not the results.

Q: The central persona in most of your written work is the black American woman. You seem to take her—and rightly so—as the quintessential survivor. Is this correct?

Angelou: The black American female has nursed a nation of strangers—literally. And has remained compassionate. This, to me, is survival. She is strong. And she is inclusive, as opposed to exclusive. She has included all the rest of humanity in her life and has often been excluded from their lives. I'm very impressed with her. I mean, if I were a Swede, or a Laplander or a Chinese, I would read about the black American woman and think: "Jesus! [She bursts out into joyous laughter.] This is incredible! [A pause . . . and the voice softens into a tone of reflectiveness.] Incredible . . ."

A Conversation with Maya Angelou

Bill Moyers/1973

Broadcast by WNET/13 on 21 November 1973. Printed with the permission of Bill Moyers and WNET/13.

Bill Moyers: A few years ago at a dinner in New York I met Maya Angelou. We had grown up in the South, only a hundred miles apart as the Greyhound bus goes, but world beyond worlds in the inner experiences that shape the childhood. I lived in the gentle and neighborly white world that opened generously to ambition and luck. She moved in the tight and hounded other world of the South, whose boundaries black children crossed only in their imagination, if at all, and even then at intolerable risk.

Yet Maya Angelou broke free. And when finally we met, at another time and far beyond those once immutable boundaries, we hardly stopped talking for hours. Two strangers from the same but different place.

For three years I didn't see her again. But I heard of her accomplishments, read her books and continued to nourish the memory of that first encounter.

On a recent trip to San Francisco I sought her out at her cottage in Berkeley, across the bay, to share with you the spirit and insights of this gifted and very human woman.

I'm Bill Moyers. (music)

Singer, teacher, dancer, poet, authoress, actress, editor, songwriter, playwright. Someone has said Maya Angelou's career has touched more bases than Henry Aaron. Yet all these categories fail to do justice to the scope of her life.

She was raised in Stamps, Arkansas, by her grandmother, and came as a teenager to join her mother in San Francisco, where, by the way, she became the first black fare-collector on the Market Street Railway.

In the early 1950's she studied dancing with Pearl Primas in New York, and later appeared as a singer in San Francisco's Purple Onion.

18

She toured Europe and Africa with *Porgy and Bess,* taught modern dance in Rome and Tel Aviv, played the female lead off-Broadway in *The Blacks,* worked with Godfrey Cambridge on *Cabaret for Freedom,* and spent a year helping to raise funds for Martin Luther King in the North.

She lived in Africa for three years, editing an English-language magazine in Cairo—she speaks six languages—and teaching music and drama in Ghana.

She came back to America to write, among several works, the screenplay for the film, *Georgia, Georgia,* and two powerful books, a bestselling autobiography and a collection of poems, *Just Give Me A Cool Drink of Water 'Fore I Diiie.*

Blacks and women are both trying to get free of cliches and stereotypes. How does a person who is both black and female come to grips with a society that doesn't know who you are?

Maya Angelou: Well, one works at it, certainly. Being free is as difficult and as perpetual—or rather fighting for one's freedom, struggling towards being free, is like struggling to be a poet or a good Christian or a good Jew or a good Moslem or a good Zen Buddhist. You work all day long and achieve some kind of level of success by nightfall, go to sleep and wake up the next morning with the job still to be done. So you start all over again.

I don't know if the society doesn't know who I am. And I mean I a woman, I a black, I human. I don't know if I quite believe that. I think it knows and doesn't itself want to cope. And that is the society's problem, not mine.

Moyers: What do you mean it doesn't want to cope?

Angelou: It doesn't want to deal with the human quality of me.

Moyers: Stereotypes are easy . . .

Angelou: Exactly.

Moyers: Categories are more manageable?

Angelou: Oh, yes, exactly. All you have to do is just put a label on somebody. And then you don't have to deal with the physical fact. You don't have to wonder if they are waiting for the Easter bunny or love Christmas, or, you know, love their parents and hate small kids and are fearful of dogs. If you say, oh, that's a junkie, that's a nigger, that's a kike, that's a Jew, that's a honkie, that's a—you just—that's the end of it.

Moyers: Are black women still wearing these myths, these labels, these categories?

Angelou: Well, black women wear them only in white people's eyes, in the white society's eyes. You see, black women have been incredibly free to struggle for hundreds of years. And the story of the black woman is about the most noble story I know of mankind, in the history of man.

We came—we were brought here from societies which had matrilineal inheritance in West Africa, which—our matrilineal inheritance still obtains in West Africa. That is, children inherit from their mother's family, so that things stay in the mother's blood line.

But in Africa there is patrilineal control, so the father can decide whether he wants his children to go to school, who he wants them to marry, and things—really important things.

Moyers: Uh, huh.

Angelou: Well, slavery obviously ruled out any chance of patrilineal control. But there was the matrilineal dominance, which went underground. And after slavery the black woman, until 1940, was the one in the family who was able to make a living, because the black men couldn't get jobs. And like . . .

Moyers: Yeah, and that—didn't that give rise to this image of matriarchal ogres, which I think is your term?

Angelou: I know. I know. It's just—and it's not fair. It's not the total picture. But it would be very valuable, I think, if the people who would use the pejorative, use matriarch as pejorative, would do some homework and see where it came from and why. The black woman at some point begins to believe her own publicity, you see? She's asked to be strong, so she's strong. And she sees how strong she is; she becomes a little bit stronger. And she becomes a bit larger than life.

The white woman, on the other hand, is—has agreed to being a victim. And a woman named Beah Richards, a great poet and a great actress, wrote a poem, "The Black Woman Speaks to White Womanhood," in which she says that white women, who were brought here many times almost as much slaves as black women—you know, to marry . . .

Moyers: Hm, hm.

Angelou: She says, "If they did appraise my teeth, they checked

out your thigh and sold you to the highest bidder, the same as I."
And yet—she goes on in her poem to say, "Yet you have settled
down, and when you saw my children sold you gave no reproach,
but for an added broach settled down in your pink slavery and
thought that enduring my slavery or allowing it to happen would
make yours less." She says, "You never noticed that the bracelet you
took was really a chain, and the necklace you accepted throttled your
speech."

Now, there's a great difference in the white American woman and
the black American woman.

Moyers: Well, do you think that women's liberation is a white
woman's fantasy?

Angelou: I—no, certainly not a fantasy.

Moyers: Not a fantasy?

Angelou: A necessity.

Moyers: A necessity.

Angelou: They definitely need it.

Moyers: Does it say anything to black women?

Angelou: Very little, I am afraid. You see, white women have
been made to feel in this society that they are superfluous. A white
man can run his society.

Moyers: Now, Maya, not superfluous in bed . . .

Angelou: No.

Moyers: . . . not superfluous in the home, not superfluous in . . .

Angelou: No. Excuse me, Bill, I didn't mean that. I mean to run
his world. He can send his rockets to the moon and the little woman
can sit at home. He can keep that camera rolling. And I love—seeing
you bring in some women in the crew, it just made me love you
more, because I really did that.

But generally, he makes the—the white American man makes the
white American woman maybe not superfluous but just a little kind of
decoration. Not really important to the turning around of the wheels
of state.

Well, the black American woman has never been able to feel that
way. No black American man at any time in our history in the United
States has been able to feel that he didn't need that black woman
right against him, shoulder to shoulder—in that cotton field, on the
auction block, in the ghetto, wherever. That black woman is an

integral if not a most important part of the family unit. There is a kind of strength that is almost frightening in black women. It's as if a steel rod runs right through the head down to the feet. And I believe that we have to thank black women not only for keeping the black family alive but the white family.

Moyers: Why is that?

Angelou: Because black women have nursed a nation of strangers. For hundreds of years they literally nursed babies at their breasts who they knew when they grew up would rape their daughters and kill their sons.

Moyers: That's . . .

Angelou: That's a fact.

Moyers: That's strong.

Angelou: I know, but it's the truth, Bill. It's the truth.

Moyers: You have done almost anything you wanted to. You have traveled a lot. You have tasted many languages and many life-styles. You have written, you have acted, you have sung. You have scored in movies. You've really been a mobile, nomadic, free person. What price have you paid for that freedom?

Angelou: Well, at some point—you only are free when you realize you belong no place—you belong every place—no place at all. The price is high. The reward is great. I feel that—I really have felt most of my life that I wouldn't live long. And now I'm doing a pretty good job, you know. But . . .

Moyers: You've lived. Prophet—somebody said a prophet is a person whose predictions have been proven wrong long after they are forgotten. Maybe that self-prophecy will prove to be forgotten.

Angelou: I hope. Anyway but . . .

Moyers: Do you belong anywhere?

Angelou: I haven't yet.

Moyers: Do you belong to anyone?

Angelou: More and more. I mean, I belong to myself. I'm very proud of that. I am very concerned about how I look at Maya. I like Maya very much. I like the humor and the courage very much. And when I find myself acting in a way that isn't—that doesn't please me, then I have to deal with that.

But—the first time I ever felt I belonged anyplace was in West Africa, in Ghana, when I went to live in Ghana.

Moyers: Why Ghana, do you think?

Angelou: Well, the little towns in Ghana, Bill, you'd think you were in Texas, really. The little towns are just like our towns—yours in Texas and mine in Arkansas. Except that the people wear different clothes and have another language. But the same mores obtain. So I could have been in Stamps, Arkansas, for all intents and purposes.

Moyers: You've lived through the era of civil rights, you have lived through the violent confrontations of the last ten years. What do you see happening now in race relations, and what's going on right now behind the curtain?

Angelou: Well, let me talk about what's going on out in front of the curtain first. And I'm quoting Cecil Williams, Reverend Cecil Williams, at Glide, who—this past Sunday, at Glide Memorial Church, said that he was asked by a non-black, "What's happening with the black movement? Why don't I see you doing anything?" And his response was, "What's happening to the white movement?"

The most positive thing that is happening in this country is Watergate.

Moyers: Watergate?

Angelou: I believe so. Because white Americans—you see, there was a period when white Americans were marching in Selma and marching to Washington, for the blacks they thought, you see. But the struggle due to Watergate is for the whites. It's for their morality, for their integrity. It's the first time since the early part of the nineteenth century that a great mass of whites have really been concerned about their own morality. In the early part of the nineteenth century there were whites who became Abolitionists and supported the Underground Railroad, not because they loved blacks but because they loved truth. And not since that time—I mean all the World War II business, where we all got together and balled up string, and so forth, was for somebody else. It was for the Jews and Europe.

But suddenly—not so suddenly—in the United States the people are concerned about their own morality, their own continuation. And it's very, very—and that, I believe, will reflect in turn and in time on the black American struggle.

Moyers: How?

Angelou: Well, I think that white Americans will freely, once they clear up their own backyards, will be able to—that is to say their own internal selves about integrity and honesty, will have no out, no recourse, except to deal with the race question, which, as Dr. Du Bois said at the turn of the century, "The problem for the Twentieth Century will be the problem of the color line." And that will be dealt with not from a paternalistic point of view, I hope. This is what I expect. Not at the sufferance of their time, their energy, or when they have—at somebody's whim, but because it is right to do. And if the country is to continue, if it is to continue to grow to be what it hopes to be, then certainly people will move because it is right to do so.

Moyers: All right, so this is going on in front of the curtain?

Angelou: Yes.

Moyers: What's going on behind the curtain?

Angelou: Well, I think that we have come to a place—black Americans have come to a place where they are taking a long, deep breath. And one sees that in history, that it does happen like that. Every so many years there is a surge forward. Herbert Aptheker wrote a great book called, *Black American Slave Revolts,* in which he starts from the seventeenth century, the slave revolts, protest movements, and actual riots, and that sort of thing. And one sees that there is a kind of rhythm to a movement. And I think that we are at a pause now while people take deep breaths and try to decide.

Moyers: You had a son, who is now 27, I guess.

Angelou: A fantastic son.

Moyers: If you had a daughter, 10 or 12 years of age, what would you say to her about growing up in this society?

Angelou: Oh, well, first, if I had a daughter—I'm at the point of adopting a child now, since I have no child in the home, and I love them—I respect all of them, white and black. My child I hope would be black because I have so much I can teach her and pull out of her.

I would say you might encounter many defeats but you must never be defeated, ever. In fact it might even be necessary to confront defeat. It might be necessary, to get over it, all the way through it, and go on. I would teach her to laugh a lot. Laugh a lot at the—at the silliest things and be very, very serious. I'd teach her to love life, I can bet you that.

Moyers: When you were growing up in Stamps, Arkansas—that's your home . . .

Angelou: Yes. Where were you growing up at the same time?

Moyers: Just 98 miles away.

Angelou: That's right.

Moyers: Same pine trees.

Angelou: Right.

Moyers: What did whites look like to an eight-year-old black?

Angelou: (Laughs) I didn't see them. I mean I didn't think that they were people. I thought whites were like ghosts, that if you put your hand on one your finger would go all the way through. (Laughs) I didn't . . .

Moyers: You know what?

Angelou: What?

Moyers: That's what we felt like. (Laughter from Angelou)

Angelou: I thought, you know, the real people were black people and the others were white folks. And they weren't—you didn't have—they didn't have kidneys and hearts, and things like that. They didn't cry. We knew that, you know, because black people—I used to see black people weep. So I knew they didn't cry, because people cried, and white folks just stayed white and floated around, like that. (Laughs)

Moyers: Did you dream?

Angelou: Yes.

Moyers: What?

Angelou: Well, at eight I dreamed once that—for a number of years, once I'd found—I'd go to the movies and I saw people like Shirley Temple and Judy somebody . . .

Moyers: Garland.

Angelou: Judy . . .

Moyers: Oh, Judy—

Angelou: And . . .

Moyers: "Wizard of Oz."

Angelou: Not Judy Garland. But anyway, those young girls who were in the movies at the time. One is now a plumber on television. You know, she does the plumbing kind of thing.

Moyers: Upward—downward mobility.

Angelou: (Laughs) Anyway, I saw them and I thought, you know, they live such rich lives. Maybe that will happen. If—maybe I'm really a white girl. And what's going to happen is I am going to wake up. I'm going to have long blond hair and everybody is going to just go around loving me and sending me off to school. And I would wait at the ranch-gate for Johnny Mack Brown and—with a little bonnet on. It's tragic.

Moyers: When did you realize it was only a dream?

Angelou: Oh, I—when I realized that I realized how lucky I was it was only a dream. (Laughter) By the time I was 14 and I lived with my mother—and she is so full of joy and life. And I was her baby. So then that became better than being anything else in the world.

Moyers: That world wasn't at all open to you. How did you manage to stay open to the world, open to hope?

Angelou: Well, I think you get to a place where you realize you have nothing to lose. Nothing at all. Then you have no reason to bind yourself. I had no reason to hold on. I found it stupid to hold on, to close myself up and hold within me nothing, to protect nothing. So I decided to try everything, to keep myself wide open to human beings, all human beings—seeing them as I understand them to be, not as they wish they were, but as I understand them to be. Very truthfully—not idealistically, but realistically. And seeing that if this person knew better he would do better. That doesn't mean that I don't protect myself from his actions, you know.

Moyers: Hm, hm.

Angelou: And dislike him for his actions. But certainly to accept that that's a human being; that too is human.

I think that when we lose the prejudices, the fearful, frightening prejudices, that say a person like a multiple rapist, a murderer, that's inhuman—when we lose that and accept that that's human, that's human.

Hopefully I'll never do it. But obviously if a human being did it, I have the potential, as human.

And then, conversely, one can say, oh, there is a great masterpiece written; it's a marvelous composition written by a human being. A human being, only, wrote that. Being I am a human being, I have that potential.

Moyers: What are you working on now, speaking of Maya Angelou as human being.

Angelou: Well, I have a new book out now. I mean "out," it will come out in the spring, called *Gather Together In My Name*. It's a continuation of *Caged Bird*. It takes the next four years.

But I've just got a new assignment yesterday to do an adaptation of Sophocles's *Ajax*, for the Los Angeles Mark Taper Forum. So I go to work on that now.

Moyers: Surely not in rhyme.

Angelou: Yes, partly in rhyme. I've decided I'm going to keep the chorus in rhyme so that there will be a downbeat (Laughs), so that people can be able to say, "Well, that's us."

Moyers: Well, as I say, if Sophocles were alive today he'd be turning in his grave. (Laughter from Angelou)

Angelou: He never had it so good. He'd be so grateful.

Moyers: Do you think that white critics have a right to judge black artists?

Angelou: Well, certainly I think they have a right. It would help if they understood what they were talking about. Quite often there are allusions made in black American writing, there are rhythms set in the writing and counter-rhythms which mean a great deal to blacks. A white American can come in and he will hear, he will understand, hopefully, the gist. And that's what one is talking about. The other is sort of "in" talk. I think that it's dangerous if we start setting up white critics as the end-all, be-all of a piece of work by a black writer, a black musician, because—there is a poem in a book of mine, called "Harlem Hopscotch." Now, hopscotch, anywhere it's done, is da-da-da, da-da-da, da-da-da.

But in Harlem, there's—that's basic. But there are other counter-rhythms that are going on, so that the kids stamp, "Dadadatadatadatam." See? So the poem says—I wrote—says, "One foot down, then hop is hot. Good things for the ones that's got. Another jump now to the left, everybody for hisself. In the air, now both feet down. Since you're black don't stick around. Food is gone, rent is due. Your cousin's drunk, and then you got two. Everybody's out of work. You call for three and then twist and jerk. Count the line they count you out. But that's what hoppin's all about. Both feet down, the game is down. They think you lost and I think you've won."

Moyers: (Laughs)

Angelou: Now, when a non-black critic approaches the word, he's going to see the social implications in the rhymes, which are there, hopefully, because the kids who are jumping hopscotch in Harlem are thinking different thoughts than those who are jumping hopscotch on Park Avenue or in the Pacific Heights, or whatever.

But he will not hear. So it cracks up a black American audience when they hear it, because it's Ta-ta-ta-ta-ta, tum-da-teh. So he loses a great deal of . . .

Moyers: Well, here we may get to the last immutable boundary, that might prove to be, it seems to me, the final frustration of people like—like us. How do you cross that boundary and get inside the skin?

Angelou: You don't have to. You don't have to. Really, being free is being able to accept people for what they are, and not try to understand all they are or be what they are. But if you're Italian and you have a certain family kind of feeling and understanding and love and love to sing and love to be, and all that, why can't I, if I were a Jew, simply accept that and you respect what mine is and we respect Mr. Chan over here and Mr. Mourisaky over there and Mrs. Brown down the street and Mr. Jones up the street, and say all of them are good? Not change them. Not at all, Bill. I think one of the most dangerous statements made in the United States, or descriptive phrases, is that it's a melting-pot. And look at the goo it's produced.

Moyers: Well, there isn't anywhere to go from there. So I thank you for spending this time with Public Television. And I wish your new segment of your autobiography great success.

Angelou: Thank you.

Moyers: And I hope Sophocles comes alive again.

Angelou: I do, too.

Thank you, Bill.

Moyers: I have been talking to Maya Angelou, who no longer needs any introduction.

I'm Bill Moyers. Good night.

Maya Angelou: An Interview

Stephanie Caruana/1974

Playgirl, October 1974, 53-55. Copyright © 1974 by *Playgirl.*
Reprinted by permission.

Born: Marguerite Johnson, 1928, St. Louis, Missouri.

Family history: Parents divorced. Raised in a shanty town, in Stamps,
Arkansas, by grandmother. At age sixteen, bore a son, Guy
Johnson. Recently married to writer Paul Du Feu.

Education: High school graduate.

Previous employment: Conductorette, San Francisco Cable Cars
(Market Street line); cook at the Creole Cafe; waitress; whorehouse
madame; prostitute; B-girl; dancer in a strip joint; calypso singer;
actress; songwriter; screenwriter; journalist; editor.

Current employment: Novelist; poet; playwright; director; Distinguished Visiting Professor in English, literature, and philosophy.

Unlikely! But the tall, brown, beautiful woman who welcomes me
to her home has played all those roles. The dancer's flash, actress's
calm, journalist's keenness, poet's vulnerability, and scholar's depth—
yes, Maya Angelou contains multitudes.

Yet in a world of suspicion, requirements, rigidities, and automatic
no-no's of all kinds, what was written on the magic passport that led
to this wild mélange of (it would seem) mutually exclusive experiences?

Her two autobiographical novels, *I Know Why the Caged Bird
Sings* and *Gather Together in My Name,* contain fascinating glimpses
of a life few would have chosen—just a life, dumped haphazardly on
one particular black girl. At the end of *Gather Together* Maya realizes
she has been tricked by a lover into becoming a prostitute; she
gathers herself and her son together and goes home to mother in San
Francisco. Okay. But how does she get from *there* to *here*?

With that question in mind, I climb into my car and careen out of
Berkeley and across the hills and valleys to Sonoma, in the heart of
California's wine country. Blundering down a maze of country roads

in the middle of an intermittent thunderstorm, I find the large, low, rambling house at the end of a well-manicured suburban street.

Maya stands in the doorway, tall and calm, saying, "Welcome," in a soft, rich voice. Inside, the rooms are large, cool, and filled with a welter of half-unpacked cartons. Maya and Paul have just returned from several months of teaching, touring, lecturing, and the premiere production of her adaptation of Sophocles' *Ajax*, at the Mark Taper Forum in Los Angeles. They are moving into a new home, and they show me the Japanese garden where golden carp huddle in a small, bridged pond under the watchful eyes of a squadron of birds; the huge swimming pool, and, past the fence, some sun-filled acres of golden grass. Hills rise toward the horizon, limned in smoky shadows of blue, purple, and gold.

"Let's sit in the sun by the pool and have a beer—like the Big People do."

Paul, relaxed and attractive in sweater and slacks, hops about with one broken leg in a plaster cast. His recently published book, *Let's Hear It for the Long-Legged Women,* talked about his brief, eccentric, but entertaining marriage to Germaine Greer, and touched lightly on his involvement with Maya. Paul is, in a way, the English equivalent of Burt Reynolds. His nude form decorated the centerfold of *Cosmopolitan*'s English edition the same month that Reynolds's picture appeared in America. (The photographer sprayed him with a light coating of gold paint, and airbrushed his navel; his genitals were coyly hidden behind an upraised knee.) He selects a book from a carton and drifts off to the living room.

We settle down in deck chairs by the pool with glasses of California wine, and I ask how it all happened.

She looks startled. "Wow! All in one go? It would be hard to say— even in a twenty-hour interview. I hope to do five autobiographical books; *Gather Together in My Name* is the second in the series. About the time it ends, I went to work in a record shop and began to learn about music. And I made my first white friend—the woman who owned the store. She introduced me to another way of life. With her help, I began to give up my ignorance and become aware. I'll never know what she saw in that twenty-year-old, six foot tall, closed, withdrawn black girl. But somehow she was perceptive enough to know she had something to give me. I began taking more dance lessons, and eventually I got a dance scholarship that took me to New

York City. Then I got a job at the Shakedown, a strip joint in the North Beach area of San Francisco. My costume consisted of two sequins and a feather.

"There were three other dancers, all white, and all strippers. But I didn't strip, because I didn't have anything on to begin with. They paid me $75 a week plus what I could make on B-drinks. When men asked me to have a drink with them, I would explain that the drinks I got were only 7-Up—so the best thing would be to buy a bottle of champagne instead. I made a lot of money because I was honest about it.

"I danced fifteen minutes of every hour, six times a night. The other ladies would go out and strip, and the band would play, "Tea for Two," or something like that, because the women weren't into what they were doing, and the band was bored with all that grind, grind, grind. But I was a *dancer,* and I loved it. Each time I danced, they *played* for me—all sorts of wonderful things, like "Caravan." And we had a fabulous time. San Francisco started hearing about this dancer in this B-joint, and gradually the nontourists, and the nonlecherous old men, started coming to see me. Then I met the people from the Purple Onion across the street.

"One night Mort Sahl was playing there, with guitarist Stan Wilson. They finished their very elegant gigs and came to pick me up. We were all sitting around at someone's house, when the singer who was starring at the Purple Onion began saying how much she hated singing calypso music. I said there was some great calypso music, and I sang one song. She said, "Oh, now I understand! You are supposed to take my place in the show, because I'm going to New York." So I took some singing lessons from a wonderful coach, and a few weeks later, I opened at the Purple Onion—as the star.

"People would line up outside for blocks, waiting to get in. In the middle of a song, I'd forget the lyrics, so I would start to dance. And they loved it. Then I joined the cast of *Porgy and Bess,* and we toured Europe for a year under the auspices of the State Department.

"It was the only time I had to leave my son Guy behind. They said I could bring him; they would have paid $125 a week extra for him to appear on stage in the crowd scenes. But I knew it wouldn't be good for him. Most of the male principals in the company were flamboyant homosexuals. When they bowed, after the performance, the audience threw roses at them. And I wondered how that would affect an eight-year-old boy. I had to do it, but I wouldn't let my son do it. I love him very much, but I have never been *in* love with him. A mother raising a son alone usually falls *in* love with him, and this screws up the young boys so badly they can't get unscrewed. But that year was difficult for both of us.

"When I came back, we went to live on a houseboat in Sausalito. It was a commune, back in the fifties before anyone knew about communes. It just wasn't done—but it was wild and we loved it.

"I was still singing, but I never had a feeling about singing professionally. Dance is different; it's like a narcotic to me. Everything dances. I haven't danced professionally in twelve years, yet when I look outside at the mountains and the trees, I think of choreography—how this would look on a stage, in dance."

"But you are a poet," I said.

She smiled, and explained, each carefully chosen word hovering softly in the air, "To me, poetry and dance are much the same. I have always written poetry, ever since I was about eight years old. It was bad, I admit, but I kept on writing. When I was nine, I fell in love with Shakespeare, and I learned a lot from him—about poetry, and theater, and about songs. I started writing songs when I was about fifteen. In the late fifties, I wrote the songs for a movie called *Calypso Heat Wave,* starring Johnny Desmond. Then I stopped singing professionally.

"I started working with Martin Luther King and eventually became the Northern Coordinator of the Southern Christian Leadership Conference. I wrote the music for Genet's play, *The Blacks,* and starred in it for a few months in New York at the St. Marks Playhouse. Then I met an African man, a diplomat, and married him, and we went off to Egypt. I lived there for two years, working as a journalist.

"How did I like Egypt? Well—they have trouble about women. When I hear Western women talking about the Muslim trip, to me it's a joke. Sexism is so much a part of their lives and their religion. Western women have no concept of the lack of stature of women in Muslim society. A woman is less important than the water buffalo. Its milk and flesh are eaten, and its muscles turn the wheels to irrigate the farms. No woman can compete with that! Women are abused there. So when I hear women say they subscribe to Muslim thought, I think, Damn! If you really saw it! But there I was, non-Arab, non-Muslim, and a six-foot-tall American female intellectual.

"But what could I lose? I always know that. The only thing I can be sure of is that I will die. I can't even be sure how this day will end. So I'm free to try anything. I took the post as associate editor of the only English newspaper in the Middle East, and I learned.

"Then my marriage broke up, and Guy and I went to Ghana. He attended the University of Ghana, and I taught there. I loved Ghana. It was the first time I ever felt at home in my life. When I was three years old, I was sent from California to Arkansas with an identification tag around my neck. And you know how provincial towns are; you can't *get* in, you have to be *born* in them.

"Until I was thirteen, when I left Arkansas, I was known as Mrs. Henderson's California granddaughter. When I went back to California, I was called the Southern girl. And when I went to New York to study dance, I was the tall girl from California. Wherever I went, I belonged somewhere else. But in Ghana, I was called the child who has returned home. I wore African clothes, and I learned to speak a few African languages, including Fanti. Because of my accent, people thought I was from the Gambia. When I said I was American, they would say, 'No, no, tell the truth. What are you, where are you from? You must be Bambara.' Then when I proved I was American, they said, 'Aah, a child who has returned home.'

"I came back to the States, expecting to work with Malcolm X. I got back on a Friday and Malcolm was killed on Sunday. I had talked to him on the phone the day before. On Sunday a friend phoned me and said, 'Maya, why did you come back to this country? These people are crazy.' And I said, 'Yes, I know.' She said, 'Otherwise, why would they have killed that man?' I hung up the phone, because I knew it was Malcolm, and I couldn't speak.

"After that, I decided to have nothing to do with politics, directly. I wrote a play, then wrote and produced a television series in San Francisco. Then I went to Algiers, and to Senegal. I haven't dared go back to Ghana because my experience there was so precious that I don't want to risk spoiling it. I got so much health and stability from that country, and the people, the way it was with Kwame Nkrumah. He was deposed and subsequently killed, and I haven't wanted to go back.

"Then I wrote *I Know Why the Caged Bird Sings* and went to the University of Kansas as Poet in Residence. After *Caged Bird* became a best-seller, Columbia Pictures invited me to come to Hollywood and write the script for Alex Haley's book, *The Autobiography of Malcolm X.* They had already tried three different writers, including James Baldwin, who is a friend of mine, a hero, and a brother. I asked him what he thought, and he said, 'If you can do it, fine.' But Columbia's attitude could be summed up by one executive who said, 'I don't know if anybody really wants a story about a colored man right now. But I wouldn't mind if you can make it into something like *Guess Who's Coming to Dinner.*' So there was nothing to talk about, really. I wanted it to be a great movie. It was finally done, almost as a documentary, and James Earl Jones played Malcolm X.

"Next, I wrote the script for a film called *Georgia, Georgia,* which starred Diana Sands. So I became the first black woman to write a Hollywood film; I wrote the score, too. We made the film in Sweden. Later I went back to Sweden and took a course in cinematography, because I am going to direct films and I want to understand the machinery—to know what the camera can do."

"Fantastic life," I sighed.

She smiled. "So far, it's a nice prologue to a piece of work that I am about to start. This summer I intend to learn to fly—there is a small airfield nearby. And I have signed on at Sacramento State College as Visiting Distinguished Professor. I will be giving classes in English, literature and philosophy. And I have just been asked to share with Shana Alexander and Studs Terkel the production of the *National Bill Moyers Journal,* for television; I will do six shows. Next year, I hope to begin directing the movie versions of my first two books. I'd like to have either Nina Simone or Roberta Flack do the music.

"Then we want to clear some of the land here and plant vegetables. Last year when we lived in Berkeley, we fed not only ourselves, but our family and most of our friends. We had all sorts of things—corn, cabbage, lettuce, onions, collard greens, potatoes. When I went out shopping today for lunch, I saw how expensive everything is. It's bad enough to feed yourself, but imagine having to feed a growing family—and kids with those great appetites. How do you explain high prices to somebody young who is hungry? We will grow great gobs of vegetables to share with our neighbors and friends, and have plenty for ourselves. It's necessary; it isn't, 'Let's join the fad and get back to the land.' It's 'Let's eat!' "

I asked about her marriage to Paul.

"We've been married for a year and a half, in the eyes of God. And we are gloriously happy. We respect each other—and we find each other most amusing. We have good, wonderful, healthy arguments. Any time he disagrees with me, it has nothing to do with his thinking that my mental machinery would not be up to handling his opposition. He is kind, but he doesn't molly-coddle me. He'll say, 'Why do you take that position?' And I say, 'Why do you?' It's stimulating. I learn something. That's what it's all about.

"Life is ruthless. Nature has no mercy at all. Nature says, 'I'm going to snow. If you have on a bikini and no snowshoes, that's tough. I am going to snow anyway.' The whole thing is about learning a lesson or a series of lessons. There is a saying, 'He who does not learn from his history, is doomed to repeat it.' Some women leave a man and they say, 'Well, I got rid of that jerk, and I've got another one. Wait 'til you meet George.' So you meet George, and in fifteen minutes you say, 'But honey, you just left him. May be a different face and a different race, but that's your old man.'

"It seems to me Nature says, 'Okay, I'm going to give you this situation. Will you learn?' And you cry. And Nature says, 'Okay, here you are, right again . . . same thing!' And you have to deal with that, and learn the lesson. *And forgive yourself.* Then you can move on. And every time you see him, no matter what clothing or what face he's wearing, or what language he is speaking, you say, 'Hi. Yes, I know you well. And I don't have to do that. No way. Thank you very much.' So you can move on to the next lesson."

"Reading your books," I said, "one of the things that struck me was that you were faced with a lot of weird situations—where you didn't have the slightest idea what the hell to do. And there were all these people, doing these things to you."

"Those *smart* people," she says with a laugh.

"Thinking back, you probably say, 'God, how could I have been so dumb?' And yet, that's where it's at."

She nods, "Yes, that's right . . . go through it all, and go to everyone clean. *Clean as a bean,* as my mother would say. And trust a lot. And let the machine work. And you'll come out. You'll get all the way through it, and come out the other side. Then you say, 'I did that. Now, what you got next?' "

"Well," I say, representing some inscrutable and nonsensical Fate, "we call this course *Life 201.*"

"Ready! Okay. Yep! And the scars that you can't help but acquire can be truly marks of beauty, like dimples or a cleft chin. You decide: That hurt. I will not deny that hurt. But I will not carry the hurt into another circumstance where I may not be hurt. But it makes your voice a little softer. When you've just been raped, abused, or assaulted in some way in the street and you walk into a room, you have no idea what has happened to the other people in that room. So if you say, 'Oooh, this happened to me,' somebody may say coolly, 'Oh, really?' You have no idea what those people have to give you. Their stories might make you understand. 'Honey, you was fishing in very shallow water. There were sharks out where I was.'

"Living life fully, fiercely, devotedly, makes you much more able to accept other people who are doing the same. All we're trying to do is to get from birth to death. And you can't fail. Even if you only live five minutes, you have succeeded. And everybody's out there, trying to do the same thing. Some don't know it, and they think they have to step on your neck to survive. It's unfortunate for them. If I ever see someone trying to do that, I try to encourage the person who is standing underneath to move away, so that ill-informed person can gain some understanding. And I certainly move away. I am not helping anybody if I allow them to use or abuse me.

"But it seems to me that life loves the *liver.* I see it in my mother. She loves life. When I was thirteen or fourteen, I remember her saying, 'Baby, if I die today or tomorrow, the world don't owe me shit!' And she's just out there, *doing it.* That's the joy.

"This morning, there was a letter in the mail from a woman who is Mexican-American and married to a Jewish man. She said, 'You don't know me, but I want to welcome you to the Valley of the Moon. There is a lot of excitement here because you have moved in. There was some difficulty when I moved in, but I rode it through.' Many of our new neighbors have dropped by to welcome us. I have a friend in Stockton, who told us that when he moved into his neighborhood, he felt he had to sit up every night for about a month with his rifle pointing out the door. That was only a few years ago. So I didn't know what would happen. Now the people are coming over, saying, 'You are welcome here.' They are making too much of a fuss for it not to be anything. But it will teach them something. They will learn something about grace, if they know me . . . about generosity, and courage, and ease. And I will learn something, too. We will have a lovely time."

I asked if she had any hard feelings about life.

"No, I don't. There are many things I wish were better for a number of people—for all of us really. We could have such a great time, sharing, laughing, growing, teaching, learning, dying. Coretta King said the greatest violence is seeing a child go to bed hungry. These are the great violences: assaults on the body and soul. Hunger, poverty, fear, dirt, and guilt—and I will not have it. That is what my life is about: highlighting these things and, hopefully, encouraging others to help make things better. But bitterness about life, no. Life is like electricity; it's just *there*. You can plug into that electricity and light up a synagogue, or a church, or keep a heart machine going; or you can electrocute a man. Life is the same way. It says, 'Okay, I'm going to be in your unit for a bit. Want to use me? Want to walk around drugged or sick? All right. It's your business. No value judgments! I'm here for you to use.' Life! When it's through with me, I hope to be through with it. I'll tip my hat, and split."

"It usually works out that way," I said amiably.

"But in that way, I disagree with Dylan Thomas and what he said in his poem, "Do not go gentle into that good night. . . ." When life is through with me, I want to say to it as you would say to a lover, or a friend, or a child: 'Goodbye! It's been a ball . . . truly. And thank you.' "

Listening to Maya Angelou

Walter Blum/1975

California Living, 14 December 1975, 12-23. Copyright © 1975 by *The San Francisco Examiner.* Reprinted with permission.

It has been said of Maya Angelou that "she makes a sorry song sing." Certainly there are few writers in America today who have managed so successfully to distill the essence of a life into a whole—into beauty and meaning, into books and poems—who has touched the hearts of so many readers with an understanding of what it is like to have been poor, female and black.

Maya Angelou has indeed lived enough for a dozen ordinary lifetimes. She speaks seven languages. She has been a dancer, a singer, a TV interviewer. She was the first black woman to run a Muni streetcar, the first to write the screenplay for a motion picture, the first to direct one. She has acted on Broadway, adapted Sophocles' *Ajax* for the modern stage, lived in Ghana where she wrote columns for a local newspaper, cut two records, produced and written a ten-part television series, been married three times and awarded several honorary degrees. Her books (*I Know Why the Caged Bird Sings* is the most celebrated) and poetry collections (the latest is entitled *Oh Pray My Wings Are Gonna Fit Me Well*) are required reading at many universities.

In person, Maya Angelou is six feet of magnificent womanhood. She wears her hair cut short. Her voice is deep and magnetic and ranges in mood from a stentorian roar to just this side of a whisper.

What follows is an extract from one full day spent with Maya and her English born writer husband, Paul Du Feu. The Du Feus live in a rambling ranch house on two acres in Sonoma's Valley of the Moon. It is a home suffused with comfort. A warm fire crackles in the fireplace. From the walls hang African masks and statues, and lovely prints and drawings of black women and children. In the combination kitchen-family room, a majestic long counter gives Maya the freedom to indulge her passion for good cooking.

What follows is Maya speaking. The oral Angelou—less polished, less organized perhaps than the skilled writer—but more relaxed, and with special rhythms and beauty that often elude the printed page.

At sixteen I desperately wanted to go to college. But at sixteen I had a child. I wasn't married, and I had to take care of my baby. My mother and stepfather said I could stay with them, and I had a scholarship, but my mother had left me when I was three and I saw her only once between the ages of three and thirteen, so I figured, if she felt that way about me—and I was her own—I'd better not leave my child with her. So I left home. I took my son and we left home, and I had no understanding about anything—I mean, utterly, so stupid that my face burns to think of it now. But I had the determination to raise my child.

How then did you acquire an education?
I read a lot, and watch people a lot, and although it's sad that all comparisons are odious, I would compare one person with another and I'd think, I'd rather be like him. I'd like to be at ease and graceful and gracious. I'd like to be like that. My contention is that we are all teachers and students, and people taught me who never even knew my name, and never even realized they had the responsibility of teaching someone.

Is it true that you would like to become a modern American female Proust?
It's my dream. There are very few American writers who use the autobiographical form for their literary output almost exclusively. I hope to look through my life at life. I want to use what has happened to me—what is happening to me—to see what human beings are like, to tell anecdotes so true, to look behind the fact of the anecdote and see what motivated this person in this action, and that person, so that people who have never known blacks—or Americans, for that matter—can read a work of mine and say, you know, that's the truth.

What was your reaction to Africa?
I really believe I felt at home for the first time in my life. See, I've been in transit all my life, it seems. When I was three I was sent to Arkansas with a tag on my wrist with my brother, from Long Beach.

We stayed there until we were seven, went to St. Louis, went back to Arkansas, went from Arkansas to California at thirteen. At sixteen I was on the road with a new baby, and no training, and I did everything except shoot drugs in my arm. Everywhere I went people would say, "Oh, there's that tall girl from California." But when I came to California they said, "There's that Southern girl." So I never felt I belonged anywhere until I went to Ghana. Then parts of me relaxed that I didn't even know I had. My soul relaxed. Of course, I could never write that line. Too purple. But that's how I felt.

Do you feel people should return to their origins?

Yes, but I suggest there is a vast qualitative difference between your returning and mine. Your people left willingly looking for something better. Mine did not. Whatever they found, whether it was better or worse, they were pulled from the land—and sold, and bartered, and all that. And then came the 300-year experience, which was totally negative, which fixes my mind and psyche with a different approach, a different outlook when I returned to Africa than when someone from Italy, say, returns to Italy. When I go back, there's a kind of pathos that really borders on the purple. I think: Now, where was my great-great-grandfather? What happened? Did they burn the whole village to get him?

How do you work?

In a very weird way, I think. I've never been able to work at home because I try to keep home very pretty, and I can't work in a pretty surrounding. It throws me. It distracts me. So I keep a room in a hotel in downtown Sonoma, and in the morning when Paul goes off to work, I go off to work at 7:15. I go to my hotel, to this tiny room and sit there on the floor, nothing in the room but a bed, which has never been made as far as I know because I've never slept in it. I work till about two, twelve sometimes if it's going badly; then I'll go downstairs and have a couple of bolts of sherry. I can't write anything with a typewriter. I can type, all right, but it doesn't mean anything to me. It loses. When it's happening I'll work straight through, but you know, those times they don't come but once a year and they last about two weeks. But when it happens, oh, it's gorgeous! It's like the flu. You can't stand to hear anybody talking. But it's such a beautiful time.

What do you do though, when it doesn't come?

Then I sit there, and I use my understanding of the craft and I write well. Sometimes I write great. I deal with the syntactical structures and I just get the work done. Of course, I may have to go back over it. The worst part is to read a reviewer's critique of my work where he says, She's such a natural writer. A natural writer! And here I've been working maybe two weeks on a single paragraph—a paragraph that nobody's going to notice at all.

Is it a different process, writing poetry?

Yes. With poetry, I try to enchant myself. When I'm working on a piece, I try to find the natural rhythm of the piece. For instance, I have a poem about hop scotch called "Harlem Hop Scotch." You know, all kids when they jump hop scotch, they have a dum-dum-dum, dum-dum-dum. But Harlem's rhythms are a bit different. They're polyrhythms. So it's dum-dum dickey-dickey, dum-dum-de-dum. And they're thinking other thoughts than the kids jumping it on Park Avenue or Pacific Heights. So if the muse is being stingy, I work on the rhythm of the piece. If I'm writing about an autumn day, I work on the rhythm. There's a flow to it. Then I try to make the content fit.

You do a great deal of lecturing at colleges. What's the most frequent question you're asked?

What's your sign? I don't even know. You know, it's so inconsequential. Here I will have spent an hour and a half speaking without notes on the complexities of heroes and heroics and how we as a species and Americans in particular have dealt with heroes and I will have quoted everybody from the nineteenth century to Servan-Schreiber, and then I throw the floor open to questions and some brute will say, "What's your sign, Miss Angelou? Oh? Oh, that's neat. That's really neat." Can you imagine? Such a distraction from the issues!

But what of the serious questions?

Well, the question asked most frequently is: How did I make it over? They've read that I was raped at seven-and-a-half, that I went through traumatic experiences, that I was an unmarried mother. Now they want to know, how did I make it over? Of course, that's a question with almost one million answers. Or no answer. I'm not sure which.

Do you feel bitter about your experiences?

No. I get angry, which keeps me from being bitter. There's an absolute difference. Bitterness is like cancer, it just stays with you and eats and eats and it comes out like lashes, like putrescent explosions. So I become angry. I think, how can I speak against the circumstance? But I know one thing: People who create problems for other people have problems themselves. I know that, you see, so I don't have to get angry or bitter against that person. So what I do is become angry with his action, and try to stop it.

How do you feel about America? There are some who claim it has become a land of greed.

It doesn't have to be. It has been rapidly turning into that. One sees what happened with the Indians first, and the black Americans second, and every other visible group. But I don't believe that's all there is, or else Paul and I would never live here. I can sell my books. I can live like James Baldwin in the south of France, or in West Africa. But I believe there's something else. There is a spirit. And it's almost like Martin Buber, a good-evil conflict. There is that lust for life, for immortality. And I don't know how that seed was planted in the American breast, but it is more virulent here than I've found it in any other country. In Asian and African cultures, people are sure they will be continued through their children, through their tradition, through their culture, through their gods. But in America everybody wants to live it all! There is a kind of lust that's wonderful to me, that's exciting as hell. Now I agree that ambition is probably the mother of all vices, and if you're ambitious enough you'll kill your mother for it, but it's still exciting. It's the American ethos, which if one could phrase it in a few words, would be: Yes I can. And all Americans believe in it. Yes, I can get a twenty-foot Cadillac. Yes, I can go to the White House. Yes, I can raise some children. Yes, I can enslave people. Yes, I can free them. Yes, I can fight for my freedom. Yes, I can be a great woman. Yes, I can. It's an amazing thing. You can see it in the way Americans walk down the street in Europe. You don't have to hear their accents, but you can say, that's an American. It's part of the mythology of the Western movement. Americans walk differently.

But along with this marvelous ethos, Yes, I can, there's also an

American need to be loved. Not respected, mind you, but loved. And that's a lot of baloney. Just respect, that's all you need. I think this accounts for the need to have a melting pot, because you can only accept the love of those you understand. And people want blacks to be just like whites, Mexican-Americans to be just like whites, Asian people to be just like whites. But people have different modus vivendi, and if we didn't insist on this same kind of cut-out look on everybody, we could really accept one another in a wonderful healthy way by saying, "Listen, so that's your thing. You're Mexican, are you? Tell me about it. That's fine." And there wouldn't be this need to essay a kind of similarity that may not exist.

Oh, of course, there is a similarity in our condition. But what makes me laugh may leave somebody else totally cold. Or the kinds of foods that please me might be just the most unattractive to another person. Or music that makes me jump might be the very kind of music that another might say, "Jesus, turn off that racket." But that's no reason to dislike. It is that other decision, that I must *love* you— not simply respect your differences from me. Well, you have as much right to yours as I have to mine, and mine is glorious, and yours is glorious to you, and then you can respect other human beings living on the same block or working on the same job—but not that need which causes the put-down, the snobbish put-down among people that what they can't understand they cannot respect. I want to *understand* you. Baloney! Baloney! I mean, how are you going to understand unless you're born to it? How? This is what caused the backlash with so many people who were so generous in the sixties— we're going to walk to Selma, we're going to walk to Washington, we're going to really understand. And then when black Americans turned around and didn't say, "Thank you so much," these people said, "What do they want from us? We tried to understand them." Why? Why not just say, you're a good human being or a bad human being? And in your thrust for being a total citizen in this country, I support you. I am not Polish. I am not Mexican-American. I do not understand all of that. I will never. I was born in this body and in this skin and in this gender.

What about the militants?
I think there is always a need in any struggle for sensationalists.

They get the headlines, they get the ear of the public, they take the race horse chances. Ofttimes they are the martyrs, but often they're not even right. You hear them speaking in your behalf and you say, "Yuch. You're not qualified. You know the rhetoric, but you're unprepared." But I don't put them down—except to their faces. If we meet somewhere quietly, say in this room, I'm ruthless. I'll say, "How dare you not take four hours to read up on W.E.B. Du Bois? What makes you talk such bullshit?" But that's privately. If I'm asked publicly, I'll say, "God bless them in their struggle."

What's your opinion of the women's movement?

The sadness of the women's movement is that they don't allow the necessity of love. See, I don't personally trust any revolution where love is not allowed. For a while in the black movement, there was a decision, especially among young black men, that the struggle, dig, was so serious that you can't waste time on the frivolities of romance. But I think that's counterproductive. I think it's part and parcel of the weaponry of our very opponents. Black women would say that women had to walk three steps behind the men to really show the brothers they supported them. Baloney! Black women were sold or bought at the same time. They slept spoon fashion in the same filthy hatches of slave ships with the men. They were put on the auction block together, they were sold together, they got up before sunrise and they slept after sunset together out on those tacky fields, and they took the lash together.

The way I see it, since we are obliged to live in a dual-gender society, then both genders are of equal importance. I suggest that's why the black American is as healthy as he/she is today. Because we've had to struggle together, both sexes out there, nobody having it easier than anyone else, so our children jump shouting from the dying loins. They walk like little kings, sashay like little queens. Why? Because male and female have struggled side by side. And I think it's dangerous—it might even be fatal—to say that the man must do it all.

What's your favorite of all your poems?

The one called *"Song for the Old Ones."* It is so important. Because again we're back to the revolutionaries and love. A number of young blacks decided that Uncle Toms are to be laughed at and ridiculed, and I feel just the opposite. We often don't realize how those people who were scratching when they didn't itch, laughing when they weren't tickled, and saying, "Yassuh, you sho' is right, I sho' is stupid," we don't know how many times their throats closed on them in pain. They did that so they could make a little money, so they could pay for somebody to go to school, to get some shoes. So that poem is for them. A lot of my work is for them, because I know they were successful, because if they hadn't been successful I wouldn't be here to talk about it.

What's the title of your next book?
I've just decided on a title. I'm going to call it, *The Singing of a Reed Stricken by the Wind.*

How do you feel about being a celebrity?
There's something seductive about a bit of celebrity, a bit of power, a bit of fame. If you don't mind yourself, you begin to believe your publicity that says you're the greatest so-and-so, whatever it is. But I know it's dangerous and I don't believe any of it. I say, "Oh, that's very interesting, very good dear, thanks a lot, by-by. I have my work to do. You can bug off." Because if you believe it—first of all, you move from the position that helped you create the work, looking in, looking out, searching, trying new things—and you begin to imitate yourself so you can continue to be popular. And that's baloney. The search stops. You can no longer be qualified as an artist.

And then greed comes in. That position of power. The power of having the searchlight move across the room and center on you. The best thing to do is stay in the back of the room. Keep working and let the searchlight pass right over you because you're behind the post. But of course, I know that I live in a society where the media dictate what's read, what's seen, what's worn. And I don't want to write any dust-catching masterpieces. I want my work read. So I've given my publishers—both hardback and paperback—a month for promotion every time I write a book. I will go about the country and tell about my work. But after that, I'm finished with it.

Are you troubled by critics who pan your work?
No. I do the best I can with everything. I have no apologies. That doesn't mean I don't do things that displease me. I do. I have automatic responses I'm not proud of, but I hope I'll work on those

and make myself a better person. But in every instance I bring all my stuff into it—whether it's cooking or dealing with Selma Berkowitz (her secretary) or my husband or new people I've never met before or at the corner shopping center—I bring all my stuff, all my equipment. Now, if you walk away from me and not like me, I give you all I've got. That's your business, not mine. I hope next year, if we do this again, I hope to be brighter, I hope to be funnier, I hope the food to be better, the house to be prettier, the fire to be warmer. I hope I will have learned by next year to be even more total. But right now I cannot be better than I am. I'm holding nothing back.

I just do the best I can. And I intend to live straight up, straight up to the last second, and be making news instead of reading it.

Maya Angelou: No Longer a Caged Bird

Beth Ann Krier/1976

Los Angeles Times, 24 September 1976, sec. IV, 1, 8-9. Copyright © 1976 by the *Los Angeles Times*. Reprinted by permission.

There is a quandary some people experience with Maya Angelou, the poet, autobiographer, dancer, singer, director, actress, playwright, film-maker, teacher, editor, and as she puts it, "small black girl from Arkansas."

As one reader complained, "Writers are always falling in love with her and you can't tell if she's really all that fabulous or not." A man who's observed her on talk shows confessed he was even more suspicious. "She's done so much—with so much passion, so much joy, so much despair—it all seems a little unreal."

To pick up the third, recently published installment of her autobiography, *Singin' and Swingin' and Gettin' Merry Like Christmas* (Random House: $8.95) is to compound such dilemmas. Sailing with her through the memories of her young adulthood, one finds Maya Angelou managing a house of prostitution, searching for a "husband-caliber" man while attempting to support her son born out of wedlock, marrying and divorcing an atheist Greek sailor, dancing clothed in a strip joint, touring Europe as the featured dancer in *Porgy and Bess,* finally returning to San Francisco and finding a son so sick she contemplates suicide to atone for her neglect. All of which happened in a relatively short period of time in the 1950s and is recalled with such astounding, bittersweet detail it borders on the surreal.

What a relief that to meet Maya Angelou is to believe. And to learn that this enormously complex woman lives ruthlessly by simple precepts. She works hard. She laughs a lot. And she trusts in the Lord.

No wonder writers are forever falling in love with her. She speaks as well as she writes, but with the added dimension of the ability to syncopate the rhythms, inviting listeners to partake in her dance of words.

She's a nonstop observer, noticing the way, for instance, the men at a table nearby have all turned to face the power of one man in particular, a film mogul she recognized who later stopped by her table.

And she's laughing and loving every minute of being here, interviewing those around her as she is interviewed. She is at once the total communicator and total entertainer.

To kick off a national lecture and book promotion tour, Miss Angelou arrived in Los Angeles this week with her fourth "and last" husband, builder/author Paul Du Feu, a charming Briton with a reputation for distinguished wives, Germaine Greer among them.

They were looking forward to the six-week tour as an adventure on which they plan to drive as much as possible. And over dinner at the Beverly Hills Hotel, they seemed to relish excursions as much as they enjoy their home in Sonoma, a big place, apparently, with a vegetable garden and a swimming pool that is shared with guests all summer.

They were still talking of another excursion, a five-week stay at the Rockefeller Foundation's Bellagio Study Center in Italy about a year ago during which a large part of the new book was written.

"They accept 15 international scholars a year and their spouses. You have to pay your own way to Bellagio but, once there, they have a staff of 48 to look after 30 people," Miss Angelou recalled, adding that yes, she thought the surroundings did have a positive effect on her writing, which seems more lyrical and less angered than in her first and best known book, *I Know Why the Caged Bird Sings*.

"It kept my tongue in my cheek most of the time. There were footmen by the score—literally. Scholars wrote notes to other scholars. And "Decca" (Jessica) Mitford—we are friends and sisters— was accepted first and she told me, 'Apply, Maya.' We keep doing this right around the country, really. At Smith, she got a degree and she said, 'Well, there is a writer, Maya Angelou, and really, I mean really, if you're going to . . . ' "

A few weeks ago, Ringling Brothers & Barnum and Bailey called to see if the 48-year-old Miss Angelou would consider riding an elephant in the animal walk on opening night. And though she was in rehearsal with a new play, *And Still I Rise,* which she was directing at the Oakland Ensemble Theater, she replied, "Of course I will do it. I haven't been asked anything so wonderful in my life. But the only thing I must ask is that I have a lady friend who is very famous and if she will ride, I will certainly ride." Then she called Decca to say she'd evened up the score again and they made their circus debuts.

It is from her friendship with Jessica Mitford—"we have a sisterness about us"—that Miss Angelou suspects another project may develop. For after her friend read her new book and told her she thought it was better than *Caged Bird,* (which was nominated for the National Book Award in 1970) and what it had done for her in illuminating the nature of black-white relationships, the two agreed to an ongoing correspondence on that subject.

"Decca has written me a letter that said, 'You know, what you've done for me, touching on the nuances of black-white relationships, friendship, love and so forth, I understand something I've never understood before. I'm beginning to understand that I can understand.' And she has two black grandchildren and asked if I would consider writing to her about all this. She'll write back and we'll examine this phenomenon, possibly with an eye to doing a book."

In the meantime, *And Still I Rise* is scheduled to open in New York early next year, with Miss Angelou directing. She's still negotiating the film version of *Caged Bird,* refusing to let a young white man interpret on the screen the memories of her youth. Two films she directed for NET will be shown on television in November. She's just finished her work on the President's Bicentennial Commission. There will always be more of the autobiography to do—originally the publishers thought of it as a five-volume series, but now, she said, it looks like it may run seven or eight, "It depends on how long I live and whether it's interesting. If it's not, I'll stop."

If she accomplishes half of what she still expects to do, this woman will have top material forever. She wants to learn to fly. For herself. And she is going to do some interesting things in film.

"I need very much to be taken seriously in film. I need to have someone who trusts me trusting myself to risk the money. Now these (film) people lose millions. I know I will have to do a number of Z (as opposed to B) pictures. I don't mind. This is again black American. The constant reminder people give you is that you have to crawl before you walk. OK. I know what the odds are. So now I'm a member of the Director's Guild of America. I will do anything that is not an insult. I hope, I expect, to be very successful. I expect it. I already accept it.

"Now it may take me a little longer than it would Joe Doe whose father has already earmarked a few million for him to try his teeth on. But that's all right. I don't mind. And I refuse utterly to use any of my energy in being bitter. Ever. I'll be angry, yes, but never that other thing. That other thing is corrosive. It just kills you, gets you sick, makes you look old and ugly. You can't enjoy anything."

She is likewise not sacrificing anything to fear. Oddly, though, for one who has dared to try so much and tried seriously enough to walk away with considerable success, she claimed not to possess much confidence in the usual sense.

"I have very little confidence about what I can do. Oh, certain things I know *now* I can do. But I do know this. All I know I have to do is die. Now that's the biggest bugaboo of them all. And yet, I will do that. So what else is there? What else is new? It's not that I have confidence but I believe that if I fail, so what? So what'cha gonna do—stop liking me? I mean, really, if you're going to stop liking me because I tried to direct a film and I fell on my face or tried to love somebody and had a divorce, I mean, I tried. Like this play, I wasn't sure I had it. It might have been laughed out (it played every night in Oakland to standing-room-only crowds). I don't know that I put all my stuff in it and if it turned into a bunch of cliches or it didn't work, it just wouldn't work, that's all. I would have learned that it didn't work."

"But Paul is going to love me. My son is going to love me. My friends are going to love and care for me. And I'm going to try again. I'm a firm believer that there is no place that God is not."

To round out her point, she started singing an old Mahalia Jackson gospel song, "Lord Don't Move Your Mountain," urging a careful consideration of the lyrics:

> *"Lord don't move your mountain,*
> *Give me strength to climb it.*
> *You don't have to move that stumbling block.*
> *But lead me, Lord, around it.*
> *If my friends start to hurt me,*

> *As I know they may do.*
> *Let me fall down on my knees.*
> *And bring me closer to you."*

Then Maya Angelou offered only one caution: "Now, not everything you do is going to be a masterpiece. But it's only in certain societies where everything you do has to be perfect. But you get out there and you really try and sometimes you really do, you write that masterpiece, you sing that classic. The other times you're just stretching your soul, you're stretching your instrument, your mind. That's good."

The Black Scholar Interviews Maya Angelou

Robert Chrisman/1977

From *The Black Scholar,* January/February 1977, 44-52. Copyright © 1977 by *The Black Scholar.* Reprinted by permission.

Maya Angelou, author of the best-selling *I Know Why the Caged Bird Sings* and *Gather Together in My Name* has also written two collections of poetry, *Just Give Me a Cool Drink of Water 'Fore I Diiie* and *Oh Pray My Wings are Gonna Fit Me Well.* In theater, she produced, directed and starred in *Cabaret for Freedom* in collaboration with Godfrey Cambridge at New York's Village Gate, starred in Genet's *The Blacks* at the St. Mark's Playhouse and adapted Sophocles' *Ajax,* which premiered at the Mark Taper Forum in Los Angeles in 1974. In film and television, Maya Angelou wrote the original screenplay and musical score for the film *Georgia, Georgia,* wrote and produced a ten-part TV series on African traditions in American life and participated as a guest interviewer for the Public Broadcasting System program *Assignment America.* In the sixties, at the request of the late Dr. Martin Luther King, Jr., she became the Northern Coordinator for the Southern Christian Leadership Conference, and in 1975 Maya Angelou received the *Ladies' Home Journal* "Woman of the Year Award" in Communications. She has received honorary degrees from Smith, Mills and Lawrence University. This interview was conducted by Robert Chrisman, publisher of *Black Scholar.*

Black Scholar: Maya, this Fall you have produced your latest book, *Singin' and Swingin' and Gettin' Merry Like Christmas,* which is the third installment of your autobiography and the fifth of your published books.

Maya Angelou: Yes.

Black Scholar: Can you comment a bit on the importance of endurance in black writers?

Maya Angelou: Endurance is one thing. I think endurance with output, endurance with productivity is the issue. If one has the fortune, good or bad, to stay alive one endures, but to continue to write the books and get them out—that's the productivity and I think that is important to link with the endurance.

I find myself taking issue with the term minor poet, minor writer of the 18th century, minor writer of the 19th century; but I do understand what people mean by that. Generally they mean that the writer, the poet who only wrote one book of poetry or one novel, or two, is considered a minor poet or minor writer because of his or her output, its scarcity. I can't argue with that. I do believe that it is important to get the work done, seen, read, published, and *given* to an audience. One has enjoyed oneself, one has done what one has been put here to do, to write. Another thing is that one has given a legacy of some quantity to generations to come. Whether they like it or not, whether the writer values the next generation, or values the work or not, at least there is something, there is a body of work to examine and to respond to, to react to.

I know a number of people who do work very slowly but I don't believe, although I have close friends who write slowly, in taking five years to write one book. Now I think they have psyched themselves into believing they cannot work more quickly, that hence because they work slowly their work is of more value. They also believe—they have bought that American baloney, the masterpiece theory—everything you write must be a masterpiece, each painting you paint must be a masterpiece.

Black Scholar: I want to talk to you more about that. I think any artist in this society is inhibited in many ways because it is not an aesthetic society.

Maya Angelou: Materialistic.

Black Scholar: I think the black writer has even more difficulty because his vision is antagonistic, it's a racist society, his whole stuff is different. Do you think that the masterpiece syndrome further inhibits the output of black writers?

Maya Angelou: To me that inhibits *all* artists. Every artist in this society is affected by it. I don't say he or she is inhibited, he or she might work against it and make that work for them, as I hope I do, but we are affected by it.

It is in reaction to that dictate from a larger society that spurs my output, makes me do all sorts of things, write movies and direct them, write plays, write music and write articles. That's because I don't believe in the inhibition of my work; I am obliged, I am compulsive, I will work against it. If necessary I will go to work on a dictionary, you understand, just to prove that that is a lot of bullshit.

So every artist in the society has to deal with that dictate. Some are crippled by it, others, I believe, are made more healthy. Because they are made more strong, and become more ready to struggle against it.

Black Scholar: More vigilant.

Maya Angelou: Absolutely. But the black writer or black artist—I include every type, from graphics to entertainment—has generally further to come from than his or her white counterpart unless the artist is an entertainer. Often this black artist is the first in his family and possibly in his environment to strive to write a book, to strive to paint a painting, to sculpt, to make being an artist a life work. So the black writer, the black artist probably has to convince family and friends that what he or she is about is worthwhile.

Now that is damned difficult when one comes from a family, an environment, a neighborhood or group of friends who have never met a writer, who have only heard of writers, maybe read some poetry in school.

But to try to explain to a middle-aged black that the life of art one wants to lead is a worthwhile one and can hopefully improve life, the quality of life for all people, that's already a chore.

Because, like most people anywhere, the middle-aged black American that comes from a poor background for the most part wants to see concrete evidence of success. So they want things. If you are really going to be a success go and become a nurse, be a doctor, be a mortician, but a *writer*? So there are obstacles to overcome, to be either done or else just given up on.

Black Scholar: Or the relationships suspended?

Maya Angelou: Right. Then the work still has to be done on the artist's psyche, because he has to keep dealing with the issue that every artist, from the beginning of time, has had to deal with, and that is, "Am I an artist?" That public display of ego on the part of artists, 99 times out of 100 only tells of the doubt he has in private, especially when one has no precedent in one's personal family history. My grandfather Jason did not know anybody who was a painter, never met anybody who was an artist, or sculptor or composer, certainly not a writer. I can talk to little white high school students and if they themselves have never met a writer in their school, Norman Mailer spoke in their school, or Eudora Welty or James Dickey visited that auditorium. Well, there have not been that many black artists that visible for black youth. There was Langston Hughes, but he was the only one and that was thirty-five to forty years ago. And men of the Negro Renaissance were not given to get outside of Harlem, really.

Black Scholar: That's true. And Langston Hughes had a very public philosophy of art.

Maya Angelou: That's right. He was one of the rare ones. So I am saying that all of the problems of artists in a mechanistic, materialistic society, all those problems are heightened, if not doubled, for the black American artist.

So as usual the black writer—I can only speak for the writer—the black writer in particular should throw out all of that propaganda and pressure, disbelieve everything one is told to believe and believe everything one is told *not* to believe. Start with a completely clean slate and decide, "I will put it out."

A great writer only writes one book every five years. Says who? Who made that rule? I don't believe it. Just because it is told to me I don't believe it; on general principle I don't believe it. And I look at a James Baldwin with those pieces of work out. If I want to read Ralph Ellison, I am obliged to reread and reread and reread *Invisible Man* or *Shadow and Art* and how many times can you reread it? You get the essence, then you get the details and there it is. But if I disagree with Baldwin in, say, *No Name in the Street,* I can pick up *Fire Next Time,* I can go to read *Blues for Mr. Charlie*—I just used a piece from *Blues for Mr. Charlie*—I can go to see *Amen Corner,* I can read a short story from *Going to Meet the Man;* I mean the work is there.

Whatever I say, I cannot ignore the fact that the man has put the work out there.

Now my problem I have is I love life, I love living life and I love the art of living, so I try to live my life as a poetic adventure, everything I do from the way I keep my house, cook, make my husband happy, or welcome my friends, raise my son; everything is a part of a large canvas I am creating, I am living beneath.

Now there is a very fine line between loving life and being greedy for it. And I refuse to be greedy, I want to walk away from it with as much flair and grace and humor as I have had living it. Okay, I am saying all this to say that when I write it would seem I am greedy to get the books done; I pray I am just this side of being greedy, on the safe side. But that determination and delight I have in working, in getting a piece done, in the achievement is delicious. I know I will have detractors who will think that I am greedy to do that—you know there will be.

Black Scholar: They want you to write a book every five years rather than one book a year?

Maya Angelou: *Caged Bird* was published in 1970 and this is '76 and the fifth book is out. In the meantime I have written *Ajax*, another play, a movie, a television production, another movie script, a lot of stuff—you know I just haven't stopped—and a monthly article in *Playgirl*. I believe that life loves the liver of it.

Black Scholar: That's for damned sure. And it loves the lover of it.

Maya Angelou: Yes, yes absolutely. Keeps you young and gay and courageous and spitting nails. It really does.

Black Scholar: Well, that is one of the things I sensed in your autobiographies, is that you have a very definite point of view about work. In a lot of ways not only work as an artist, but in the general effort of life. Would you discuss that with me now?

Maya Angelou: I believe my feeling for work is something other than the puritan ethic of work.

I do believe that a person, a human being without his or her work is like a peapod where the peas have shrivelled before they have come to full growth. I have very little to say to people who don't work. I don't know what to say, I mean not that I want to discuss sewing dresses with a seamstress but if she or he respects her or his work we have a jumping-off place because we at least separately know something about respect and respect for something outside our own selves. Something made greater by ourselves and in turn that makes us greater. And that's pretty fantastic, so that I honor the people who do what they do well, whatever it is. I feel that I am a part of that.

Black Scholar: Black people are a working people and the sense of work pervades your autobiographies, your mother's rooming house, your own growth as a child, you were always around a working situation. One of your own primary motivations for work in autobiographies seems caring for your child.

Maya Angelou: Yes, that's right. Well I can't imagine what life would be like for me without having work that I cared about. I suspect that I have been a "liberated" woman in the sense that that term is now used most of my life. There may have been a couple of years in my life when I did not choose how I would live my life, who would pay my bills, who would raise my son, where we would live and so forth, but only for a few years.

I am so "liberated" that except on rare occasions my husband does not walk into the house without seeing his dinner prepared. He does not have to concern himself about a dirty house, I do that, for myself but also for my husband. I think it is important to make that very clear.

I think there is something gracious and graceful about serving. Now, unfortunately, or rather the truth is, our history in this country has been the history of the servers and because we were forced to serve and because dignity was absolutely drained from the servant, for anyone who serves in this country, black or white, is looked upon with such revilement, they are held in such contempt while that is not true in other parts of the world. In Africa it is a great honor to serve, to be allowed to serve somebody is a great honor. You can insult a person by not accepting something from him. In Europe from the great family traditions, work patterns are the patterns of the waiters and the maitre d's and the chefs and so forth. Generation after generation of servanthood. I don't mean to say that class issues are not at issue here too but there is something beyond that, when people have been made to serve or because of their economic circumstances, they have found within that some grace, some style, some marvelous flair.

Well, I refuse, simply because I happen to be born in this country, to take on the coloration of the larger society which says to serve, to take off your sister's shoes as she walks into the house, is really belittling yourself. I don't see that and ladies who travel with me, my friends, if we get into the car and it is only the two of us, I open the door for the ladies, and see them in and lock the door. Most women are made uncomfortable when another woman serves them. It's unfortunate. I happen to be 6 foot tall, I can push a door stronger than somebody who is, say 5 foot 2, you know, and that is just the truth. And if somebody is helping me shop I'll carry the bag. I am physically stronger, if I were not I would certainly say, "Sister, would you take it," and feel no compunction at all.

So there is something about the way people look at work that I think is completely off. I believe I know why there are the negatives about work, especially in the black community, but I refuse to get out of one trick bag and get caught in another. Now that I know why it means that I don't have to fall into that.

Black Scholar: Yes, there is that element, at the same time, of the disdain for work, there is the mystification of excellence so that people will talk about the inspired genius of John Coltrane while they forget he ran scales—

Maya Angelou: —for five hours a day.

Black Scholar: Right. Hard work was at the base of Trane's revolutionary music—and the courage to be audacious.

Maya Angelou: Audacity is fine; it's splendid. I'd like to pursue that a bit. True revolution in music took place, as far as I can see it, took place only a few times, three times in this century. One was the revolution that took place aided and abetted if not instigated by Louis Armstrong. Louis Armstrong did something with the trumpet that had never been done. Things that have become so casual, so common to our ears now, Louis Armstrong introduced. One can say that for European music the innovation of Stravinsky was revolutionary because again, Stravinsky and that whole group of European composers who introduced African tone into European music. In "Afternoon of a Faun" and "The Rite of Spring" and all of that you can keep hearing, those notes, that pentatonic scale.

Then bebop was the third. Truly revolutionary; it did something to all of our ears and that has happened with those three, I believe. Now, of course, musicologists know more but I mean for me, I would say these were the three truly innovative times in modern music. Rhythm and blues or rock & roll, or blues or spiritual or popular music, all that's been around; there's nothing new to that. Dizzy admittedly brought in Bossa Nova, but that was no real revolution whether it was Calypso or Bossa Nova, cha cha cha, no.

Black Scholar: Sure. Bop changed the whole basic premises of the music.

Maya Angelou: And our ears. Amazing, when you think of the music as it was played until Louis Armstrong came up to Chicago, when he was down in Louisiana, New Orleans, he just put notes in that nobody had ever heard and he split notes and he did things that we think of as being there forever.

Black Scholar: Yeah, improvisations in each of the major instruments.

Maya Angelou: Exactly, and 8 bars or 2 verses, a bridge and a verse. That's like a stanza in AB,AB,ABC in poetry. Again we come back to your earlier question about work. When Louis Armstrong, according to a few of his biographies, came to Chicago he was wearing a suit, the pants of which were about three inches too short, his white socks showed, he had these brogans on and he wore a derby hat. He got up on the stage and all the musicians laughed until he started to play. When he finished playing, the next day all the musicians went out and bought some pants three inches too short, some white socks and some brogan shoes and a derby hat, you understand. Louis Armstrong was on J—and never got off his J— never, never stopped. I mean for all intents and purposes, died with his trumpet in his hand. So did Duke Ellington, all those people who inspire one, who inspire me. Duke was still going on the road right up till the last. Louis Armstrong still on the road till the very last.

I appreciate that, I respect it and I am grateful for it. I am grateful, in the name of my grandson I am grateful.

Black Scholar: Has the example of these men influenced your own development as a writer?

Maya Angelou: Well, certainly. I tell you one of the most aggravating things of all is to pick up a review of a work of mine and have a reviewer say, "She is a natural writer." That sometimes will make me so angry that I will cry, really, because my intent is to write so it seems to flow. I think it's Alexander Pope who says, "Easy writing is damn hard reading," and vice versa, easy reading is damn hard writing. Sometimes I will stay up in my room for a day trying to get two sentences that will flow, that will just seem as if they were always there. And many times I come home unable to get it so I go back the next day, 6:30 in the morning, every morning, 6:30 I go to work. I'm there by 7:00; I work till 2:00 alone in this tiny little room, 7 x 10 feet. I have had the room for two years and they have never changed the linen. I've never slept there. There is nothing in the room except a bed, a face basin, and that's it. I write in longhand. If it is going well I might go to 3:00 but then I pull myself out, come home, take a shower, start dinner, check my house, so that when Paul comes in at 5:30 I have had a little time out of that, although my heart and mind are there, I still try to live an honest life. Then when you go back it looks different to you. I think that a number of artists again, or people who have pretensions that in order to be an artist you must have the back of your hand glued to your forehead, you know, and walk around and be "terribly terribly . . . " all the time, thinking great thoughts of pith and moment. That's bullshit. In order to get the work done and *finally that is all there is,* it's the *work!* all the posturing, all the lack of posturing, none of that matters, it is finally the work. You don't really get away from it but you try and I think that is very healthy. So it's good to take a swim and relax in some way.

Black Scholar: You mentioned some of the attitudes toward life that one gets in this society. When you were abroad did you get a different perspective on being a black American?

Maya Angelou: Well I came to, if possible, regard my people, black Americans, even more affectionately. Once out from the daily pressure of oppression, hate and ridicule and all, the negatives that permeate this whole frigging air we breathe, just being out from under that, not having to use 30 to 40 percent of my energy just kicking that crap out of my doorway before I can even get out and go to work, it was amazing. First off I didn't know what to do with myself. I was so geared to struggle, when I was living in Ghana, for the first year, I had my fist balled up for nothing, it was like tilting at windmills. I was absolutely so highly sensitive as to be paranoid. Any time anything happened I would say, "Oh, yes, I see. I understand why you are saying this; you are saying it because I am black."

Well, of course, everybody around me was black, so for the first time in my life, my defenses not only did not work they were not necessary, not those particular ones. It took a year for my son to unball his fists.

Once I did relax and realize that if I was rejected from the job or whatever, it was not because I was black, now it may be because I was black *American,* which is another thing, but it wasn't because of the color of my skin.

Then I began to examine my people and I thought, my God! How did we survive this! Good Lord! It's like growing up with a terrible sound in your ears day and night. Terrible, a kind of sound that is unrelenting, that pulls your hairs up on your body. And then to be away from it. At first you miss it, naturally, but then when you get used to the peace, the quietude, the lack of pressure, then you begin to think, my God, how have my people survived that crap and still to survive it with some style, some passion, some humor; so living in Africa made me even more respectful of black Americans. That's one thing.

I suppose too my family directly and my people indirectly have given me the kind of strength that enables me to go anywhere. I can't think where I would be afraid, apprehensive about going in the world, on this planet. I have had some very rough times in my life . . ..so what else is new, you know. Many things that really are so gruesome I wouldn't even write about them, because writing about them just makes it melodramatic. There are places of course I would not like . . . a Siberian salt mine or a Georgia chain gang, there are things I would rather not experience.

Black Scholar: Going to another country allowed me to see what is permanent about human nature and what is imposed upon it.

Maya Angelou: I was very pleased actually to see so many Africanisms or to be in Africa and recognize what I thought were black American mores, but then to recognize them as Africanisms, to see them at their source. That was lovely because I grew up until I was thirteen in a small town in Arkansas and once I was married to a man who was an African and he came to the States doing a post-doctoral tour for UNICEF. He went down to Tuskegee and he told the professor down there he was looking for Africanisms still current in American lives. The professor told him, "Why don't you go to a small town in Arkansas called Stamps," and I have no idea why that is, but my husband at that time, certainly I had never mentioned Stamps to him so he didn't recognize that, he didn't make that up. But that is the town I grew up in and I was back there about two months ago, first time in 30 years and it's true, absolutely. The town looks African Village, the people in it.

Black Scholar: Well, some of the Africanisms are present in church services, dancing and celebration.

Maya Angelou: Body language and black people anywhere from any place in the world can hold whole conversations without saying a word. Um um *um*. Um hum. Um hum. *Ummm* or take the words, auntie and uncle. That really boggles my mind because I knew that Aunt Jemima and Uncle Tom came from somewhere, but I didn't put it together. I thought white people had imposed those names. But in my town where I grew up, you had to call people Uncle or Auntie so and so, cousin; Tura, sister; bubba, brother, absolutely. For example, in raising my son Guy, or say, my grandson. He can say, "Hello, Mr. Chrisman," but it is too cold. On the other hand, he cannot call you Bob. That doesn't give him anything. If you are equal—he's seven and your equal—who the hell does he run to? So then properly as a friend of the family he is supposed to call you "Uncle Bob." That's the way I grew up, that's the way my son was raised, even though I raised him in the North so that Max, until Guy was 18, Max was Uncle Max and that was absolute, with all my friends, Uncle Jimmy. Until Guy became 17 or 18 and then they arranged, "Guy, call me Max," on an adult basis. If you encourage that particular distance, children can feel they have some shelters; each one of those aunties, uncles, sisters, all those people become shelters and when one lives in a threatening society, not only threatening but actively oppressive, you need as many shelters as possible. This is the way the African thinks and the way Southern blacks where I grew up think. So that's why it continues in the South. Well, seeing that in Ghana . . . there are so many Africanisms . . . that gave me another sense of continuity. I used to say on soap boxes in Harlem that slavery removed, stole our culture. But that's baloney. And I had to admit, I had to say, "Look, I was wrong."

Black Scholar: In some respects it might even have reinforced it.

Maya Angelou: It might have. Certainly the prejudice, racism and Jim Crowism reinforced it, kept us from moving into the mainstream as the American Indians have done in many, many cases. So many Americans that have more than one generation of their family in this country will say, "I am Cherokee and so and so, or Blackfoot and so and so." So many American Indians married into the white race and then, by the second generation, lost identity. We haven't done so.

Black Scholar: I had marked one passage in *Singin' and Swingin'* in which you mention your dilemma. Let me read it here. "I hadn't asked them for help . . . Nothing would bring me bowed to beg for aid from institutions which scorned me and a government that ignored me. It had seemed that I would be locked in the two jobs and the weekly baby sitter terror until my life was done. Now with a good salary my son and I could move back into my mother's house."

I am impressed throughout the autobiography with the dedication to the rearing of your son. You said earlier that in a sense you were a liberated woman but that, of course, obviously for you didn't mean not raising your child.

Maya Angelou: I think that one has to be liberated to do so. To bring up a person healthily you have to be liberated. You have to be liberated from all sorts of things, for one, from being in love with the child. A number of parents fall in love with their children and thereby wait either vicarious or true existence through their children. And that's baloney, that hampers, imprisons and cripples the person, the small person. He doesn't want all that weight on him; he's got his own stuff to do. I had the good fortune of never being in love with my son. That was one of my greatest blessings.

I really loved him, he amused me and tickled me and pleased me and still does. But I have never been in love with him, so that meant then that I could try to keep him as free as possible. And I don't know how I knew that. I can't say, because I was very young when he was born; I really don't know.

He was telling a story recently. We lived in Cleveland, he was seven so I was 23. I rented a top floor in a private home. The woman had a terribly rambunctious rooster, a few hens and a rooster in her back yard which was the only place for Guy to play. He went out to play and this rooster ran him, so he came inside and said he couldn't play. I took him back out and I gave him a long stick and said, "Whenever the rooster comes, you run him away." He played for some time and I came out and said, "Well, the rooster hasn't bothered you yet so you can break the stick in half." So he played and had the stick and broke it in half again, until finally the stick was about four inches long. He said, "Do you really think this will keep the rooster away?"

But how I knew how to do that, I don't know. But I do know that I was concerned to see him stay healthy and balanced and it was damn difficult because I knew too that I was 6 foot tall and had a very heavy voice and for a small person, who is a foot and half tall I must have looked like a mountain.

So I was aware of that and I managed to speak softly. He trained me more than anyone else. I spoke softly and quietly and moved, hopefully, not too fast so as not to frighten him. I remember hitting him when he was seven and realizing that that just didn't do. I felt so embarrassed, I felt, "Well, now that is the last time I will ever do that," and that was the last time. But to raise a healthy black boy without a father . . . I was aware that he could end up being a homosexual or a bully; somewhere between there was what I wanted. I mean a bully in any kind of way, and that includes players, hustlers, pimps and so on.

Black Scholar: Well, in this respect the kinds of things that you talk about as a developing black woman don't always seem to be the same concerns as those the feminists have.

Maya Angelou: Yes, I know.

Black Scholar: On the other hand, you are an egalitarian and an activist?

Maya Angelou: Absolutely. You see, there is one major difference between white American women and black American women. And it is this. White men have been able to say to white women and have said: "I don't need you. I can keep my factories running at top speed, I can send trains down silver tracks, and ships out to rolling seas. I can keep my institutes of higher education going without you, my banks going without you; I can run *wars* without you, I can go to the *moon* without you. I need you in the bedroom, the kitchen and the nursery."

Now black men have never been able to say that to our women. There's a qualitative difference in our approach to our men and our approach to life and our approach to our children and our approach to ourselves. A total difference, because although white men and white women may say that to me in effect by the way they treat me, my own fathers and brothers and uncles do not say that.

But for a white woman to have her own brother, father, nephews and uncles say that to her—"I don't really need you in the areas of my life of greatest importance, I don't need you"—has got to boggle the mind. I just *know* that this is what has happened and it is because of it that I support the women's liberation movement. Because I am for every person, or groups of people who intend to make it a better country for everybody, a better world for everybody. I mean I would be a liar if I said I thought I could enjoy my freedom without this white woman across the street enjoying hers. I cannot. She might be able to, or think she can—and obviously through slavery a number of people thought they could enjoy their freedom because I was enslaved. I don't make that mistake. So I am for it, but I see what the difference is between me and the average white woman.

Black Scholar: So white male chauvinism willfully excludes women from all the important aspects of life.

Maya Angelou: Right. For example, let's say we're sitting with our gentlemen friends at a table or around a fire or something and I said, "It has occurred to me that I would like to talk to you about something that happened in China the other day. I really would like a clarification." If all my gentlemen friends, my brothers, said, "Oh yeah Maya, why don't you go and make some coffee?" If, historically, they did that to me, what would happen?

Black Scholar: It would be impossible, you'd be alienated . . . angry . . .

Maya Angelou: No work . . . the sense of having no work, no seriousness. Naturally then I would begin to use those things I could use, my sex, sexuality as such. Hysteria. You rarely see black women hysterical. Angry, yes, but that, no, and the way a black woman usually uses sex is in a way to enjoy it herself. I really have a lot of sympathy for white women. We don't have the same struggle.

Black Scholar: That is a very complex thing—the moral, social and political enforcement of slavery did not come from white males alone. The white female also had complicity.

Maya Angelou: Bea Richards has a poem; it's so great. It's called "Blackwoman Speaks to Whitewoman" and she says,

You were brought here the same as I and if they praised my teeth they praised your thigh/they sold you to the highest bidder the same as I. But you snuggled down in your pink places and gave no reproach, accepted an added vote thinking that forgetting without realizing that the bracelet you accept in order to keep quiet about my house . . . and the necklace . . . and the man was your husband by law but mine at night and yet you stood there and watched him tell my son that what your husband did. Thinking that it's nothing just keep quiet and your slavery would be less. It's sad. It's sad.

Like most things it's the person who perpetuates the evil who is usually more crippled by it than the person upon whom the evil is perpetrated. There is something very healthy about struggling against evil. It's very positive, puts a little spring in your step.

Black Scholar: In the theater and performing arts again, I think you are one of the few modern women today directing and producing television shows and theater. What kinds of problems do you encounter there?

Maya Angelou: The problems are the old-time ones of being the first black woman. In many cases the crews with which I am obliged to work are composed of middle-aged, middle-class white men who have never worked with a black *man*, for that matter; and I have been very fortunate. I have met some nice men, I try to give little pep talks, like saying, "Gentlemen, you have a chance to be really generous. I need to learn something and I work very hard and if you don't teach me I will learn anyway. It will cost me more, the project will be endangered, but I will learn." That is why I went to Sweden and took a course in cinematography, just so I would know something, I wouldn't have to be completely ignorant. But it gets results; all kinds of people will rise to heights greater than *their* expectations if you expect it of them. It's fantastic; the same people who would be very difficult if you said, "Gentlemen, I really need this and I know you can teach me and I will be very grateful, if you would, I expect you will." Many times they are made greater, they try to live up to other people's expectations. The same way people will live down to expectations.

Black Scholar: I think that probably gets back to your philosophy of work concept, an honest effort or venture made stands a chance of success.

Maya Angelou: Exactly. And none can come if it's not tried.

Black Scholar: Right . . . . Have you ever considered dramatizing parts of your autobiography?

Maya Angelou: Well, I hope to. I wrote out a screenplay to be done but I couldn't get the backing I wanted. The big companies wanted to buy it from me, *Caged Bird,* for an incredible amount of money but they wanted to provide their own directors and I said no. I wouldn't have it directed by anybody but me.

That's not really quite true, there are a couple of other directors I would consider, Gordon Parks Senior, Dick Williams, he's a brilliant actor/director, lives in New York. Those were the only two I would consider. My producer begs me to do it for the Broadway stage; I can't see it right now.

Black Scholar: What are your plans for 1977?

Maya Angelou: Well, I will be writing and directing a musical drama, *And Still I Rise,* this January in New York. It is exciting to direct and I hope to be doing much more. This spring I hope to compile a kind of omnibus of plays, articles and short stories and poems of mine. The omnibus would contain, say, *Ajax;* the screenplay of *Georgia, Georgia;* and short stories, the scenario of a little short film called *All Day Long,* some articles from *Playgirl,* some of those, and some things I did for the *New York Times.* That would be the book for 1977.

Black Scholar: Thank you, Maya Angelou.

Maya Angelou: And Still She Rises

Curt Davis/1977

Encore American & Worldwide News, 12 September 1977, 28-32.

Both feet flat, the game is done.
  They think I lost. I think I won.

It is Maya Angelou speaking in "Harlem Hopscotch," the last poem in the volume *Just Give Me a Cool Drink of Water 'Fore I Diiie.* It is little Marguerite (pronounced Marg-you-reet) Ann Johnson, a far too big, flat-figured and flat-featured lass growing up in Stamps, Ark. It is Maya Angelou, renowned writer-poet-actress-director-composer-lyricist-dancer-singer-journalist-teacher-lecturer, having the last laugh and savoring a deep, chillingly cool chug of water.

The water flows like the Nile now for Maya Angelou. She is preparing to write the script for a television movie based on the life of civil rights activist Fannie Lou Hamer, to star Della Reese and to be directed by Vinnette Carroll. She has already scripted the miniseries for CBS of the first installment of her autobiography, *I Know Why the Caged Bird Sings.*

Her immediate project is a theater evening of some of her poetry set to her music, choreographed by George Faison. Called *And Still I Rise,* it empties pockets of Black life, and will open in Washington, D.C. late this month prior to Broadway later in the season. Besides writing and composing, Maya Angelou is the lyricist and the director. And still she rises.

To rise, one must have been low. Born 49 years ago in St. Louis, Mo., Angelou was so low ostriches gave up the search. At 3, she and her beloved brother Bailey were herded off from their squabbling California parents to their paternal grandmother and uncle in Stamps, Ark. There they were raised strictly, southernly, religiously. Little Marguerite (Maya was a diminutive bestowed by Bailey) knew nothing of White people (except "powhitetrash") or of the best things in life that are not free. Her physical plainness ravished her childhood and awakened her from her dreams, but the family unit was a circle of love that grew concentrically through the years.

On a vacation at 8 to visit her mother, Maya was raped by her mother's boyfriend. She returned to Arkansas, where she and Bailey stayed for five more years. Then they tried the West Coast again and began to discover their mother as a real force in their lives. Maya took refuge in books and built her A-frame house in the country with insular romanticism. Personal or societal horrors mattered not when there was another, printed, guaranteed world to escape to. That current injustice, too, shall pass.

As a teenager, she felt ambitions creep into her soul with the regularity of insecurities. Maya became San Francisco's first Black cable car conductor; the following year, because she was afraid of lesbianism and wanted a sexual experience with a male, she became a mother. And the indifference of that sexual encounter was transformed into an intense, unyielding, but not smothering love for her son, Guy, now 30. The phoenix rises from the ashes.

Maya's wings were just being tested. She became a short-order cook, a dancer, a madam at 18, she went into prostitution briefly to earn money for her lover. She flitted back and forth between the Golden Gate City and Stamps with as much facility as she jumped jobs, wearing sadness as a chiffon robe and loneliness a tiara.

Finally she settled into dancing in dives, until discovery after discovery, she worked her way up and in her mid- to late 20s toured Europe as a lead dancer in *Porgy and Bess*. The public Maya Angelou was born and it is through this point that her autobiographies have brought the reading public.

I Know Why the Caged Bird Sings (1970), *Gather Together in My Name* (1974) and *Singin' and Swingin' and Gettin' Merry like Christmas* (1976) are responsible for Angelou's literary reputation. She was nominated for a Pulitzer Prize for her poetry, but it is this trilogy—two more to come, she says, desirous of being America's Black female Proust—that has opened hearts among America's readers.

The quality of the three works varies. The first—*Caged Bird*—is easily the finest. Its tough, tactile tribute to a little girl forced to be a woman before she's through with childhood intoxicates the reader with life juices. Hilarity balances heartache; wisdom's ancestors are both calm and chaos. In *Gather Together,* the late teenager has blossomed into worldliness, and thus the book is far more cerebral than the earlier one. *Singin' and Swingin'* often wallows in indulgence—stylistic and emotional—but all three books are special because we need know nothing about Maya Angelou, the professional singer-dancer-actress, in order to discover Maya Angelou the person.

Also, her ability to characterize is a gift to her and a gift from her. Her brother Bailey expands your heart as you read the three volumes. There would be no need to be introduced to him at a party; his sensitivity and vulnerability would tug your humanism across a crowded room the way oil can direct a drill. The sophisticated mother shivers with restrained love and shimmers with axioms ("If you decide to be a whore, all I can say is, be the best. Don't be a funky chippie. Go with class.") Grandmother Annie Henderson is the cornerstone of Maya Angelou's life and the building shall not crumble.

Maya Angelou speaks in the tongues of men and of angels, but has love.

Her experiences have, as anyone who has read her or seen her perform knows, given her compassion and sensitivity, and her romanticism lends omniscience. But after her childhood, after three marriages—two ending in divorce, one going strong—after recent familial developments, her life and her world view cannot be peaches and cream.

"You never really know how the toll is taken. The toll is exacted in different ways. Most often the ways you think it's being exacted don't matter. That is, if you can't sleep at night, loneliness, that kind of bare, terrible loneliness where you question what life is about, what is your responsibility, not just to yourself but to your race, to your gender, to your species.

"But the other ways—the unexpected illnesses" (she has had a series of minor nervous breakdowns) "when the back goes out and the feet swell up, the arguments that you either solicit or begin or initiate. All those subtle ways when you can never actually put your finger on it, those are the ways how the toll is taken.

"The sensitivity is shown not in saying, 'I am my brother's keeper,' but in saying 'I am my brother.' So that everything that happens around you glues itself to you. Somebody plays the fool and kills nine people, slap somebody, rape somebody—whack, whack, whack, like *decals.*

"You have no idea how the toll is taken so you learn to operate in the familiar—get up, brush your teeth, put on your clothes, 'How do you do, very nice to see you, fine thank you.' What is really happening you can't even look at, if in fact you can know."

What Maya Angelou did know in the 1950s was that she had to dance. And dance she did, with Pearl Primus, Martha Graham, and Ann Halprin as well as in clubs and in *Porgy and Bess.* She later taught dance and drama in Rome and Tel Aviv.

While abroad, she spent the mid-1960s in Africa, working as a journalist in Cairo and writing and teaching in Ghana. While there, she contracted an acute case of self-discovery and self-joy. In that way, she was an ancestor of her friend Alex Haley, and when she played Kunta Kinte's grandmother in *Roots* there was a sense of *déjà vu.*

She was being considered to direct an episode or more of *Roots,* but the producers were on a tight schedule and budget and people with more television directing experience were chosen. But the people ultimately chose Maya Angelou. "After it was done," she says, "I found that people knew me. I walked down the street, especially the first month. I've written five books, I can't say how many plays, movie scripts, music, and poetry, and so forth. I walk down the street and people say, 'You're the actress in *Roots.* What's your name again, and what have you been doing all this time?' "

She had acted often before. Besides the appearance in *Porgy and Bess* and off-Broadway with Godfrey Cambridge in *Cabaret for Freedom,* Angelou was nominated for a Tony three years ago for her performance opposite Geraldine Page in the two-character *Look Away,* which closed opening night (the nomination "was a little like giving a person a Band-Aid three months after his throat was cut"). And last season she was the wife of a drunken Richard Pryor on the latter's NBC special in a segment Angelou herself wrote.

One of her most important performances was in Genet's *The Blacks,* off-Broadway in 1960-61. There has been talk about its revival. Angelou comments: "It was a very important play. It still is an important play. It implies that, come the revolution, Blacks will be as bad and as greedy as Whites have been. What goes around comes around, which is a very Black statement, an African statement, too.

"Working for me as a young woman, with the cast of *The Blacks*, was an incredible experience. The original cast included Cecily (sic) Tyson, James Earl Jones, Raymond St. Jacques, Roscoe Lee Browne, Lou Gossett, Charles Gordone, Helen Martin, Cynthia Belgrave, Jay Flash Riley, Lex Monson, Godfrey Cambridge, Ethel Ayler, and me. It was the thing to go into; if you were out of a job, go try out for *The Blacks*. It was wonderful to break down the play together. Obviously it fed all our artistic growth.

"It would be interesting to see it today with some new people. All the [original] actors have done so many things since [that they] would bring so much other equipment to it now. Just like the time—instead of 1960-61, 1977 has its own rhythm and its own impetus. I think the words would be loaded, freighted, now, for us [the originals]. I think young Black actors today would do it totally differently from the way we did it, in terms of what they see of their world, from what we saw of our world.

"In '60-'61 there was an incredible aura—air, is better—of hope. Martin was out there and Malcolm was out there and the Southern Christian Leadership Conference was doing its business. SNCC was about to be born. The young people in the country, Black and White, were involved in sit-ins, freedom rides; there was a dream that we could change this country. I think that was a hope that died aborning.

"So young people should do *The Blacks* today. Most of the original actors have had some success, so the same anger . . . would be manufactured. I wouldn't trust it."

Maya Angelou was not just an observer in the era of hope. She worked with Martin Luther King in the SCLC and believes that when the final history book is written then King "will be known as one of the great minds and hearts of the 20th century. He was *human*—he was never superhuman, and people tend to imbue him with that and that's not fair."

He can still be a hero, however, with all his human foibles and all his humanism. And Angelou says that people live in direct relation to the heroes they have. Three years ago, for the Mark Taper Forum in Los Angeles, she adapted Sophocles' *Ajax*. "I began to see the likenesses in modern-day life, heroes who we've allowed to die and give no quota to their contribution except some big mouthing much later. So I thought I'd write this hero and make the character who was his enemy into Odysseus, into the person who must speak for his burial, and at one point Odysseus at the end says, 'If we allow the dogs and the vultures to pluck the bones of our heroes, what will our children have?'"

They'll have none of the impetus that Angelou had as a child. She'd often quote Shakespeare or Langston Hughes and now adds Gwendolyn Brooks, Mark Twain and Edna St. Vincent Millay to that list. But those writers, those dreamers, gave her a chance to develop Maya Angelou from Marguerite Johnson. They told her—even if her White neighbors denied her—that she had a chance, that there was something in her that could be molded, shaped, developed, something of beauty that would make people forget or look beyond the physical and later see the physical as this marvelous house sheltering a precious part of the universe. Those writers—some physically dead, some physically alive, all spiritually alive in her— made Maya Angelou pretty.

And they made *her* write to carry on the inspiration. She writes alone, imprisoned in her thoughts as her body is solitary in a bare room. "Once I start to work, that's all there is. There is no audience and I have no outside thoughts. I'm always nervous before I start to work, even writing. I'm afraid I'll show myself up to be totally talent-less, conceited, just a bag of hot air. The work gets me out of it. I just give myself to it.

"I tend not to have loyalty to work; my loyalty is only as long as I'm working on it. When I see other people hold on tenaciously to a piece of work, sometimes to its benefit, sometimes to its detriment, I sometimes wish, oh, I wish I could feel that way. I, Maya, don't feel I'm any more important to the work than the vessel out of which it comes. Once it's out, then other people have to go work on it.

"Quite often I don't recognize my work when other people do it. That's one of the qualities and also one of the flaws in my personality, in that once I'm finished with a piece, I'm totally finished. I can really hear it as a finished work and if it doesn't hold up, it doesn't hold up.

"It's like a painter. Once he or she has finished it, and it's on exhibit, the first viewer who comes along changes the nature of that piece, because he comes along with his equivalent, with his frustration, his successes, and suddenly the piece has a whole other meaning. The painter may have painted a watermelon, but the viewer says, 'That's a green grape, one of those striped grapes in magnitude, and isn't that magnificent. It reminds me of a glass of wine I had one summer in San Diego.' Suddenly the piece is completely different."

After five morning hours of writing in, for example, buddy Jessica Mitford's home, Angelou would "read the work to see if it jelled. Around 6:00, I'd be out, I'd get out of myself, make a decent dinner, take a bath, watch Walter Cronkite, and face the rest of the word." She'd cook French, Italian, Black American, Mexican-American, or Japanese cuisine, or perhaps one of her specialties—Arkansas country soup. That's a big soup bone and some beef, with fresh tomatoes peeled, and leftover vegetables, potatoes, okra, corn, packages of mixed vegetables, handfuls of fresh noodles; San Francisco sourdough bread heated and a good bottle of wine.

She'd be cooking for, besides herself, her third husband, Paul Du Feu, a writer (*Let's Hear It for the Long-Legged Women*) former husband of Germaine Greer, and now primarily a mason. He is White, foreign-born, less outgoing than she but still far more than civil, the brawn to her brain, and the love of her life.

Maya Angelou's countenance becomes virginal as she recalls Du Feu's acceptance into her family. "My mother says I have married a few times, but this is the first time I've given her a son-in-law. At the ceremony my brother took his glasses off and tears were on his face and said, 'I want to go on record and look Paul Du Feu in the eyes and call him brother.' " She literally breaks down, unable to speak, thinking of the communion between the two men she loves most in the world.

Her first husband was Greek—Enistasious Angelos, an electrician to whom she was married for a couple of 1950s years. Their shared time is chronicled in *Singin' and Swingin'*. That of her second husband is not—anywhere.

He was a high African official and Angelou has yet to name him publicly. In all likelihood she wed him about 10 years after her first and about 10 before Du Feu. "My second husband is African and Africa, Africa, has a profound and long memory. There's an African statement that says royalty does not weep in the streets. If I speak about my husband—my second husband—I have to speak about some problems and that would not be gracious. It wouldn't serve anyone well. He's a fine man; he just wasn't my husband.

"My mother has a theory that most people marry other people's mates and never know it. None of the people involved know that that man's love is in Des Moines, Iowa; that woman's mate is in Barbados; and *those* two people are married to two different ones. So I married a wonderful man, he just wasn't my husband. Paul is my husband. He's the husband I've looked for all my life. It's strange that my husband would be English and all the things that he is. . . . "

Maya Angelou found Paul Du Feu, but when she was with Angelos she lost her grandmother. "I hadn't gotten to the place where I appreciated her apart from herself. I never got a chance to tell her all the things I'd have liked. Because of that loss, I have an eternal love affair going with old Black women.

"I remember as a child how huge she was—a mountain. And I remember her hands very well, they were very hard. The skin on my grandmother's hands was hard, but the way she laid her hands on you was soft."

Maya herself is a softie when her 19-month-old grandson is mentioned. "I just talked with our son day before yesterday and I was telling him our plan that when our grand is six years old, we're stealing him, that's all, moving to the mountains somewhere and I'll change my name. Paul will change his name and then we'll just go incognito. Guy says, 'Mama, you can change your name, and even the way you look. Paul can become Black and you can become White and you both get short, but you can never change your style. So all I have to do when I go looking for my son is go to any village, any city, anywhere, and go to the most elegant place and then say, 'Have there been two, who drink quite a lot and sing "Danny Boy" and a spiritual?' "

She indeed beckons the angels when she discusses her beloved Bailey. The siblings were one as children; over the years they grew and traveled apart, but, as he called her "My," short for "Maya" and for "my sister," so did they belong inseparably, irrevocably to each other. Knowing Maya Angelou Du Feu, one is sure he knows Bailey Johnson Jr. And there's a luminosity about her when she discusses why she doesn't discuss him now.

"He's made that qualitative change in his life. I don't want to waken the dragons. For years I did my best to protect him from prying eyes, because he was a drug addict, and now I protect him from a different reason altogether. I just have every prayer that he's going to make it and we love each other very very much, always have. He was in prison by the time I went to *Porgy and Bess,* but I'm still really—it's too precious. Last June he signed himself into a program and he's been clean ever since, the first time in 25 years, and I don't want to wake it up, I don't want to wake up that demon. Five years from now, when he's solidly on the road, it'll be different. He's an excellent writer, excellent. A brilliant man. He's spent years and years in Attica and everywhere, and he's never been in prison for assault against a human being. Never."

She's been attacked by her own dragons, possessed by her own demons. She has slain many and exorcised most of the others. Ease is promised to none and Maya Angelou doesn't ask for it. She doesn't need it. She's got a sense of serenity through her own indomitability. She quotes from the title poem of *And Still I Rise:*

> You may write me down in history
>   with your bitter, twisted lies
> You may trod me in the very dirt, but
>   still, like dust, I'll rise
> Does my sassiness offend you, why
>   are you beset with gloom?
> Just 'cause I walk like I got oil
>   wells pumping in my living room?
> Just like moons and like suns, with
>   the certainty of time
> Just like the hopes, springing high, still
>   I rise.

Westways Women: Life Is for Living

Judith Rich/1977

Westways, September 1987, 44-47, 78. Copyright © 1977 by
Westways. Reprinted by permission.

The Township of Sonoma dozes in sun-drenched contentment as we
pass; stirred mainly by day-trippers wandering through its restored
colonial square, exploring the white-bleached stone mission and
army barracks, the postcard quaint restaurants and shops selling
bridles, bric-a-brac, antiques and local wines.

Out of town on the way to Boyes Hot Springs, the road slips softly
into an avenue of trees, skirted with gardens and lawns; a country
club belt bathed in emerald light and undisturbed calm.

A turnoff near the golf club leads into a suburban country lane and
the house where Maya Angelou has settled after a turbulent life of
chance.

A long way from the dry, dusty, cotton-pickin' South; trailer parks,
junkyards, teeming city ghetto streets, pool halls, gambling and
prostitution dens, greasy short-order cafes, boxing gyms, nightclubs,
theaters, television, films, Africa, Europe. . . . Maya has known so
many realities; she has moved through extremes.

Not far away is the lush countryside and picturesque Glen Ellen
village of the Valley of the Moon—this is Jack London territory, where
the legendary adventurer-writer came to seek a similar peace. It's
fitting that Maya Angelou, another celebrated writer of raw experience and a folk hero in her own right, has found a nature-blessed
oasis here.

The house has large, open spaces, light flooding in through glass
walls looking out on a swimming pool and garden (which she loves to
tend), adjoined by a field where horses sometimes roam.

Maya is a handsome, statuesque woman in shirt and long skirt,
with a scarf on her head. She carries herself with grace, and is
barefooted. Her voice is rich, melodious, deep. She chooses her
words elegantly. Her feelings flicker always somewhere close to the

surface; her eyes brim with tears as she recalls someone dear, or she laughs her full, throaty joy.

It's her capacity to transmit this warmth and humor, together with the inherent pain, through her work, that has made her a leading figure in writing and the performing arts.

Maya has found her expression in many forms—books, plays, poetry, dance, films and television. She is a Renaissance woman, who has always dared, both in her life and work, to do more. She became the first black woman to make the nonfiction bestseller lists with her acclaimed autobiography *I Know Why the Caged Bird Sings,* followed by the success of *Gather Together in My Name.* Her recent *Singin' and Swingin' and Gettin' Merry Like Christmas,* which traces her launch in show business in the Fifties, went into a second printing even before publication date. She's published two books of poetry and a handful of plays.

Maya was the first black woman to direct a major motion picture, *Georgia, Georgia,* and has been responsible for television plays and specials, including the ten-part series on African traditions in American life for National Educational Television, "Blacks, Blues, Black," which she wrote, produced and hosted.

She's a journalist, songwriter, singer, dancer and actress, with a Tony nomination for her supporting role in Alex Haley's "Roots." She was honored this year as "Woman of the Year in Communications" by the *Ladies' Home Journal.*

Maya has always thrown herself passionately into whatever she does. "Life is going to give you just what you put in it," her street-wise mama told her. "Put your whole heart in everything you do, and pray, then you can wait."

Maya is not one to rest. Even in the peaceful Sonoma retreat, she keeps a strict work schedule. This morning, as her long, generous hand reaches out a greeting, she has been at work since a quarter to seven, working on revisions for the off-Broadway production of *And Still I Rise.* She keeps a room at the hotel in town, holed away from the distractions that surround her at home; cut off from the sentimental flights of her mind as it alights on a painting of dancing black women or the sculpture that was a gift from director Michael Schultz and his wife.

In her "grim, drab, mean little room" at the hotel she keeps nothing but playing cards, crossword puzzles, a dictionary, thesaurus,

Bible and a yellow pad, on which she writes in longhand. She usually works till two in the afternoon, or three if it's going well. The intensity she gives to her work brings on all sorts of physical reactions. Her knees swell, her back goes out, her eyelids swell completely closed and huge clumps come up on her hands.

"They had to lay me out last night," she said, "I was in such bad shape; I simply couldn't move. At the starting of each piece of work it eludes me; I think, oh God, it's gone! My body comes up with fantastic things."

She pushes herself to the limits of her ability. "I have always got to be the best," said Maya. "I'm absolutely compulsive, I admit it. I don't see that that's a negative. Oh no. I'm not competing with anybody else but myself. I love to be excellent."

Maya has learned to overcome in the course of the harsh lessons dealt to a black woman trying to make her way in the world. Her childhood as Marguerite Johnson (born forty-eight years ago) was molded with a downhome, wise, hardworking grandmother in Stamps, Arkansas, where revivalist religious meetings and flares of racial violence scored her education.

Then she and her brother Bailey, who shared her love of literature, would be summoned to live with Mother Dear in Saint Louis and San Francisco, among a colorful cast of low life characters, who more often than not survived through crime.

Here she learned a new morality: the black ghetto ethic by which "a hero is the man who is offered only the crumbs from his country's table, but by ingenuity and courage is able to take for himself a Lucullan feast."

Her flash spade daddy popped in and mostly out of the picture, charming and disappointing her.

From the time she was a schoolgirl and became the first Negro hired on the San Francisco streetcars, her determination never let her give up. Her first two books are full of the courage bred of these early experiences and in her latest the caged bird soars to higher realms, as Maya wins the approval of white folks as a sassy dancer in night spots and tours Europe with the musical *Porgy and Bess,* going on to teach dance in Italy and Israel. The hard times have tested her character and talent and now they begin to flower. "Preparation," she reflects at the backstage warm-up, "is rarely easy and never beautiful."

"When I went to write this last book I had to almost hype myself into remembering," explained Maya. "Which is what I have to do to work. Almost enchant myself. Get back, so the book does not become an As Told To . . . but really so the reader's there."

It was during that European tour in the mid-Fifties that Maya began writing—long detailed letters sent to her mother. Her mama dug them out after *Gettin' Merry* was complete and found that Maya has remembered events and people exactly as they'd happened so long ago.

Maya first book, *I Know Why the Caged Bird Sings,* which rocketed her to fame, was published in 1970.

"The story is that James Baldwin took me over one night to Jules Feiffer's house," recalled Maya. "The four of us, Jules and his wife then, Judy, and Jim and I, sat telling stories and drinking Scotch till three o'clock in the morning. And the next morning Judy Feiffer telephoned the man who was to become my editor and said: 'You know the poet, Maya Angelou? Well, if you could get her to write an autobiography, you'd really have something.' So he phoned me."

Maya, who was living in New York at the time and was busy on the West Coast producing a television series, refused the offer. Until . . . "He did something that made me know he'd spoken to James Baldwin. He said: 'Well, Miss Angelou, it's probably just as well that you don't attempt an autobiography, because it really is the most difficult of the literary forms.' I said: 'I'll do it, of course! Are you kidding? Of course.'"

Maya's friends know she can't resist a challenge. Give her a mountain and she'll climb it. Take her journalist career in Africa. After writing short stories, plays, poems and songs, she married an African diplomat and went to live in Egypt for two years.

"When I arrived in Cairo I said I wanted to go to work. I just couldn't sit. My husband said that would be utterly impossible; in Egypt nice women didn't work and because of his status I would not be allowed to work. But I had a friend, a black American who was working in a feature news agency. He told me about the *Arab Observer,* the only English news weekly out of the Middle East at the time. He said maybe I'd like to take a chance with that. I got the Africa Desk-Politics. It was really interesting, because I was, at once, a female, non-Muslim, non-Arab, American, black and six feet tall. All I needed was that I should be Jewish! It was a shock to the community. It was really terrifying, that each time I spoke, each time the magazine came out, there was the question of: Was that my point of view, or was I speaking for my husband? But anyway I lasted. All the other journalists were male and the idea of having a woman even work there, let alone a woman as boss, was ridiculous. But we worked it out and everyone worked when I went there."

Then Maya married again and went on to Ghana, where she worked as a journalist and assistant administrator at the University of Ghana.

Maya has never let an opportunity go by, when things were tough or even since she's been successful and could afford to sit back.

"I kept getting breaks and I still haven't found my niche. I'm still daring everything all the time."

It is Maya's unfailing capacity to see the positive side of life that has spurred her on to rise above even the most difficult situations.

"I've been very fortunate. . . . I seem to have a kind of blinkers. I just do not allow too many negatives to soil me. I'm very blessed. I have looked quite strange in most of the places I have lived in my life, the stages, spaces I've moved through. I of course grew up with my grandmother: my grandmother's people and my brother are very very black, very lovely. And my mother's people were very very fair. I was always sort of in between. I was too tall. My voice was too heavy. My attitude was too arrogant—or tenderhearted. So if I had accepted what people told me I looked like as a negative, yes, then I would be dead. But I accepted it and I thought, well, aren't I the lucky one!"

She has a rare ability to see goodness, in even the darkest periods. "What I tried to show in *Gather Together* was, all through people were good to me. People were pretty bad to me too. But, more important, they were pretty good. Those acts of generosity that people showed me saved me a great deal."

Maya never forgets the kindnesses. There was her first husband, a white man who managed a record store and gave her a sheltered life staying at home, reading, playing word games, cooking and taking care of her son; cut off from the world and forbidden to have visitors. "He was an isolationist, absolute introvert; very very bright and who felt I was very very bright. So he provided a climate for me and I figuratively climbed into his armpit and sort of curled myself around and got healthy. He provided the climate for me to examine

myself, to heal all those scars. I will never stop thanking him, being
grateful to him. At first it was exactly what I needed. I'd been very
much brutalized by life. But after two and one-half years I began to
see that one could not live that kind of life."

There was also the heroin addict, Troubador, who warned her off
drugs. "It's very hard to be young and curious and almost egomani-
acally concerned with one's intelligence and to have no education at
all and no direction and no doors to be open," said Maya,
remembering the murky escapism that claimed her own brother and
nearly tempted her.

"To go figuratively to a door and find there's no doorknob at all. I
understand young people very well. But that man, Troubador, was
extremely kind to show me himself at his most debased."

There was the Jewish rabbi she went to see, when she was a
young girl dabbling in religions, searching for some faith. She writes
of his sympathetic counsel (which led her to find some direction in
the philosophy of Martin Buber) and many years later he turned up
at her hospital bed after a serious operation.

"Those were the kindnesses and I never forget them. And so they
keep one from ever becoming bitter. They encourage you to be as
strong, as volatile as necessary to make a well world. Those people
who gave me so much, and still give me so much, have a passion
about them. And they encourage the passion in me. I'm very blessed
that I have a healthy temper. I can become quite angry and burning
in anger, but I have never been bitter. Bitterness is a corrosive,
terrible acid. It just eats you and makes you sick."

For all the experience she's been through, Maya has always
retained a certain innocence and an ingrained sense of religion, going
way back to her Methodist Episcopal upbringing in the South. The
peculiar street morality she found in the life of the ghettos presented
her with no conflicts.

"One always knew that there were things you didn't do to other
human beings," she said. "You see, morality for the most part is
influenced by culture, as much as it influences culture. What is
acceptable in one culture because of the pressures might be amoral
or immoral in another. You can see for instance that prostitutes
ofttimes are not looked upon with the same kind of revilement and
contempt as generally happens in our society. In some cultures it's

just a very real part of surviving. And the con men, they use other people's greed. If people are greedy they'll pay for it. And that is still not looked down upon in the kind of sections where I grew up. But there are certain classes of blacks who forget the particular onus, the stench of poverty: try to anyway, and so begin to take on the morality of middle-class whites. Fortunately it sticks out as awkwardly and ungainly as peacock feathers hastily stuck on a turkey."

The status and security of success have not qualitatively changed Maya. She still feels the same compassion and roots among her people, but denies she speaks for black consciousness.

"What I represent in fact, what I'm trying like to hell to represent every time I go into that hotel room, is myself. That's what I'm trying to do. And I miss most of the time on that: I do not represent blacks or tall women, or women or Sonomans or Californians or Americans. Or rather I hope I do, because I am all those things. But that is not all that I am. I am all of that and more and less. People often put labels on people so they don't have to deal with the physical fact of those people. It's easy to say, oh, that's a honkie, that's a Jew, that's a junkie, or that's a broad, or that's a stud, or that's a dude. So you don't have to think: does this person long for Christmas? Is he afraid that the Easter bunny will become polluted? . . . I refuse that."

Maya aims her work at audiences of all colors and creeds. Her concern, however, is for a certain backpedaling of the black cause. "It's been dangerous the last few years. There's a threat of polarization that blacks must oppose unless we are ready to have life narrowed into a tiny alley. There was a period in the Sixties when the lines of demarcation seemed to be melting. It looked at the time as if the country could have healed itself quite a lot. Then the backlash came, and it's become something else. I simply refuse to have my life narrowed and proscribed."

With her reputation established, it came as an unlikely shock when Maya married an Englishman, Paul Du Feu. He's younger than she and had written a book about his short-lived marriage to Women's Libber Germaine Greer (of The Female Eunuch). They met five years ago at a literary party in London, where Maya kept an apartment to write. It was the kind of occasion she usually steers clear of, she so avoids any kind of pretension. She and Paul have been inseparable ever since.

He followed her to America and in California met the person most dear to her, her son Guy, whom she describes as "my monument in the world. Six feet four . . . 240 pounds . . . looks like a wall . . . very very handsome and erudite." Paul had never known any black Americans, but he hit it off with Guy and the rest of Maya's family: her brother Bailey, who was her rock as she grew up, the genius of the family, but ended up in Sing Sing for stolen goods; her mother, always an inspiration to her, who is now in the merchant marine. (Her father died while she was writing her first book.) The wedding took place at the multiracial Glide Community Church in San Francisco.

Despite their greatly different backgrounds, Maya says she and Paul are very much alike, with a similar sense of comedy about life's melodramas. "We hopefully, both of us, wear all those cloaks life demands, wear all those hats and all of them as lightly as air."

Everywhere she went, from universities to TV interviews, Maya was asked about her marriage to a white man. "The difficulty, of course, was the sensation-seekers, who tended to make my marriage a focal point," said Maya. "Before I said, yes, I went to talk with Baldwin. And he said: 'Now Maya, you talk courage and you encourage us all to dare to love. You love this man and you are questioning . . . what?"

With Paul, who is a builder and also a popular cartoonist and columnist in Britain, she first looked around the London area for a house. Then, deciding that they really wanted to live in the wine country, they drove around France looking in vain for the appropriate setting. They finally settled on California and Sonoma as the perfect choice.

Today is going to be a small family lunch. Maya's daughter-in-law is coming with the newest pride and joy of the Johnson clan, her baby grandson, Colin Ashanti. Close friend and helper Sam Floyd collects them from the station. Maya, who boasts a collection of 150 cookbooks, launches into preparations with characteristic zest. "I shall cook today a quiche for lunch," she announces. "I shall cook a quiche that'll be the lightest, the crust will be the flakiest, and I will do it with one hand, you see, so that it seems effortless. So they will sit to eat and they will say—Ahh! Excellent! But, in fact, I have been planning it."

Maya busies herself in the kitchen with Sam, while tiny Colin Ashanti gurgles away with his mother on the carpet. Her heart is full and as we drive away from the scene of her well-earned content, Maya's power still resonates: "I've always had the feeling that life loves the liver of it. You must live it and life will be good to you, give you experiences. They may not all be that pleasant, but nobody promised you a rose garden. But more than likely if you do dare, what you get are the marvelous returns. Courage is probably the most important of the virtues, because without courage you cannot practice any of the other virtues, you can't say against a murderous society, I oppose you murdering. You got to have courage to do so. I seem to have known that a long time and found great joy in it."

Maya Angelou Raps
Jeffrey M. Elliot/1977

Sepia, October 1977, 22-28. Copyright © 1977 by Jeffrey M. Elliot. Reprinted with permission.

One of the most celebrated writers in America, Maya Angelou is the author of the best-selling three-volume autobiography—*I Know Why the Caged Bird Sings, Gather Together in My Name,* and *Singin' and Swingin' and Gettin' Merry Like Christmas*—and has been praised widely for her insight and sensitivity. In addition, she is an accomplished poet, having written two touching and witty volumes entitled, *Just Give Me a Cool Drink of Water 'Fore I Diiie* and *Oh Pray My Wings are Gonna Fit Me Well.*

Miss Angelou has equally impressive credentials in the entertainment world, where she has produced, directed, and starred in *Cabaret For Freedom* in collaboration with Godfrey Cambridge at New York's Village Gate. She also starred in Jean Genet's *The Blacks* at the St. Marks Playhouse, and wrote a brilliant adaptation of Sophocles' classic work, *Ajax,* which premiered at the Mark Taper Forum in Los Angeles in 1974. Her most recent play, *And Still I Rise,* is scheduled to open on Broadway this year.

In addition, Miss Angelou wrote the original screenplay and musical score for the film *Georgia, Georgia,* and wrote and produced a ten-part television series on African traditions in American life. Not long ago, the Public Broadcasting System asked her to participate as a guest interviewer for the program *Assignment America.* In 1975, she was named "Woman of the Year" by the *Ladies' Home Journal.* She holds honorary degrees from Smith, Mills, and Lawrence University.

When I arrived at Miss Angelou's picturesque but unassuming home in Sonoma, California, I was greeted by a tall, striking figure with a deep contralto voice, a joyful laugh, and an effervescent spirit. After a bountiful lunch, which consisted of homemade quiche, pate, ham, string beans, peas and French bread (Miss Angelou is a gourmet cook and recipe-collector), we settled down in the living room amid objects of art collected from her travels all over the world, particularly African art. We drank wine produced in the Sonoma Valley, and discussed the events of her remarkable career.

Sepia: Tell us about your childhood in Stamps, Arkansas.

Angelou: The first picture that flashes in my mind was our store in Stamps. It was a glorious place. I remember the wonderful smells; the aroma of the pickle barrel, the bulging sacks of corn, the luscious, ripe fruit. You could pick up a can of snuff from North Carolina, a box of matches from Ohio, a yard of ribbon from New York. All of those places seemed terribly exotic to me. I would fantasize how people from there had actually touched those objects. It was a magnificent experience!

Sepia: Was it your mother who propelled you to excel as a youngster?

Angelou: No. My mother has had a more profound influence on me since I've been an adult than she did as a child. In fact, I've come to the conclusion that some adults are not really qualified to be parents of young children. They make much better parents of adults. My mother is that type. Today, we have a much closer relationship. She knows how to be a friend, and when to stay out of my business.

However, I felt very little positive influence from her as a child. I owe much more to my grandmother and my brother, whom I credit with saving my life—both my mental and spiritual life, as well as my breathing-in and breathing-out life.

Sepia: Was religion a major factor in your life then?

Angelou: Its importance was primarily through music. The church was a central meeting place where one could listen to and participate in the music. Actually, the first poetry I ever knew was the poetry of the gospel songs and the spirituals. I knew that blacks had written that music. I thought it was marvelous stuff! I loved the songs. I also loved the sermons. However, that God with the long hair, the One who sat on a throne in Heaven, He scared me to pieces.

But the music of the sermons inspired me then and still does today.

Sepia: Are you a religious person?

Angelou: Yes, I believe in God. I believe in whatever people call

God. I believe in life. I believe in will. I believe in good. I believe that right wins out. It may sound naive, but I believe in those things.

Sepia: Can you recall your first love?

Angelou: Yes. I think that I've been treated rather gently in my life. I was extremely fortunate to have an older brother who loved me, but who was not in love with me. We shared a very special type of love, although there was no physical or incestuous love involved. His love was a precious gift that I can hardly put into words. I was really quite blessed.

Despite the fact that I was six foot tall, and only fourteen, he kept telling me that size had nothing to do with being female. His advice kept me ready, as the Catholics say, in a state of grace. I never became rude or tough, at least not on the surface.

And so I was ready when Curly came along. I was ready to accept his gentleness; and he was very gentle. I've been very fortunate since then. My search has always been for the man who is at once strong and gentle. Curly taught me to expect kind treatment. I haven't always received it, but I certainly look for it.

Sepia: As you grew up, you had a rather traditional view of marriage. Do you still see marriage that way?

Angelou: No. I grew up with the idea that I had to be the weak person in a relationship. I thought it would be magnificent if I could be the June Allyson-type—you know, have a big house, a station wagon, and lots of kids. I would stay home, of course, and do the cooking and the cleaning. My husband would have a good job and bring home the money. He would tell me what to think and how to act. I thought that would be heaven.

I found it to be sheer hell!

I am now in the process of discovering that real love relationships, whether they involve friends or lovers, are those that are built on mutual respect. A typical marriage, or one in which one person makes compromises for the other—usually out of laziness, idleness, or greed—is the last kind that I could endure.

Sepia: How significant was being black, as you grew up?

Angelou: It was very significant. I decided many years ago to invent myself. I had obviously been invented by someone else—by a whole society—and I didn't like their invention. I just didn't. So I continued to invent myself every day.

I would have liked, of course, to be pretty, or petite, because everyone seemed to love those girls. Being black, and female, and six foot tall, I was forced to play "Momma Heavy." I didn't like that role. Therefore, I reached into my race memories to find those positive things that I could use to help myself and raise my son. I rejected those things that were negative; and not just the negative from the white community, but the negative from the black community as well. I still reject both of them. I want no part of them.

I know that many people use the term "nigger." They don't use it in my house, however. I know that some people say they use the term as an endearment. Baloney! You cannot throw a lie into a person's face and ask them to accept it as an endearment. It is still a lie. It is a statement made to demean. I reject it totally. Being black has strengthened me, and in the process I've become alienated from this type of negation. It's just not in my life. I refuse to accept it.

Sepia: Your first marriage, which came at an early age, was to a white man. Was race a problem in your relationship and subsequent divorce?

Angelou: Well, in a strange way it played a part. I began to be ashamed of my husband.

Originally, though, it didn't enter into our relationship. If anything, it drew us closer. Tosh loved me, and I became stronger thanks to his love. However, as our relationship developed, I wanted to spend more time with other people. He was a total introvert. He opposed every effort I made to make friends. He wouldn't even allow my son to play with the other children. He was a true eccentric.

At first, our relationship was marvelous. I just crawled under his umbrella for a few years and got well. I discovered later that I didn't need him anymore. He refused to change, and I couldn't stand it. But come to think of it, I would have divorced him at that point, even had he been black.

Sepia: As a young girl, you were very wary of whites. In fact, in one book you stated, "Never let white folks know what you really think. If you're sad, laugh. If you're bleeding inside, dance." Do you still feel that way?

Angelou: Yes and no. Some whites look at me, at all black people, and expect us to entertain them. My outlook really depends on my mood. Generally, I try to be courteous to everyone. I like myself better when I'm that way. I just like to be nice. If laughter will avoid a confrontation, I might laugh.

Sepia: Throughout your life, you have often expressed doubts about your own physical beauty. Did those feelings significantly affect your relationships with men?

Angelou: Yes. To begin with, if you're black and every model of beauty is either white or dark-skinned black, then it has to create some insecurity in a person like me, who couldn't possibly conform. But I was blessed with the advantage of anger. It was a kind of hauteur. I could withdraw from such plebian company and stand tall and sneer.

As I became older, and found some success in other areas, I was fortunate enough to discover that I looked all right. When I was young, however, it was awful.

Sepia: While you were growing up, you worked as a cook, a bus girl, and a waitress. How did those experiences make you feel about the value of work?

Angelou: Although I don't want to sound like a puritan, I think that hard work, especially when one likes and respects it, can be a tremendously satisfying experience. There is no pay so sweet as the accomplishment of a job well done. I know that if I was broke, I could make a decent living as a cook, or a waitress, or a dancer. I could do so without feeling that I was stepping down. That's a good feeling.

Sepia: How important is music in your life?

Angelou: I don't know what life would be like without music. In my lonely times, music has been my closest friend. It has also been my doctor—and my lover, in the sense that I sometimes listen to music and dream of a lover that doesn't exist. Late at night, when I don't feel sleepy, I'll play music—all types of music—and lose myself in its mystery. I might decide to play Stevie Wonder, or Debussy, or Tchaikovsky. It depends on my mood.

Sepia: You have danced all over the world—in Italy, France, Greece, Israel . . . Did you derive satisfaction from dancing?

Angelou: Oh, I think that I was meant to be a dancer; however, I never had an opportunity to develop my talent. There's something marvelous about writing—it frees the mind. But when you dance, you free the body as well. Suddenly, the body is lifted and born again.

Sepia: Did you enjoy performing for audiences?

Angelou: No, not particularly—but it's difficult to talk about dancing. It was so many years ago. Dancing was the only thing, other than writing, that I ever really loved. When I started, I was only fourteen. I had a child two years later, so I didn't have much time for dancing. Although I studied, it wasn't really sufficient, and I had no chance to ever become a "great" dancer. I simply didn't have the training.

But I had the heart of a great dancer. I still feel the dancing.

Sepia: Do you ever think how your life would have been different had you had the training?

Angelou: Oh, yes. I longed for it years ago. However, it wasn't given to me. I was busy living my life and raising my child.

I have a good life. I really do. I wouldn't exchange it with anyone. But when I was younger, and used to watch the great dancers perform, I would weep. I really would. I would have been a marvelous dancer.

Sepia: At a point in your life after several disappointments, you sought to enlist in the Army. Why did you decide to do that?

Angelou: Basically, I saw the Army in terms of security. I was nineteen, with a young child and a host of problems. The Army seemed like a good answer: I would sign up for a two-year hitch, save my money, and buy a house when I got out. Then I would go into something really exciting, like real estate. Oh, I could see it so clearly.

I lied like the dickens to get in. Although I wasn't caught in any of the lies, they found out that I had attended a school that was listed as a "Communist front" by the House Committee on Un-American Activities. I had studied dancing at the school at night. I didn't know whether the school was Communist or capitalist. No one ever talked to me about those two states of mind—or maybe one state of mind. When the Army rejected me, I thought I was an excellent American. I was going to really snap and salute that flag. I was going to make the whole country proud of me. It was a very disillusioning experience.

It also came at a particularly bad time. I had tried so many other things. I thought to myself, "I'll never get anywhere." It was just terrible!

Sepia: For a brief period of time, you ran a house of prostitution.

Why did you become a madam? Weren't you afraid of getting caught?

Angelou: Actually, I didn't mind running the house. I was hardly ever there. I merely came each night to collect the money. In fact, I thought I was terribly clever. After all, I had conned these two women, who had tried to exploit me, into working in the house while I made most of the money.

One night, however, I came in and saw a man there. I was stunned. It was the first time I'd ever seen one of the men. I couldn't believe how cruel the women were. So I decided to run away. I took my son and went to Arkansas.

Sepia: Several times in your autobiography, you expressed an unabashed flag-waving patriotism. Do you still feel the same about your country?

Angelou: Yes, I still love this country.

Unfortunately, patriotism has become an ugly word. It has been used and abused by flag-waving conservatives to oppose all change. They are tradition-bound, and often bound to a tradition that never did exist. When it did exist, it meant the slaughter of the Indians or the slavery of blacks.

However, I am inspired when I see this country in light of the other countries in the world. To think that this country, which was literally built upon the slaughter of human beings, still believes in the dream of "the land of the free and the home of the brave," is an incredible thing. It may take hundreds, or perhaps thousands of years to realize, but to dream it, just to dream it, is in itself an elevating experience.

Sepia: Are you interested in any political issues?

Angelou: Yes. I was always interested in fair play, probably from reading the works of Paul Dunbar, Langston Hughes, and Charles Dickens as a child. I was always concerned about justice and injustice. To the extent that I could understand the issues, I was always on the side of the underdog. I'm on the same side today.

Sepia: How do you feel about the women's movement?

Angelou: I'm involved in the movement. However, the women's movement is primarily oriented toward white American women.

That is true for several reasons. White women have been told by their men that they weren't needed. The white American male society states that it doesn't need the white woman to run its banks, build its rockets, plan its cities—only to stay in the bedroom, the nursery, and the kitchen.

Black American men have never been able to say that to black American women. While there were other problems, they at least thought of themselves as equals. In fact, one of the problems is that black women here may be more than equals: They're sassy, tough, tender, humorous, giving, and independent. White women, as a general rule, are not quite as independent.

There are, however, several important goals that the women's movement aspires to that will not only serve black and white women, but black and white men as well; these include equal pay, equal respect, equal responsibility. These things have got to make this a better country.

The women's movement has made tremendous progress, and I trust it will continue to make important inroads.

Sepia: How did you first develop an interest in literature?

Angelou: As a young girl, I read every book in the Stamps library.

At one point in my life, I had stopped speaking. I literally stopped speaking for four years. During that time, a lovely black woman came by the store and invited me to her home. When we got there, she read to me. She knew that I wouldn't speak. She read from Charles Dickens' *A Tale of Two Cities*. Her voice was like listening to a church sermon.

One day, she took me to the local school. Somehow she had a key to the side door of the library. She told me, "I want you to read. Start at 'A' and read until 'D' by the time I get back to town." And so I did.

When she came back, she said, "Now, I want you to read from 'D' until 'G.' Don't stop until you've finished all the books." And so I read every book in the library.

I didn't understand all of them, but I read them anyway. I thought I was being singled out. You can't imagine how excited I was when I saw her come down the road with a big bag of books in her hand. I knew they were for me. And so I read everything; I still do.

Sepia: Did you think about how the books got written?

Angelou: Oh, no—I thought that was pure magic. I mean, no one typed that. It was probably like a baby—God and the writer got it together and a book came out. It came from some orifice which only writers have.

Sepia: When did you decide that you had the talent to become a professional writer?

Angelou: I don't know, maybe today. When I say today, I mean that today I can say I'm a writer. I rarely say that. When I'm asked what I do, I usually say that I'm a poet or an autobiographer. I belong to writing; it doesn't belong to me.

I started to work as a writer, or live by my writing, in 1968.

Sepia: How would you assess your writing?

Angelou: I'm grateful for having been blessed with self-discipline. That means I'm not afraid to try new things. I can see, therefore, that I'm making more progress. I would love to see more.

However, I believe that I have a particular kind of brain. Some people have what I consider to be original thought. They may not be able to develop it, or care much for it, but they are able to think, as black people sometimes say, "off the wall." I don't have that kind of brain. I've accepted that fact. I have original thought, but it's only twenty per cent of the time.

I work by taking someone else's original thought and tearing it to pieces. Then I go through the methodical process of trying to remember what I've read. Once that's done, I try to think it together so that it works. I have a good mental machine. I'm grateful for it. It seems to work.

Sepia: You've been called a Renaissance person—that is, you write books, plays, essays, and poetry, as well as sing, dance, act, and direct. Doesn't that require a special kind of talent?

Angelou: No, not really. I think that we've done young people a disservice by making those things seem special. Every human being is born with talent. It's very much like electricity. Anyone can plug into it. It can be used to heat a house, or light up a cathedral, or put someone to death in the electric chair. It's all a question of how it's used.

Our society says to people, "If you're a doctor, you shouldn't love poetry," or "if you're a brickmason, you shouldn't love ballet." That kind of thinking seems to be unkind—dangerous. I don't think it's wrong to enjoy many things. That's what life is about.

It's not that I care so little about poetry, or so little about acting, or so little about directing, it's that this is my life. It's my one time as me. I want to experience everything.

Sepia: Were you surprised by the public acclaim of your autobiography?

Angelou: I was surprised at first. It was really thrilling. I'm still thrilled.

I hope I'm not becoming blase, however I expect it now. But I still get a thrill when I pass a bookstore and see one of my books in the window. It makes me feel good.

Sepia: At the request of the late Dr. Martin Luther King, Jr., you became the Northern Coordinator for the Southern Christian Leadership Conference. What were your impressions of Dr. King?

Angelou: I think that he was a magnificent spirit. He could only have happened in the United States. Although he was inspired by Mahatma Gandhi and Bertrand Russell, he was an American phenomenon. He was a great spiritual leader and an extraordinary man.

Sepia: For a period of time you lived in Africa, where you worked as a writer for several newspapers in Cairo and as a faculty member at the University of Ghana. Did you learn anything interesting yourself there?

Angelou: I learned much more in Africa than I expected. I discovered many Africanisms that I had thought were black Americanisms. In Ghana I found myself at home for the first time in my life. I had always lived such a hectic life that I was never really able to call any place home. From the time I was three until I was thirteen, people called me "Mrs. Henderson's California grandchild." Then when I came to California, I was known as "that girl from the South." When I moved to New York, I was known as "that little girl from California." Living in Ghana, it was the first time that I felt at home. I loved it!

Sepia: Has your life changed since becoming a well-known writer?

Angelou: I'm not sure. It's certainly different in the sense that I can afford to live more comfortably. But I've been fortunate to keep my friends, those I knew before I was better known. And my life hasn't changed that much in a qualitative sense. I'm living pretty much as I did five years ago. I still work hard, laugh as much as possible, and try not to cry too often.

Sepia: You live a rather secluded life in Sonoma. Why did you choose to settle in Northern California?

Angelou: I like country living. I like the ease of it. I like to live in a working community where people care about the quality of life. They take an interest in their schools. They're concerned about the environment. I like the sincerity of the local mayor. I like to have a say in how the hospital is run. I get a feeling that I'm important in the town, that I'm building something here. When you live in a community, you ought to share in that community. I want to be part of my community, and that's why I live here.

Sepia: How have you managed to maintain your own happiness in a world filled with so much sorrow?

Angelou: Well, the most honest answer is to say that whatever I've learned, I'm still in the process of learning. What has worked for me until this afternoon, may not work for me this evening. One must learn to adjust, to be flexible, to cope as well as possible.

However, I've come to certain basic conclusions in my life. I don't love life so much that I would rather live it under all circumstances. That means I won't allow any person, or any circumstances, to drive me beyond my limits. I won't allow myself to become a slave to anyone or anything.

Sepia: Your second book, *I Know Why the Caged Bird Sings,* is dedicated, "To my son, Guy Johnson, and all the strong black birds of promise who defy the odds and gods and sing their songs." What does it take to defy the odds—to make it—to win at life?

Angelou: One of the first things that a young person must internalize, deep down in the blood and bones, is the understanding that although he may encounter many defeats, he must not be defeated. If life teaches us anything, it may be that it's necessary to suffer some defeats. Look at a diamond: It is the result of extreme pressure. Less pressure, it is crystal; less than that, it's coal; and less than that, it is fossilized leaves or just plain dirt. It's necessary, therefore, to be tough enough to bite the bullet as it is shot into one's mouth, to bite it and stop it before it tears a hole in one's throat. One must learn to care for oneself first, so that one can then dare to care for someone else. That's what it takes to make the caged bird sing.

Maya Angelou

Arline Inge/1978

Bon Appetit, March 1978, 74-77. Copyright © 1978 by Bon Appetit Publishing Corporation. Reprinted with permission.

NOVEMBER 7, 1977. Her "Declaration of Sentiments" for the National Women's Conference is being carried by relay runners 2,500 miles from Seneca Falls, New York, to the opening session of the Conference in Houston, Texas. In the next two days she will fly to Washington, D.C., to be honored by the National Council of Negro Businesswomen. Then it's on to Durham, North Carolina, to scout locations for the television feature film she is writing. On her desk lie notes for her narration of a 30-part educational TV series. Three unfinished poems are "working" in the back of her mind.

But here, in the everyday suburban kitchen of her Los Angeles home on a hill above the Pacific, Maya Angelou is cooking. With the insistent joy that marked her passage from impoverished childhood to a queen of American letters, this stately woman stands in African head-tie and Givenchy T-shirt, holding back the clamor of tomorrow with a wooden spoon. She pokes the spoon into the depths of a pot of fragrant Kontumre, and inhales with satisfaction. "It's smelling very nicely." Then, offering a dab to her husband, Paul Du Feu, she tells him, "Taste."

Maya is preparing a trio of West African dishes she brought home from her years in Ghana as a journalist and educator in the early 1960s. "There, this meal takes a day to prepare," she explains, "with the children and servants peeling, seeding and chopping the tomatoes for the Jollof Rice. It takes at least two hours just to pick enough wild mustard greens for the Kontumre, another hour to wash them and another to chop them fine. But here at home, I just pick up some canned tomatoes and frozen spinach for greens, and I season with cumin and chilies in place of the native spices. It takes almost no time to put the ingredients together." Maya turns her attention to a pan of simmering peanut sauce for her golden Groundnut Stew. Now it's her turn to taste. "It's not bad, is it!"

Beaming, she unmolds the coral Jollof Rice onto a hand thrown pottery platter and arranges the chunks of tomato and onion, fried banana, avocado, papaya and pineapple in a brilliant ring of side dishes around it. "West Africans don't serve salad. These condiments and the cooked greens take its place," she explains. Between sips of chablis from a blue-stemmed glass on the counter beside her, she adds that West Africans would usually drink beer with this meal—but she will serve California wine.

White wine is Maya's delight. It also satisfies her sweet tooth. "I don't do a special dessert because I prefer wine, and besides, my guests seem to like fruit and cheeses," she says, "but in Ghana a typical dessert for this meal is pineapple fritters. The fruit is soaked in coconut milk and a little rum, dipped in the batter made from cornstarch and egg, then fried in coconut oil. A warm cream sauce of coconut milk and rum goes with it."

Maya delivers this information in the measured tones and deliberate accents of a veteran performer. She is indeed actress, singer, dancer as well as theatrical director and filmmaker, and as a distinguished visiting professor of literature, she has lectured widely in university classrooms. Her books, required reading on many campuses, include the autobiographical *Singin' and Swingin' and Gettin' Merry Like Christmas* (Random House, New York, 1976, $8.95) and her first two autobiographies, which were Book of the Month Club selections. A volume of collected poems, *Just Give Me a Cool Drink of Water 'Fore I Diiie,* was nominated for a Pulitzer prize.

As chief beneficiary of her infinite gifts, not to mention her cooking, Paul Du Feu is visibly proud of his prodigious Maya. He leads us to a small study where the walls are hung with his wife's honorary doctoral degrees from Smith College, Mills College and Lawrence University; a certificate proclaiming her a Chubb Fellow at Yale; framed parchments announcing her appointment by President Ford to the Bicentennial Council, by President Carter to the International Women's Year Commission; and her Tony Award nomination for best supporting actress for *Look Away* in 1972. (She also played the Grandmother, Nyo Boto, in *Roots.*)

Opposite this imposing display is a wall-to-wall bookcase crammed with assorted literary works. She has a collection of more than a hundred cookbooks. "I read and read and read—that's how I learned to cook—from M.F.K. Fisher, Julia Child, James Beard," she tells us upon our return to the kitchen. But once having made a recipe her own, Maya says, she goes back to measuring ingredients in the palm of her hand "like my grandmother did." And apparently it works.

Some years ago she mailed her mother a recipe from Ghana with quantities expressed in terms like "take a pinch of that and a right smart bit of this and enough of that." The dish turned out "marvelous." Maya, herself, had learned how to prepare it by watching the cook in her own West African kitchen. "The household servants (who are usually men) thought I was a freak for wanting to cook."

In other cultures, Maya's culinary fame has made her a welcome belowstairs guest. She spent November and December 1975 as a scholar-in-residence at the Rockefeller Foundation's elegant Bellagio Study and Conference Center on Lake Como, Italy.

Though the luxurious Rockefeller retreat maintained a large staff of servants to care for about thirty resident scholars, it was Maya to whom the staff turned for an authentic dressing for Thanksgiving turkey. First they asked her to write out the recipe, but since the problems of converting handfuls into grams were insurmountable, she was formally invited into the kitchen to produce a perfect American dressing before a battery of white-toqued chefs.

Paul tells us that story with relish. British born, he is an author and raconteur in his own right. He pops up to refill Maya's blue-stemmed glass "so she can get through the cooking." "He's a born maître d'," Maya calls from the stove, "always emptying ashtrays, even in other people's houses."

Paul is, in fact, a faithful *sous-chef.* His chopping knife is at the ready when extensive preparations are afoot, such as the big family celebrations in Northern California, where Maya's mother and son Guy Johnson and his family live. The guest list can number a hundred "including all the people we call aunts and uncles," Maya says. She and Paul will do all the cooking, and need extra hands only for serving.

Maya's holiday menus are unpredictable. One year as a change for Thanksgiving, she did a Brazilian *Feijoada* which she considers also "fantastic" for Easter because it incorporates the Easter ham along with sausage, white rice and beans. "And it's very pretty."

A good part of Maya's year is spent away from home on lecture tours. "Whenever we're at home," she says, "we sit down to a proper dinner." Among her specialties are Twelve-Boy Madras Curry (twelve is the number of condiments) and Chinese dishes.

As a serious cook, Maya prepares ahead. She saves chicken necks, wings and feet, freezing them until she has enough to fill her stock pot. Then one evening before settling down to television, she'll put them up to simmer. When friends call unexpectedly, there's always frozen stock ready for almost any dish. And there's fresh fruit.

"Paul often craves something sweet around 11 at night. That's why I keep fruit. I peel an apple, put it into a small pot with a little brown sugar, perhaps some cinnamon, and butter. While the apple cooks, I whip up an egg with a tablespoon or two of flour and pour out a crepe. It's easy."

Now before calling her guests to the buffet table laid with an African cloth and pewter, Maya retires to drape herself in a billowing *Grand Bou Bou,* a self-embroidered Senegalese caftan of palest lavender that whispers as she walks. Allowing the neckline to drop over one shoulder, she informs us archly, "Senegalese women are the most beautiful—and they always manage to show some shoulder. Before a party they will ask one another, 'What color are you wearing?' The mix of lavender, turquoise, orange, gold and white *Bou Bous* adds to the beauty of a West African party." Then she binds her short-cropped hair anew into a high, festive head-tie ("Hair is a sex symbol in West Africa; married women cover their heads") and swirls into the dining room with its English sideboard and African masks.

Maya has dressed for our benefit. Normally she greets her guests in what she calls "my uniform"—a floor-length skirt or flowing pants. She became accustomed to long gowns as the wife of an African diplomat 17 years ago. Pointing to her long legs she laughs. "I feel like a kid in short skirts now. I only have one in my closet." As for her guests, they may dress as they please. "If somebody turns up in jeans at my party, well . . . I wouldn't feel dishonored."

An authentic West African dinner. The hostess in Senegal silk. Is it a return to roots? Maya is shaking her head. For her, nostalgia food is "lovely Southern black cooking." "I prepare it much as I approach all food, with respect and with a tenderness for the people who will consume it. Southern black cooks had to deal with the parts of the hog and the cow that other people threw out, the entrails and feet, for instance.

"And they were successful, so successful that black Americans, even two or three generations removed from poverty, still treat themselves to soul food. When I go to Houston I will stay with the great black American painter John Biggers. I phoned to tell him I was coming and he said, 'I know—you want my wife to cook some greens.' And she'll cook mustard and turnip for me and we'll have a lovely meal of greens and probably spoon bread. That's exotic to me now."

Southern black food, as admirers of Maya Angelou's lyric prose well know, is woven into the fabric of her earliest memories. As a child, she, with her brother Bailey, helped tend her grandmother's general store in the dusty cotton town of Stamps, Arkansas.

"Weighing the half-pounds of flour, excluding the scoops and depositing them dust-free into the thin paper sacks held a simple kind of adventure for me. I developed an eye for measuring how full a silver-looking ladle of flour, mash, meal, sugar or corn had to be to push the scale indicator over to eight ounces or a pound. . . . If I was off in the store's favor, the eagle-eyed woman would say, 'Put some more in that sack, child. Don't you try to make your profit offa me.'

"Then I would quietly but persistently punish myself. For every bad judgment, the fine was no silver-wrapped Kisses, the sweet chocolate drops that I loved more than anything in the world, except Bailey. And maybe canned pineapples. . . .

"Momma used the juice to make almost-black fruit cakes. Then she lined heavy soot-encrusted iron skillets with the pineapple rings for rich upside-down cakes. Bailey and I received one slice each, and I carried mine around for hours shredding off the fruit until nothing was left except the perfume on my fingers. . . . "—*I Know Why the Caged Bird Sings* by Maya Angelou

An Interview with Maya Angelou

Dorothy Randall-Tsuruta/1980

Ambrosia, October 1980, 3-8.

Visible only from shoulders up, Maya Angelou, leaning out from the practically opened back door of her hillside home, calls out to me as I trek along the pebble path which runs parallel to the shrubbery from the rear carport to the front door. A motorist, cruising that scenic Oakland neighborhood on a Saturday sightseeing or house hunting jaunt, might easily register the sight of the two of us as the human complement to an idyllic setting. While in truth ours is no routine garden visit, the neighborliness of our backyard meeting could have inspired a painter with euphoric impressions. Upon introducing myself to her, Ms. Angelou directs me to continue on to the front door. She closes the back door, still inside the house, and proceeds to meet me at the front threshold. To the eye of someone passing by, she could be identified as the lady of the house—and I, perhaps, as a next door neighbor come to borrow a cup of sugar. Only next door is San Francisco, and the cup of sugar, an interview with Maya Angelou.

With a gracious spontaneity, she consents to my request to invite my husband, Kaz, who waits in the car with camera equipment, to join us for the purpose of photographing her. In the ease with which she establishes rapport with the camera and questions, she accommodates us in our effort to capture her and her views which penetrate issues crucial to Black Americans.

She leaves us to set up in the living room. When she returns seconds later, she explains that as we pulled up in the car, she was on the phone in the kitchen and thus had noticed our approach from that entrance. Her air is casual and comfortable. She wears no make-up, and her hair is tucked under a print headwrap. Her knit pullover and floor length skirt are of brown and tan earth colors. All about her countenance encourages an eager eye and ear to expand as called to attention.

Before we begin, she conducts a swift and unsuccessul search for cigarettes, then waves off immediate hopes of finding them. Upon assuming seats in the living room chairs situated just opposite, but facing each other, we settle into the business of the interview. I explain that the theme of an upcoming issue of *Ambrosia* is the Black family, and that the editorial staff felt that her understanding of the Black family—as gleaned from reading her autobiographical novels and her poetry—could direct minds to reexamine what family really means. Then turning to notes based on essences of relationships discerned in *Gather Together in My Name,* I commence with questions:

D.T.: You mention in *Gather Together* that since you were not Daddy Clidell's blood daughter, your child was his grandchild only so long as the union between him and your mother held fast. Is that one way in which the mind accounts for stepparents?

Maya: Stepfathers—ideally—are part of the extended family; however, human beings rarely experience the ideal. In the Black family landscape, everyone is available and useable—family members, church members, small store owners, teachers—everyone is grist for the mill.

(Then, noticeably pensive and with a touch of sadness)

It is a tragedy that we have become so Anglicized, so gentrified; we are losing fast the very material that held us together as a nation within a nation—that's really unfortunate: we've lost the cohesive.

With that said, she rises again in search of the cigarettes. As she excuses herself and walks calmly back to the kitchen, I am impressed with the way her movements *do not* suggest that she is pressed for a cigarette. There is a naturalness about her bearing that one senses could be drawn upon to mitigate life's discomforts.

After disappearing into the kitchen, Ms. Angelou calls out that she has found the cigarettes. Momentarily she reappears in the hallway, and offers us tea. We accept. To maximize our time with her, but more importantly, to get to know her, in as hang-loose a fashion as possible. We propose to join her in the kitchen as she prepares the tea. She consents with a gentleness that captures our spirits in harmony with her own. Yet there is a unique strength to her gentleness. It is the same self-will unveiled in her works. Relocated, I continue

with a question built on her comment about the "cohesive" that has
held Black people in a family mold.

D.T.: Could you describe the cohesive in terms of qualities?

Maya: That quality can be seen in a relationship I shared with a
woman who was my very first adult friend. We helped each other in
raising our children.

D.T.: In what ways?

Maya: The way friends do!

(Pause)

We were both about 20 . . . I guess 21 when we met. She had a
daughter and I had a son. If her daughter had teeth problems, and
she had no money, I'd see to her getting her teeth taken care of. If
my son needed glasses—he lost his glasses often—and I had no
money, she would see to his getting new ones. So in many ways, we
were sisters.

Upon that answer, and with the tea now ready, we turn back to the
spacious living room. There Ms. Angelou serves us delicious helpings
of English tea. Resettled in our thinking chairs, we let the tea ease
though in a refreshing aromatic break. After a bit I start in again with
questions:

D.T.: In your books you write about your relationship with your
blood brother. For instance in *Gather Together* you describe how
your brother came to your rescue after Curly's exit from your life. Do
you think it likely that you benefitted from your brother's masculine
strength—the way some women with brothers seem to distinguish
themselves compared to some women without brothers?

Maya: In *I Know Why the Caged Bird Sings* I describe my
relationship with my brother. We spent our young lives together. I
credit him with whatever sanity I have. He was a wonder as a brother.
He was funny and bright . . . he said that I was very beautiful.

D.T.: Hum . . . nice. What about extended family?

Maya: You know that until the age of 13, I was raised by my
grandmother and Uncle Willie. But the people around us also helped
raise us. They watched us when we were out of the house. They
knew that Mamma was getting up in age and Uncle Willie could not
get around easily, so they watched us and reported our actions to
Mamma and Uncle Willie.

D.T.: When you return to your grandmother and Uncle Willie in

Stamps after about 5 years' absence, you run into a childhood acquaintance, L.C. He tells you how his dad drinks up the food money, and that your grandmother knows about it and lets them run up credit at her store. Does her participation in his life attest to the reciprocal nature of the extended family?

Maya: Yes. Just as others helped raise my brother and myself, she helped raise L.C. (whose mother died when he was young).

D.T.: What about your family life in San Francisco?

Maya: Bailey and I lived with my mother and stepfather for three years.

D.T.: During the years when you were 13 through 17?

Maya: Yes, then we went out on our own.

D.T.: Was there any extended family in San Francisco, outside the home, such as there was in Stamps?

Maya: Oh yes. In San Francisco there were aunts and uncles— there were friends of my mother. They were observant.

D.T.: Did they, in their role as extended family, encompass any of the qualities of your grandmother?

Maya: No. My grandmother was rural and very devout. These people were worldly. (Pause) There was one aunt [in San Francisco] who is still very close. She's still my Aunt Bert. My brother and I used to say, 'she's gold plated!' And she's still gold plated.

(Pause—sipping tea)

The importance of familial love and responsibility can be under- stood when one experiences defeat. One may encounter many defeats but may not be defeated. It is important that one encounters defeat—in order to best oneself. It demands precision in order to develop the brilliance of a diamond . . . a steadfast family helps.

D.T.: Are you speaking of blood family?

Maya: I never mean blood family because they can be most exasperating.

D.T.: Yeah!

Maya: I've just written a movie script that deals with the Black family. It will come out in the Fall, and will star Diahann Carroll, Roselyn Cash, Paul Winfield, and Robert Hooks. In the film I look at the Black family. I look at how you can develop relationships that are stronger than family. Friendship is what's important. It is what you look for in a love affair, in a marriage.

D.T.: And you are concerned with this in your work.

Maya: In my work I'm trying to show the development of a mind's impact upon the world. I'm trying to show that particular linear connection in my work. When writing about the past, you have to enchant yourself—yes, that's the word, 'enchant' yourself back to that time. When I write about how I felt at 12, I have to feel as I did then, not as I feel today at 50, but as I felt at 12!

And then to write. . . .

D.T.: (Sigh) Ms. Angelou, you spoke of a female friend with whom you shared an extended family relationship, what about males? Please comment on the brothers that make up part of your extended family.

Ms. Angelou picks up my copy of *Gather Together* and reads the inscription,

Maya: "This book is dedicated to my blood brother, Bailey Johnson, and to the other real brothers who encouraged me to be bodacious enough to invent my own life daily: James Baldwin, Kwesi Brew, David Du Bois, Samuel Floyd, John O. Killens, Vagabond King, Leo Maitland, Vusumzi Make, Julian Mayfield, and Max Roach."

D.T.: Will you share a glimpse of the role they played in your life?

Maya: These brothers helped me in many ways. They helped me raise my son. They were constantly at the end of the telephone. I could call Max at two in the morning. James Baldwin would meet me in the street if necessary. I had a son who I wanted to grow up healthy in a weak society.

D.T.: Hum . . . yes!

Maya: They advised me on how much allowance he should have, although he had his own job. (That last she adds with parental pride.)

D.T.: And your other brothers?

Maya: All of them took responsibility. Kwesi Brew, a Ghanian Ambassador and a great poet, was a brother of mine who took responsibility. He defended me and protected me in many foreign countries. When he was told that after all I was not a Ghanian citizen and could not come under Ghanian protection, he replied, "She may not be a Ghanian, but she is a sister."

Apparently holding onto the thought, Ms. Angelou gazes sentiently out of the engulfing picture window that separates us from fawning trees. She seems embraced by the gentle touch of kind memories.

And she has a way of taking you into her reveries: a pinch of content, a hint at the sentiment, and you are with her in mood and sensitivity. You grasp her strongholds in life. Now she focuses back on my last question, this time speaking of her ex-husband, Vusumzi Make.

Maya: Vusumzi Make was my brother/lover. He is South African.

D.T.: Did you live in South Africa?

Maya: Oh no! We lived in the United States and Europe.

D.T.: (Pause)

Maya: David Du Bois is another one of my brothers. He is always there in critical moments. He is still courageous and supportive. He is never afraid to tell me when I'm wrong—never reluctant to give me compliments.

Now Ms. Angelou relaxes in her chair. An hour has passed. We become mindful of the time. I put away my paper and pen to signal that I'll not stretch the hour, however tempting it may be to do so. As I close up, Ms. Angelou leans forward, thoughtfully, with some parting conversation now that the official interview is over. She shares how she has spent the day up until our arrival. After returning home from work (writing) she enjoyed a phone call with a friend, and gave some thought to exploring antique shops.

And then, almost as an epilogue to the interview, she recalls a "hair trigger" friend she'd not mentioned before. She laughs roundly as though wholeheartedly amused just thinking of him. She says, "He is the friend that will call at 4 a.m. for help out of one jam or another— always promising that it won't happen again." She explains that she and Hair Trigger have been friends since 1959 and in fact just yesterday had a long phone conversation. Then elaborating she states, "The calls in the early morning reveal just one side of him . . . he's kind, brave, and loyal."

I relax again in my chair. I tell her that as we've talked I've felt the presence of close friends dear to my own life. We nod our heads at the same instant as though bent upon a common conjecture. We exchange thoughts on the importance of blood ties, and extended family. Then lightheartedly, Ms. Angelou quips, "Just as I have brother/friends, I also have sister/friends." I hastily reclaim my paper and pen from my purse, then query for a final note.

D.T.: Even with your writing schedule, you are able to visit with your friends?

Maya: Just yesterday I had lunch with my sisters Ruth Love and

Jessica Mitford-Treuhaft. I also see friends at church . . . friends who love me and who I love.

D.T.: Does the number of friends increase the responsibility?

Maya: The size of the family does not determine the amount of stress; the nature of the people involved does.

D.T.: You are available to your family and friends?

Maya: I make an excellent aunt, sister, daughter; I'm not perfect, but I'm pretty good.

She smiles at that. Then, as though hit upon an understanding, Ms. Angelou, almost wistfully, concludes: "While a number of people bemoan the passing of an extended family, many of them are not prepared to accept the responsibility."

Maya Angelou: Resolving the Past, Embracing the Future

Esther Hill/1981

The Student, Spring 1981, 6-9. Reprinted by courtesy of The Student Literary Magazine, Wake Forest University, Winston-Salem, North Carolina.

In 1931, two small children, ages three and four, were delivered like packages to their grandmother in Stamps, Arkansas. Tags around their wrists addressed "to whom it may concern" listed their names, address, and destination. After their parents' divorce, the children were shipped from Long Beach, California to the small southern town, where they soon blended into its quiet life. Maya Angelou vividly recalls that arrival in Stamps in her first autobiographical book, *I Know Why The Caged Bird Sings*. Her life has carried her far beyond the Arkansas of her childhood. Ms. Angelou, now an internationally known writer, recently returned to Stamps with Bill Moyers as the subject of a television special. As part of the filming, Ms. Angelou also visited Winston-Salem where she sat in on a question and answer session with Wake Forest students. While here, she granted *The Student* this interview.

Student: In a *New York Times* article you said, "No man can know where he is going unless he knows exactly where he has been and exactly how he arrived at his present place." You were speaking of history, but would you say that in your life writing has been this defining process for you?

Angelou: Yes, it has. Sometimes I've been conscious of the learning, or relearning. Sometimes the process is so subtle that it's only maybe a year after I finish a book that I have a realization of this learning. Something happened that was quite strange on this trip with Bill Moyers. I remember Stamps, Arkansas, as tiny and closed-in, mean, with very little natural beauty, except the changing seasons.

But all my life I have loved a softly rolling landscape, and any time my husband started to build a fine house for me, he looked for that softly rolling landscape. I appreciate and admire the harshness of mountains and the sound of the sea, but my heart sings when I see the hills, whether it's in England, California, or Italy. It so pleases me that I've asked my husband and my son that should I become really ill, terminally ill, at any time, please get me out of the hospital and take me to some place where I can see the rolling hills. Two weeks ago, when I drove from Texarkana into Stamps, there were the hills. I had grown up around them and had no remembrance of them. If anyone had ever told me before two weeks ago that there were rolling hills around Stamps, I would have said it's flat and tight and mean. So, in the process of this filming, I found out how I reached this particular preference for that particular topography. It was the first I ever saw and I must have liked it, but it's something I had totally forgotten. So now it will compound my loving of that look, that vision. So in subtle ways, writing these books helps me to find out where I'm coming from.

Student: In your writing there's a distinctive rhythm; how did you find this? Was it from the speech patterns you picked up from your family in Stamps? Or do you think it was an innate sense?

Angelou: I don't know. I listen for rhythm; I don't know why I do. But every situation has a rhythm or rhythms. Cocktail parties, for example. There are sultry flirtations in one corner which are legato, and intellectual arguments around a table which may be adagio. Old friends remembering an old, really sad story, this may be lento or grave. I listen for them, no matter what I'm writing about. I listen for the most pronounced rhythm, and I think I find it. But first I write everything I know about the subject. And then I try to enchant myself into that particular situation I want to write about, just cover myself in it, and keep listening for the rhythm. Then, when I am satisfied with what I've done, I make the content clear. So the rhythm is first in my stories, in the poetry, always.

Student: In the interview for the Bill Moyers special, you spoke of your particular ritual when writing. Could you describe that?

Angelou: Well, I don't like to have any clothes touching me, so I wear voluminous things, some flannel gowns. Anyway, they don't intrude, they just hang about. I used to wear hats, then head ties for a number of years. I still have those, and sometimes I like to tie them nice and tight—I guess to keep my brains in. I work in longhand. I can't seem to work on a typewriter; the words don't look right. I just got a scrapbook which an old man in Arkansas presented to me on this trip. He said I did it when I was nine years old. It was marvelous. But the handwriting has not qualitatively changed since then. When I read one of the pieces, I thought, nor has my style of writing very much.

Ms. Angelou slowly turned the pages of the scrapbook and laughed at the occasionally inept phrases of her nine-year-old self. This was one of the better memories in a strangely mixed assortment of good and bad. Her memories of childhood include both the violence of rape and the strong, protective love of her family. After the brutality of being raped when she was eight years old, Ms. Angelou withdrew into silence for a time, speaking only when necessary. Her family's love and acceptance, along with an increasing interest in reading literature and writing, helped her surmount this difficult period.

Student: So this was a type of journal?

Angelou: Yes, it was from the time I didn't talk. I was given a B−, and I understand why. Since the other students would talk to supplement their reports orally, mine had to be the best, with photographs and all sorts of things. But this certainly couldn't have been written past the time I was ten. [*She reads:*]

Such jolting, rumbling, squeaking and creaking! Such ringing of cowbells as the cattle plodded along! And dust—dust so thick that your mouth was full of grit, your ears were—oh, very dirty, and your hair was powdered with the reddish Arkansas dust. The sun was hot and the sweat was streaming down your face streaking through the grime. But you were happy, for you were on a great adventure. You and your father and mother, brothers and sisters, and many of your neighbors were moving from your old home in the East. You were going to settle on some of the rich land in Arkansas. And you were going there not on a train of railroad cars—there weren't any—but in a train of covered wagons, pulled by strong oxen.

Student: That's very good.

Angelou: The actual script has not changed a lot, and I do like the way words look on a page.

Student: When did you actually begin to write?

Angelou: I started writing when I was about nine, because I wasn't able to talk. It was my way of keeping in touch, I guess. And I loved poetry, oh my dear, I just loved it. I must have been the most tiresome kind of child—you know, not talking, and weeping over poetry, which I half understood at that. I just think I must have been a nuisance! Grandmother was very good about it. And people in Stamps said that they'd walk into Grandmother's store, and if I was tending it, that I was always reading or writing. Sometimes they'd have to rap real hard on the glass counter, and then I would do their business. I wasn't purposely trying to ignore them.

Student: In an interview you said you think it is possible to lead a poetic life. Have you?

Angelou: I try. Leading a poetic life for me means being existential, to the extent that any human can be responsible. By this, I mean being immediate. I have set aside in this day an hour for you. All my equipment is here, everything I know, everything I dream, all my wishes, all my fears, my losses, defeats, are here and available to you. *That* to me is being immediate, and that is being poetic: to take responsibility for *each* moment. To accept no man-made or human-made barriers between human beings is poetic, to absolutely refuse to accept barriers because of history's tragedies or assaults, because of differences in languages or customs, age or race. Brick masons can lead poetic lives; clergymen, nurses, doctors, domestics can. I try to also write poetry, which adds to it. To be aware of the imminence of death as one lives with a great love for life is to be poetic. Not to be so in love with life that you will live it at any cost, but to love it, not to be in love with it.

Student: And laugh a lot?

Angelou: Absolutely. Laugh a lot, absolutely. External events, colleagues, associates, friends, and hostile forces will bring enough to cry about. So as often as possible laugh, and hug somebody.

Student: Who are your heroes? You said once, "Everyone lives in relation to their heroes."

Angelou: And she-roes!

Student: Yes, she-roes.

Angelou: There are so many, some living and some dead. I admire courageous people who have the courage to live and to laugh and be tender. People who have the courage to control the element in all of us which is destructive, which strives for utter chaos. We all have that demon in us. I admire people who have the courage to struggle daily to control that demon. Certainly the world may deserve it, but a person does not have the right to let it loose. I admire those who don't take themselves too seriously—who don't go around as if they put glue on the back of their hands and pasted them to their forehead. [*She places her hand on her forehead in an attitude of mock despair.*] I've never trusted those ones. Serious people want to survive, and realize that in order to do so they have to have some humor in their lives, some warmth in their lives, and some giving. I can't name any particular heroes.

Student: Have you ever played the dinner party game? If you could invite any three people from any age, past or present, whom would you invite?

Angelou: Again, that's hard. I can't do it with just three. I'd just throw away the dinner party: I wouldn't have it. I could fill a table . . .

Student: Who are some people you might invite? I'm curious.

Angelou: Well, my grandmother, for her gentle strength and perseverance. My mother for perseverance and wit and loyalty. Paul Laurence Dunbar for poetry, along with Joseph Johnson, Edna St. Vincent Millay, and Shakespeare. I would invite Frederick Douglass for his grandiose grandeur and magnificent generosity. The only living person I would have is my mother. For all the other living people I'd just have to have a ballroom. There are so many marvelous, powerful people. James Baldwin would have to be there, Dolly McPherson, my husband . . . the list goes on and on.

Student: What would you say has been your most fulfilling work? This could include not only your work as a writer, but also your work in theater, film, and public service.

Angelou: Well, my writing. I think *Gather Together in My Name* was the most painful and hardest writing, and I think the best one. It was a hard story to tell dramatically without melodrama. Some of the poetry, some music. But the writing, that's where I'm gratified. Other things which I do please me and I'm grateful for them, grateful to have the chance to do them and that they turn out all right. But in my heart, I'm gratified most by the writing.

Student: How do you choose the next work? You have something to say and . . .

Angelou: Sometimes work chooses you. You don't know it at the time maybe. If something bears on my mind, I may write a poem. Then if it still bears on my mind, I'll look around and see if I want to do an article for a newspaper or a magazine. And if it *still* bears on my mind, I might have to write a short story. At present I'm not thinking of doing anything since I finished my book yesterday.

Student: Congratulations.

Angelou: Thank you. I'm not going to do anything, I say this, for months, maybe years. I'll probably be working in two weeks.

Interview: Maya Angelou

Judith Paterson/1982

From *Vogue*, September 1982. Copyright © 1982 by The Conde Nast Publications, Inc.

Editor's note: Maya Angelou is a woman who creates her own force field: A writer (her four autobiographical novels include *I Know Why the Caged Bird Sings* and, most recently, *The Heart of a Woman*, published by Random House), an actress, and a political activist. Here, Maya Angelou speaks out—in a voice alternately soothing and razor sharp—on courage, spirit, surviving and thriving now. . . .

Judith Paterson: I have often taught *I Know Why the Caged Bird Sings* in Women's Studies courses and been an admirer of yours for a long time. I guess you hear that a lot these days.

Maya Angelou: Never enough.

JP: Never enough?

MA: No, never enough admiration. *Never.*

JP: When Southern white women like myself read your books, we identify with you as women and at the same time feel guilty because of the racial history we share. We have been the enemy. You have said that black women and white women have different struggles. Could you elaborate on that?

MA: As I see it today, all the struggles are one. The armaments we use and the battle arenas for black women and white women are different. The struggle, I hope, is to make this country a better place for everybody. And one has to start at home, like charity. You know, make it better for your own self and, once you do that, automatically life is better for everyone—in a very oblique way. But once one's own struggle is enjoined—and maybe overcome—then one can get about the business of struggling other people's struggles. Frederick Douglass says, "He who is struck must *himself* cry out."

But white women and black women are basically very different, and we're different because of our histories. One of the things I see about white women is that their husbands, and fathers, and brothers, and sons, nephews, uncles, and male lovers have told them, either implicitly or explicitly, that they really aren't very important—except in the kitchen, the bedroom, the nursery, and maybe in elementary schools. White fathers, uncles, nephews . . . have shown white women that they can run their countries without them—run entire societies, go to the moon, philosophize without them.

Black women have never been in that position. While the white men in the society say the same thing to black women—and worse— at least the people who are saying those things to us are not our uncles and fathers and brothers and sons. In the black community, black women are very important.

JP: In what ways?

MA: We support the church and all the social organizations. The ministers and the presidents of universities and the principals of high schools, they have to have our support. Nobody wants to anger the black American woman. No black man—I mean *en masse*; that's where he gets his support. We look after the children and not only our own; we have had the strength to nurse a nation of strangers and look after white folks' children as well, and still have some pizzazz left. Style! But I think that one of the reasons we have so much style— such insouciance—is just that. The men in our lives have *not* rendered us negligible.

Given the burden of work, when it's not a joy, having to work sometimes at very lean jobs—everything from picking cotton to picking up somebody's dirty drawers—given sometimes very lonely homes—husbands gone, fathers gone—we have, as a group, not turned into a bunch of whiners. Black women seldom whine. *Rage*, yes, but very seldom *whine*. And I don't mean to say that makes us superwomen, because nobody wants us to be too much. Everybody wants us to be enough. But it makes us "other." And black mothers expect so much of their daughters, you know. Mothers and daughters in black families remain quite close. And we do not, as a rule, blame our mothers for society.

JP: I can't help comparing the optimism and energy of your biography with the sometimes self-pitying, self-indulgent tone of the white feminist writers of the early 1970s, Erica Jong, Marilyn French, Gail Parent, Sue Kaufman, all the "Mad Housewives." Of course, the best have moved beyond that. Erica Jong's *Fanny* is a marvelous, robust, funny book.

MA: Yes, it is. Wonderful. But I know. . . . Well, I don't want to imply that I, or black women, don't cry bitter tears and as Georgia Johnson said "beat against the bars at night." That is where the title of my new book comes from. A black poet, Georgia Douglas Johnson, who lived here in Washington, whose son, quite aged now, still lives here, wrote a poem called "The Heart of a Woman." She says: "The heart of a woman goes forth with the dawn, as a lone bird, soft winging, so restlessly on . . . The heart of a woman falls back in the night and enters some alien cage in it plight, and tries to forget it has dreamed of the stars while it breaks, breaks, breaks on the sheltering bars." Well I mean, they *all* do.

And maybe leisure affords people time to be introspective and reflective. Usually, black women haven't that kind of time for looking at what seem to me to be the smaller issues in life. If the woods are on fire, you don't worry if your slip is showing. You know, you just don't have time. We are being assailed and assaulted on every level *all* the time.

Our beauty even is not the beauty of the society. Our features are different; our bodies, in fact, are different. Black women are obliged, unless they can sew or have somebody sew for them, to wear clothes that are really designed for the white female frame, which usually does not have that rising behind, or the high calves, the small waist and the wide hips. You understand?

JP: I do. I hadn't thought of it. . . .

MA: Those are small issues, but they're issues. Take makeup. Just in the last ten years have they started selling makeup for black skin— all those shades, "cinnamon," "toast," "nutmeg," "licorice"—all those beautiful colors. Black women had to use white powder before, and the darkest white powder usually was "suntan." On our skin, some of us, that's as light as talcum powder. Those small issues mean something. But the larger issues are getting a job, being able to eat and sleep, trying to raise children, trying to keep peace and love in a home, and meanwhile maintain those strong relationships in families, so that if all hell breaks loose, you always have somebody. And hell is threatening to break loose *every minute* for the black American. So . . .

JP: But you sound so . . . what is it, optimistic, in your books. There is such gusto.

MA: Right. It *is* optimism and it's right there before this book. There is a spiritual that says: "Through many thousand toils and snares I have *already* come." I mean—there it is.

JP: That brings me to a question about endurance. When my daughter, Beth, was sixteen, she read *Caged Bird* and reduced her admiration to one word—*guts*—said like that—*GUTS*. The guts to strike out on your own, to bear, love, raise, and support a child when you were just sixteen yourself, and not just to try it, either, but to succeed at it. I think of words like "courage" and "prowess," but the black survivor and the black artist have often been saddled with Faulkner's label, "enduring." How do you react to the difference between "prowess" and "endurance"?

MA: Well, there's nothing noble in enduring pain, just enduring. I'd better not say that; no, I don't mean that. But the human being is not at his or her best when he or she simply endures. Still, it is important, at a stage, to endure so you can overcome. Surviving is important, but thriving is *elegant.* So there are few things that can really stand against gusto, very few things, very few people. It's a wonderful word; I hadn't thought of it in a long time until you mentioned it. If you enter a room of hostile strangers with gusto, there are few who can contain, preserve, their hostility. First, what they see, not consciously maybe—but sense—is something that is really in them. And maybe they put it behind their kneecap. But it's there, and it speaks immediately to the gusto in other people.

I appreciate your saying "prowess"; I have learned to do a number of things I didn't know how to do. I think I did approach every challenge wth gusto—actually. I know there are the documents in some library to teach me to design the Lincoln Center if I wanted to. They were created by human beings and are being preserved by human beings and I'm a human being. We have allowed ourselves, I think, too much laxity in the use of our brains. The brain will do anything. If we are not physically handicapped, we can do the most wonderful things. We can do almost anything.

You know, I never expected to live very long; I never did. I really

thought I was going to die at twenty-eight, but I expected to be a
very successful real estate broker before I died. Honest to God!

JP: Why in the world did you expect to die so young?

MA: I have no idea, but I always thought it. I'm always, anyway,
prepared for it. Or I *think* I am. But until that time, I will not allow
*any*body to minimize my life, not *anybody*, not a living soul—
nobody, no lover, no mother, no son, no boss, no President, nobody.
I have to *die* by myself! I mean, if somebody came along and said: "If
you don't do this, we will do this" and if I capitulated, when it came
to drawing that last breath—alone—I wouldn't be ready to do it.

JP: When did you begin to realize all that?

MA: A long time ago. I know that most restrictions are set up by
somebody else at their whim and for their convenience. I think I must
have been very young when I first understood that.

It happens in jobs. I think if one has a job where the employer or
boss or the job itself really gives nothing, you just have to throw it in.
Or what? Crawl and eke out some miserable existence where you
become mean because the situation is mean. You become mean and
narrow and small to your children and friends and lovers. I'd rather
be dead. And try to the next time around. You see?

JP: Strong women have obviously been very important in your
life—teachers, mentors, but especially your powerful grandmother
and, of course, your mother. How did they influence you?

MA: My mother, really, she is remarkable. I was just thinking about
phoning her. She called yesterday.

When I was twenty, she told me I was a great woman. Now, she
was very pretty and had money and was about 5'4" tall. I was six
feet. At the time I had a job in a record shop and another in a diner—
they called it a dinette—as a waitress, trying to make ends meet
because I wouldn't take money from her. I mean I *couldn't*. I was a
woman; I had a son. We walked down the street, down Fulton Street.
I'll never forget it. There was a mayonnaise and pickle factory nearby.
I still remember that smell. And she said: "Baby, let me tell you
something. I think you are the greatest woman I have ever met." I'm
still amazed and I can still cry over it. So I asked her why she said
that. She said: "Because you are intelligent and merciful. Those two
things don't often go together." I walked across the street and got on
the bus *in shock*. And I thought, she's not a liar; she's much too fierce

to lie. She's intelligent, so maybe she sees something, maybe, just maybe. . . .

She called me yesterday in New York, and she said, "Now, I will come to you anywhere. I hope you aren't overdoing it." I said, "I'm not." She said: "Because, Baby, we have cemeteries filled with dead heroes. And our people need you alive. Now I will come, and you know it." I said: "Yes, Ma'am." [*laughs*] And you know—always around her all my friends who know me in other circumstances. . . . They can't believe it. You know?

JP: The "Yes, Ma'am" says it all.

MA: Right! And I remember years ago. I was doing a film in Sweden. I was having trouble with the actors, and the director was playing the fool. I composed the score and had to use the Swedish radio orchestra director, who kept telling me it was impossible to do what I wanted to do with the music. And I *hear* the music, but I'm not trained in music. I begged him: "Please just play it. I've sung all the parts one at a time, and I know it works, please play it." I was having a horrible time. So I called my mother. She was on the beach, and that is home for two months. I told her: "I need some mothering. I'm going to send you a check today and as soon as you get it, come to Sweden." She said: "Well, Baby, I'll have the postman hold my mail; because I suppose when I return, your check will be in it. But if anything is leaving for Sweden today, you can pick me up at the airport tomorrow. You just go to the airport tomorrow to meet me." I said: "Yes Ma'am." So I went to the airport that night and sat in the bar and drank. At about nine o'clock I met her and I just, oh, cried. She always takes me in her lap, as little as she is. I just get in her lap and melt.

I said: "Let me get your bags." And she said: "No, you take me to the bar. I think you know where it is; take me to the bar." She said: "I'll have a drink, my baby will have a drink, and give everybody in this place a drink." Then she said: "Baby, Mother came to Stockholm to tell you one thing—a cow needs a tail for more than one season." I was drunk and tired and I thought: "What the hell: I've spent all this money to get this obscure advice." She said: "Well, the cow that thinks because summer is over, it can drop off its least needed and most laughed at part and stomp on it, is a fool; because if it lives, spring will come and the flies will be back, and it will want nothing so much as that very tail." She said: "Now, they're treating you like a cow's tail. You do your work. If they live, they will be back to you."

I tell you, it was prophetic. Diana Sands was the star. She died. Sometime later my husband, Paul, and James Baldwin and I were in a restaurant not far from Lincoln Center. And in trooped those same actors—I mean like *snaking* around our table. Well, usually when people see Jimmy and me together, they go to Jimmy. And he not only is a great artist and all that, he's also very generous about setting people up in booths, and ordering drinks, and picking up the tab. So I was prepared for them to surround him. And they said: "Hello, Jimmy. Lovely performance tonight." And then they were all over me. And I was right back in that bar on the second floor of the Stockholm airport. And I saw my mother standing there saying: "If they live. . . ."

JP: Your mother really comes across powerfully in the books. I admire the relationship between the two of you all the way through. The way she was able to reestablish you and your brother in a family after all those years you spent in Arkansas with your grandmother is remarkable.

MA: Well, she was a poor mother for a child. She didn't know what to do with kids, except feed us and things like that. She and my stepfather taught us to play cards, which was very important. And when my son was about five or six, we taught him to play pinochle, whist, bridge. You know, it is marvelous for the brain.

JP: It seems to me that the most important black writers these days are women, people like you, Toni Morrison, Alice Walker. Is that true?

MA: I think things go in cycles. There was a time when there were just black men writers. One read Ralph Ellison, James Baldwin, John Killens, Julian Mayfield, you know. Julius Lester. And then there are periods like now, which is certainly not to say that there are not some wonderful male writers. And this too is a wave, and there'll come waves of black male writers again. I pray so. I know they're out there, because I read bits of manuscripts from time to time. It's very hard to sustain oneself as a writer, though. You usually have to lecture or take a post at a university, and that immediately cuts down on the time one needs to write.

JP: You are doing that at Wake Forest University, I understand.

MA: I am. I've taken the chair for one semester a year until 1985, so that gives me the spring and summer to write.

JP: That sounds ideal.

MA: I think so. You can be sure that Mr. Baldwin is writing. And he's been posturing to me about being the aged writer of the group and all that. But I won't hear it. He's fifty-seven. Nothing! Year before last he had *Just Above My Head*. He continues to turn out the work, which is very inspiring to me. I hope inspiring to a lot of other people, too, writers, because he does essays, novels, short fiction, plays. . . .

JP: But you can't speculate about why black women seem to be in the forefront now?

MA: No, I can't.

JP: Themes of relationships run through all your books—relationships between parents and children, men and women, blacks and whites. You seem to get things worked out between the generations. But where are we now, all of us, in terms of the other two—the sexes and the races?

MA: Let's take love first, romantic love, erotic love. I think there is a cynicism in the world now, in the air we breathe. We breathe in cynicism and exhale cynicism. Too many of us do. And that puts a terrible, high barrier between the giving and accepting of love. And by cynicism, I don't mean that condition of the lover frustrated. I don't mean that, I mean true cynicism—lack of belief, lack of trust.

I find more and more people, either meaning love and talking about sex, or meaning sex and talking about love. That's unfortunate. Not just erroneous, but unfortunate.

JP: Some people are accusing the Women's Movement of causing a breakdown in the relationship between men and women.

MA: If what they mean is that the Women's Movement has done in those old out-of-balance, destructive, stultifying, suffocating relationships, we should herald that, because they weren't working. Nature abhors imbalance and will not live with it very long. And all one has to do is see that 90 percent of all the species that have lived on this little glob of spit and sand have become extinct, because they got out of balance. So, I mean, it's a good thing that something came along. But, it will take a little time to adjust to the responsibility for women and for men, the responsibility of being partners. It's a hell of a responsibility.

JP: I thought you might be alluding to that when you used the word "cynicism."

MA: Oh, no! If that were all, it would just mean that this is a time when we are lying fallow, with the bulbs and things doing whatever they do in the heart of the darkness; that's fine, that's a good time. Unfortunately the cynicism is superimposed on this time so we can't seem to see anything glorious happening.

For me personally, I hope, I've prayed, that I will be in love again. It's a marvelous condition . . . fighting . . . flattering. I don't know— I've been in love and been loved a lot, and it's very nice. I don't have a lot of time to bemoan my outcast fate.

JP: Back to the question of race. How are we doing?

MA: We're not doing well at all. Not well at all. Whites are too ready to abide by the teachings of their ancestors rather than take the rash step of evaluating things for themselves. When it comes to other people—black, Hispanic, Native American—whites are generally afraid and lazy. And those two afflictions are hell together [*laughs*] It's worse than a trembling finger on that red button. I mean, damn, you won't want those two together.

Blacks, I think, are disappointed and frustrated by the residue of the "dream deferred," and that's a hell of a condition to live in. I don't know really what's going to happen, but I have a feeling something pretty wonderful is going to come out of it all, finally.

JP: How much harm do you think the New Right and Reaga-nomics is doing to blacks and women?

MA: Blacks *and* Asians *and* women *and* Hispanics *and* Chicanos *and* poor whites. Well, I think it is hurting quite a lot now, but not as much as it's going to.

California is a case in point. When Proposition 13 passed overwhelmingly in California, Californians were very pleased. And they felt no pinch at all, not knowing that, thanks to Jerry Brown, there was an incredible surplus in the coffers. So life went on as it always had, with the sunshine, and orange trees, and smog—and everything sort of went on. And about a year ago, the truth had to be revealed, that the surplus had been used up. And now the cuts are taking place in services that people took for granted. That's the California way of life. And people are having to come to grips with what that means—for the handicapped, the aged, the poor, the children, and the minorities.

JP: Still, you expect *something wonderful* to happen?

MA: Yes. Something wonderful *is going to happen*. That is in the air too. That is why the dynamic of the time is fabulous.

JP: In America?

MA: In America.

In Maya Angelou, A Caged Bird Sings

Marney Rich/1982

The News and Observer, Raleigh, North Carolina, 7 November 1982, sec. C, 1, 16. Reprinted by courtesy of *The News and Observer.*

"If growing up is painful for the Southern black girl, being aware of her displacement is the rust on the razor that threatens the throat. It is an unnecessary insult."

From *I Know Why the Caged Bird Sings* by Maya Angelou.

WINSTON-SALEM—At the crack of six dawns out of seven, Maya Angelou leaves her spacious home tucked away in the woods and drives to an undisclosed motel room.

She locks herself for six hours in the room she rents by the month. At her request, the management has stripped the walls, and the maids do not clean the room.

In the room are a Bible, a dictionary, "Roget's Thesaurus" and a bottle of sherry. She writes, she prays, she sings, and sometimes she mutilates a deck of cards.

The room is an involuntary asylum—a necessary confinement—so that Maya Angelou can bleed her life onto yellow lined legal pads.

Maya Angelou, autobiographer, poet, singer, actress, dancer, professor," says her motel room makes her feel "at once anonymous. I love it and am frightened by it."

Maya Angelou is far from anonymity. At 54, she has published four autobiographical volumes (*I Know Why the Caged Bird Sings, Gather Together in My Name, Singin' and Swingin' and Gettin' Merry Like Christmas* and *The Heart of a Woman*), three collections of poetry (plus another not yet published) and several screenplays. She is widely known—an author read worldwide, a regular of both the television talk show and university lecture circuits. She is a Reynolds professor of American studies at Wake Forest University.

Thursday evening in Durham, Ms. Angelou will speak on "Women of the Harlem Renaissance" as part of the New Negro Renaissance

Program sponsored by the Duke University Office of Continuing Education and the Durham County Library. Her readings and remarks will center on the spirit and voice of Harlem in the 1920s. The program begins at 8 p.m. in the B.N. Duke Auditorium at North Carolina Central University. Admission is free.

Harlem has tremendous social significance, Ms. Angelou says. "Harlem was Paris to the lost generation at the turn of the century," she says. "Some of these women, who have never been heralded, must be saluted."

The talk is one of many for Ms. Angelou. She sits on her couch amid the African sculpture and paintings she cherishes, counting on two hands the number of planes and campuses she has been on in the last two weeks—University of Tennessee in Knoxville, University of North Carolina at Wilmington, University of Chicago. . . . In January she begins another 25-city lecture tour.

She is almost indifferent to her public life, saying she wishes she could just push a button to recite the lectures. In her private life she is a distinct and separate Maya. There are no cross-overs. She is vivacious, witty and profound onstage, but quiet, calculating and mysterious at home. She is haunted by her past.

Becoming a prisoner to her own words in that motel room every morning is the essence of her. "When I approach the door, it is with utter apprehension and anticipation," she says, her large black eyes widening like those of a hunted fawn. "It is frightening. It is what I am."

She is the same frightened Maya Angelou who, at age 3, was placed like a package on a train in Long Beach, Calif., by her divorced parents to cross the United States wearing a tag on her wrist bearing her grandmother's address.

She is the outcome of rape at age 8, motherhood at age 16 and the saving grace of books read past bedtime. She is the product of cotton pickers' bitterness and the religious fury of revival meetings.

She is still passionately bitter. She overcame pain, but was never softened by it.

There is no praising her. "I learned long ago to take no praise to heart nor criticism," she says. "It is baggage which simply slows one down from achieving their goals. My goal is to become a great writer, professor, dancer, lecturer, and performer."

It is little wonder that Maya Angelou is sought after. She has an

illustrious and complicated background. In her younger years, she
studied dance with Pearl Primus in New York and toured Europe in
the U.S. State Department production of *Porgy and Bess*. She has
received four honorary degrees. At the peak of her singing career, she
played in Harlem's famed Apollo theater and appeared in major city
nightclubs.

She was appointed by the late Martin Luther King Jr. in the 1960s
as the Northern coordinator for the Southern Christian Leadership
Conference. Later, she became disenchanted with the mildness of
King's philosophy. "Redemptive suffering has always been the part of
Martin's argument that I found difficult to accept," she wrote. "I have
seen distress fester souls and bend people's bodies out of shape, but I
had yet to see anyone redeemed from pain, by pain."

That philosophy spurred her to help lead a screaming, shouting
demonstration from a good chunk of Harlem that marched in one of
the most volatile demonstrations the United Nations had ever seen.
The protest was staged after the killing of an African leader whom
radical black Americans supported.

In New York she fell in love with and married an African freedom
fighter who took her to Africa, where she edited and wrote for several
newspapers and administered the School of Music and Drama at the
University of Ghana.

In 1977, she won the Golden Eagle Award for her PBS documentary, "Afro-American in the Arts." In 1979, *I Know Why the Caged
Bird Sings,* her first autobiographical volume, was shown as a CBS-
TV special. Other television credits include the PBS study course
called "Humanities Through the Arts," and the screenplay for
"Sisters" (pre-empted by WPTF-TV in Raleigh earlier this year),
which drew a larger viewing audience than "Dallas."

Her best-known work, however, remains *Caged Bird,* which
Christopher Lehmann-Haupt of *The New York Times* called "a
carefully wrought, simultaneously touching and comic memoir. . .
whose beauty is not in the story but the telling."

Ms. Angelou's early childhood was spent in the dusty desolation of
Stamps, Ark., where Marguerite ("Maya" as her brother called her)
was raised by her grandmother after her parents' divorce. She and
her brother, Bailey, worked in the general store, a shelter from white
bigotry.

When Maya was 8, she and Bailey moved to St. Louis to live with their mother. The stay was temporary. Maya was raped by her mother's boyfriend, and the man was later found dead in a slaughter-house lot. Maya blamed herself for the death and, out of repentance and fear, did not speak for months.

Maya and Bailey returned to Stamps where Maya learned of Shakespeare, Charlotte Bronte, and Edgar Allan Poe through her mentor, Mrs. Bertha Flowers, the aristocrat of black Stamps, who took Maya under her wing.

When she entered her teens, she and Bailey moved to San Francisco to the home of her mother. She graduated from high school at the age of 16 and took jobs as a cook, waitress, stripper. She took up a career as a singer and actress. But they never measured up to her desire to write.

Baby Guy was born to an adventurous Maya, the result of a night she asked the most popular boy in town if he wanted to have sex with her.

She married three times, first to a man of Greek origin named Angelos. Her marriage to Vusumzi Make, the African freedom fighter, took her to various homes in New York, London, Egypt and Africa, but then tore apart at the seams. She later married Paul Du Feu, a builder in San Francisco, but now that marriage has dissolved.

She came to Winston-Salem 11 years ago. "I was separated from my husband, from a marriage that was never to end," she says. "I needed to give California a rest. Winston-Salem is physically very beautiful, and I love Wake Forest. They offered me a place here and I came."

She keeps her distance from the press and is known for being gracious but curt in interviews. She is 6 feet tall and her elegant bearing, deep voice and pensive pauses in conversation enhance the impression.

But yes, she nods, she knows that. "Because I have chosen to be an autobiographer, I was forced to make certain decisions," she says, taking a long pull on her cigarette.

"Because I have chosen to be profoundly intimate with the public, I am private otherwise. I am a very private person. I am extremely formal. I hope not starchly so, but I do not encourage familiarity. I encourage closeness, but not familiarity."

Even her friends have vivid memories of Ms. Angelou's shutting herself away from them. Longtime friend Dolly McPherson of Winston-Salem lived doors away from Ms. Angelou in New York when she was writing *Caged Bird*.

"I had to take it upon myself to see that she was fed," Ms. McPherson says. "She would lock the door for days at a time, and she would not let me in her house. I'd knock and knock and knock until she let me in.

"She does have an honesty one seldom experiences in literature. The readers think they know her so well—they know Maya. It's as if Maya is more than human. And they don't. Her son, Guy, has that from his mother, too. He keeps the distance his mother keeps.

"As a friend, she's very loyal. But I grow impatient with her when she's working. One has to tread very lightly. She will say or do things she does not mean. She can be very short and sometimes not very understanding if she's involved in her work."

Yet, Ms. Angelou will respond to some questions with the same candor she reveals in her books. On her present relationship with her brother, Bailey, who lives in Northern California: "We are not as close as we used to be," her eyes staring at the floor.

And on Guy, "the powerful axle of my life," now living in Sonoma, Calif.: "I just saw him last week," she says, her face at once relaxed and bright. "I talked with him on Sunday and I'll talk to him this afternoon. He's a fine poet, a fine, fine poet. He's just finished his first book."

She stands by the window in the living room, agreeing to pose for a photograph. She talks about her new book of poetry.

"The title will either be 'Sing Me to Sleep, Savannah' or 'Shaker, Why Don't You Sing?' It's from a John Henry song."

Then she bellows out the song in a deep voice. "Isn't it wonderful?" she says with a broad smile.

Then the bright mood changes. "I've had enough," she says to the photographer.

The phone rings for the first of four times within one hour. It is a call from an NBC-TV producer interested in doing a documentary on her trip to West Africa. She is planning to take 10 white students and 10 black students there for a semester in 1983.

"I think it will be fascinating to see young people come face to face with what they thought was exotica and find out that this is where their affectations come from."

She loves teaching and conveys the impression that she is extremely harsh on her students. "I have brilliant students," she says. "Brilliant. I'm a very hard teacher. I am a very good teacher. I use any ploy to do anything to convey my message. I will sing. I will read Shakespeare. They must read. They must debate. No one comes to my class on time. They must be early."

The president of Wake Forest University, James R. Scales, says: "Secretly, I think she is a softy with them."

The phone rings again, and she rises to go to the kitchen. "Good afternoon," she says. "Oooh, so good to hear from you. How are you? I want to hear everything."

Minutes later, she re-enters the living room, hands in her pockets, and walks over to stare out the window. "I have good news," she says. "That was my publisher at Random House. She's just heard that my new book (the unpublished one) is hot. It is HOT! That is good news. Yes."

She remains at the window, her eyes become wistful. Her mood has changed again. "Come over here and look at that tree," she says. "Is it an oak? Aren't the colors beautiful? Do you remember how you used to take leaves in the fall and put them between wax paper? I have a friend in California I want to lure here. I should send her those leaves."

Abruptly she turns and says, "You must go now. Go well."

Angelou: The Caged Bird Still Sings

Paul Rosenfield/1983

L.A. Times Calendar, 29 May 1983, 7. Copyright © 1983 by the Los Angeles Times. Reprinted by permission.

Hollywood moments count for a lot. When times are hard, or conversations dull, a really good Hollywood moment is something to treasure. Recently in Beverly Hills, there was one such moment. It revealed a lot about the town—and about Maya Angelou. For the uninitiated, suffice it to say that Angelou wears more hats than a milliner. She's an author, actress, poet, professor and a dozen other things.

But back to that Hollywood moment. The occasion was the annual benefit for the starry charity Neighbors-of-Watts. Angelou, who's six feet tall, was immediately—and lavishly—greeted by the petite wife of a local producer. Angelou, who's black, and the wife, who's white, touched cheeks. "Maya, darling!" the woman bellowed. "Do you know how much we love you? Do you have any idea?" Angelou had no idea—she'd never met the woman. But that's not the punch line. When the women parted, each wore a trace of the other's makeup. Thus entering the Beverly Wilshire ballroom were two women with black-and-white faces.

"Integration!" roared Angelou recently, being typically succinct. "Hollywood is not a town I understand, even remotely. But—that moment! A stranger who loves me! Or does she just *need* me to be Maya Angelou? To be somebody who writes books and appears on TV and so on?" Angelou means, of course, that she's a kind of very busy cult figure. She represents, especially to empathetic blacks and whites, a woman who never stops *doing*. One of the first black women to write a major film (*Georgia, Georgia,* 1972). The author of four volumes of autobiography and four volumes of poetry. A saloon singer in the '50s, a Tony nominee in the '60s—and on and on. She can talk extemporaneously on any subject, bar none. And, over white wine and guacamole in a bungalow at the Beverly Hills Hotel, she recently did just that. It was a one-day visit to Hollywood, but Angelou completely filled the time.

"People who get a lot of work done," she said firmly, "are people who give themselves permission. Look at (author) James Baldwin. He has something like 18 major pieces of work to his name. It's because of Jimmy that I became a writer. One night at dinner he and Jules Feiffer convinced me my story was worth telling. So I sat down and wrote *I Know Why the Caged Bird Sings*. Then another book, and another. Whatever I do, I'm reaching into the same pot. Call it energy, or faith. The point is, you've got to submit to it, that's all. And let me tell you something else."

Here the self-possessed woman turns into a child-woman. Enveloped by a velvet sofa, she hardly seems six feet tall. Angelou still wears her vulnerability like a badge.

"You never get over the fear of writing," she said, looking into space. "The fear never goes away. I go off to a room to write, and I take legal pads, a dictionary, a bottle of sherry, a solitaire deck and a lot of prayers. Then I give myself permission."

Lately, that permission led to her most recent volume of poetry, *Shaker, Why Don't You Sing?* (Random House). The publication of her work seems to be almost arithmetical. Every 18 months or so we get another Maya Angelou book.

It sounds neat, and it obviously isn't. There's a cost to everything, and Angelou has paid—constantly—for her freewheeling life. For part of her childhood, she was a voluntary mute. Barely a teen-ager, she gave birth to a son, Guy (who now lives in San Francisco). And Angelou's adult life has been one endless globe-trot, with stops in the Soviet Union and Egypt and Harlem and Hollywood. The woman who played the grandmother in "Roots" only last year became rooted herself. And she got a plum position to boot. Angelou has life tenure as a Reynolds professor at Wake Forest University in Winston-Salem, N.C. There she lives, and writes, in a big Southern Gothic house framed by flowering trees and tranquility. The go-go woman of the '60s and '70s has finally found home.

"It's absolutely beautiful—and, yes, I still get terribly lonely," she confessed. "Last week I got so lonely I called a friend to come over. So I could cry on his shoulder, and he could hold me in his arms.

Instead, we had a drink, and talked about my book tour. Then he went home, and I went to bed and just bawled."

It's the familiar cry of the female overachiever. The need for companionship often resolves itself with a manager-husband. Angelou, twice divorced, doesn't put down the idea. "I certainly long for that. Sometimes I think I'm too old or too fat. Or I wish I was prettier. Being strong and daring doesn't mean you don't cry yourself to sleep at night. But if I had to give up a quarter of my devotion and excitement for a man . . . well, I cannot do it."

There, finally, an admission. To the cynics who say, "Maya Angelou cannot possibly do *everything*," the lady would agree. She also could not "do" Hollywood, and her failure-of-sorts here is instructive. Four years ago, NBC committed itself to a series pilot called "Sister, Sister," which Angelou conceived. The pilot sat on the network's shelf for two years before airing in 1982.

"They had such excitement when the idea was new," Angelou remembered, wistfully. "Then what happens?" Although networks have always shown interest in her writing, Angelou never became a TV fixture—except on talk shows.

"Hollywood," she said, "seems to be a community completely in search of money. But even that isn't entirely true." She paused, puzzling over the thought. "Yet money, you must know, is very important here. Because it's the currency they use to buy anything. This is a community that adores youth, then misuses it horribly."

After "Sister, Sister," Angelou left Hollywood for San Francisco. There she lectured, visited her close friend, author Jessica Mitford, and contemplated her fate. Such contemplations don't last long with Angelou, however. She's as adept at changing careers as Ronald Reagan. Yet with all of her surface calm, there seems to be a restlessness at the core. Was it always there? At age 30 was she even more restless than she is at 50-plus?

Angelou's laugh was throaty, and happy. Then she tried for total recall. "At 30 I moved abruptly to Egypt," she answered matter-of-factly. "I had never before been a journalist, and so I became one." The newspaper was the *Arab Observer*, then the only English-language paper in the Middle East. Angelou went rapidly from reporter to editor—to expatriate. Back in America, she found a home

off-Broadway with some of the best black actors of her generation
(Louis Gossett Jr., Cicely Tyson, Roscoe Lee Browne); the play was
Genet's *The Blacks*, and the production was a landmark in black
American theater. Even now, Angelou seems more than anything else
an actress. In public, there is always the sense of performance. One
would have to assume she misses the footlights.

"No, no," she countered. "I loved acting, but I never need to do it
again. The lectures now fill my need for public approval. I only did
Roots because (author) Alex Haley and (producers) David Wolper
and Stan Margulies called me. It was a four-way phone call, and it got
hard to say no." But can the woman who sang for her supper at San
Francisco's Purple Onion and danced across Eastern Europe in *Porgy
and Bess* really be happy not performing?

"Oh, absolutely," she said without a flinch. "What I do best, and
love most, is writing. I cannot be stopped from writing. Poetry sinks
me down into concrete, it seems, but I can't stop. It's part of my
survival apparatus. I have no fear of stretching."

But what of the danger of self-promotion? Can the writer really go
out on the road and promote—and still come home and write? It's a
contradiction, to be sure, but Angelou understands it. Looking
straight ahead, she said slowly, "I don't want to sound falsely modest.
Because I'd like to think I have humility. But really, finally, it's not that
I'm unusual. . . . It's just that what I try is unusual."

Maya Angelou: The Heart of the Woman

Stephanie Stokes Oliver/1983

Conducted by Stephanie Stokes Oliver, this interview appeared in *Essence*, May 1983, 112-114, 116. Copyright © 1983 by Essence Communications, Inc. Reprinted by permission.

Maya Angelou is moving fast! About two years ago, after living in bustling cities from San Francisco to Accra, Ghana, she moved to low-key Winston-Salem, North Carolina. One might think that would mean a newfound, settled-down lifestyle—but not so! Maya may be on quieter turf, but her force as an author, poet, actress and political activist still abounds. In 1981 she gave us the continuation of her powerful autobiography, *The Heart of a Woman,* published by Random House. Just released by the same publisher is a volume of poetry called *Shaker, Why Don't You Sing?* Here she steals a private moment to give us this sister-to-sister interview.

Sister is a word that is close to you. Sister, Sister was the name of your television movie, and you call your friends sister-friend. What does sisterhood mean to you?

Well, I don't believe that the accident of birth makes people sisters or brothers. It makes them siblings. Gives them mutuality of parentage. Sisterhood and brotherhood is a condition people have to work at. It's a serious matter. You compromise, you give, you take, you stand firm, and you're relentless. The only thing is you just don't have sex to further complicate it. But all the responsibility, all the courtesy, all the soft and sweet words, all the teaching words, are called for in those relationships as much as in a love affair. So it's a serious matter. It's big stuff.

But some people are not able. They're not prepared to put in the investment. And it is an investment. Sisterhood means that if you happen to be in Burma and I happen to be in San Diego, and I'm married to someone who is very jealous and you're married to somebody who is very possessive, if you call me in the night, I have to come. Whatever I have to pay, I have to be there. So really, it's no small matter.

You have white women friends. Can they be our sisters?

With those I know to be sisters, we have all paid dues for our sisterhood. What I find more awkward is when a teenager who hasn't been through anything walks up to me and calls me sister. Only equals make friends. Otherwise the relationship is out of balance, out of kilter. Without the parity of investment, loss, triumph, bravery, cowardice, fear, the relationship is essentially paternalistic, maternalistic, condescending.

Jessica Mitford [an English author] is a sister of mine. If I had to go into a room with a leopard, I wouldn't hesitate to ask for her. And if they told her, "Maya can only have one person and she's called you," it wouldn't occur to her to stop from coming. I mean we would vanquish that leopard too! I'd pay like hell after, though, because she'd run me crazy with "Why the hell were you in that damn room in the first place?"

I have many sisters, Black and white. But then I've lived a long time. My mother told me early on: if you want to have a friend, you have to be a friend—and I make a good friend.

From the things you write about your relationship with your mother, it's obvious that you make a good daughter, too. Tell us about her.

Some years ago someone wrote that success had made me haughty. My mother read that and said, "Those people should have asked me. You haven't changed. The only things you've changed is last year's socks."

My mother, Vivian Baxter, is 72 and lives in Stockton, California. We visit often. I have to see about her and she thinks she has to see about me. But it's a curious thing because since I was taken from my mom [to be raised by her grandmother] when I was 3, and except for a disastrous, bitter visit when I was 7, I didn't see her again until I was 13. I'm often asked how I got over that without holding a grudge. I see her as one of the greatest human beings I've ever met. She's funny and quite outrageous really. She said a long time ago, "They spell my name W-o-m-a-n." And that means nobody takes advantage of her. When I was about 18 she said, "Now, you were raised when you left my house, and no man, no woman, no white people, nobody, can raise you." She's something.

I can tell some Vivian Baxter stories. I wrote *Georgia, Georgia* and when I was shooting the movie I had to write the music score. I'm not a trained musician, but I can hear very well, so in order to do the score I had to sing all the parts into a tape recorder. I'd sing the piano part, sing the first violin part, the second violin, cello and bass. Then I'd put the whole score in a shopping bag for the transcriber. And the guy couldn't figure it out. This Swedish television orchestra fellow said, "Oh, you can't have this E minor seventh!" I didn't even know the names of these notes—and it was just horrid. So I called my mother.

I said, "I'm being treated badly and if you've ever done any mothering, I need some now." I told her, "I'm going to put a check in the mail and as soon as you get it you get your ticket and come to Stockholm."

She said, "Baby, what time is it there?" I told her and she said, "Well, it's early in the morning in San Francisco, and if anything is coming to Stockholm today, you pick your mother up at the airport tomorrow." So the next night I went to the airport and stayed there, and the next day my mom arrived! The wonderful thing is she doesn't see how I can get so old that I don't need her.

Has your relationship with your mother helped you in being a mother?

I suppose. My son, Guy . . . The greatest gift I've ever had was the birth of my son. From the very first, I've always respected him as a separate person. I've expected to be entertained by him and I expect to entertain him.

But because when he was small, I knew more than he did, I expected to be his teacher. So because of him I educated myself. When he was 4, I started him to reading because I loved to read and he would interrupt when I was reading. So I taught him to read. But then he'd ask questions and I didn't have the answers, so I started my lifelong love affair with libraries. He would ask questions and I would say, "I'm not prepared to answer that now, but later this evening when you come from school we'll talk about it." And off I'd go to the library. I've learned an awful lot because of him.

Your 5-year-old grandson, Colin Ashanti, has been missing for two

*years, kidnapped after your son won custody of him in a bitter battle.
I know your heart must ache. What does being a grandmother mean
to you?*

My son is most important, and certainly his son could only compound my love. I was raised by a grandmother, so I know what a
grandmother can give a grandchild. If the grandmother is loving,
warm, close and reasonably wise, it's wonderful. So I want my
grandson to think of me as I think of my grandmother.

*Maya, you've been married more than once. Will you tell us about
your marriages?*

Well, I was married—I never say how many times. The reason is
that the number would make me appear to be frivolous. But in each
marriage I brought all of myself and put in all my energy and loyalty,
excitement, fidelity and hard work. The only thing is, when the
marriage doesn't work I am one to say, "Hey, I'm unhappy, and it's
not given to me to live a long time. So I've left a number of men, but
I've been loved a great deal and I have loved a great deal.

You've married white men.

I've married white men. I've married Black men, Africans. I've
never married an American white. That's not to say that I won't
tomorrow. But I hope that the next man who takes my fancy will be a
Black American—just for life to be simpler. I adore Black men.

*Can you give us some insight on sharing that closest of relation-
ships with a white man?*

No, my closest relations are with my son and my mother. Those
are the closest.

It would have been easier to have married the boy next door, but
for the most part I didn't appeal to him. By the time I was 17, I had a
son. I put him on one hip and hit the road, and we lived sometimes
in hotels. I don't know. I might have been willing to have become
somebody's handmaiden and helpmate, but nobody asked.

So the men I have found who loved me, whom I have loved, have
been very strong men. Incredibly strong. And when I found a man I
admired who was brave, fun, intelligent and loving, I had to try and
rustle up enough courage to stand by my love.

Yet, no matter how close the relationship, it doesn't go away, the fact that the person is white. Sometimes an argument, which would simply be "Why don't you pick up your socks?" suddenly becomes a racial argument because of my history. I say, "What do you think I am?" I mean, "Pick up your own damn socks!" It weighs and burdens the relationship unfairly, but that's a part of racism.

Did the breakup of your last marriage contribute to your decision to move here to North Carolina?

Yes, I decided to give California a rest. And I love Winston-Salem. I was offered the Reynolds chair at Wake Forest University. It's an endowed professorship to which someone is usually appointed for two to five years. I am fortunate to have the position for life. It's an honor, although it didn't sit well with some of the white male professors.

I'm just finishing a one-act play called *Theatrical Vignette,* and I have a new book of poetry coming out. In May I'll be setting up the structure for the next book of my autobiography and starting to write late in the summer.

These are hard times for Black writers. Not many Black books are being published now. We're fortunate that yours continue to be published and that we are able to read them.

Thank you. I would write if the books were published or not. There are so many fine writers who are not published or who are published and not promoted. But we must continue to make our contribution.

Maya Angelou: The Serene Spirit of a Survivor

Lawrence Toppman/1983

From the *Charlotte Observer,* 11 December 1983, sec. F, 1-2.
Copyright © 1983 by Lawrence Toppman, Arts Writer, the
Charlotte Observer, Charlotte, North Carolina. Reprinted by
permission.

WINSTON-SALEM—West African masks hang, proud, implacable and
serene, in the foyer of Maya Angelou's suburban home. Weathered
by time and the passions of their creator, they are ghostly reminders
of a distant, almost forgotten world.

So, too, is the face of their owner. Maya Angelou has long outlived
her childhood in Stamps, Ark., a town she once described as
"swollen-belly poor." Yet it left her with a fierce dignity and the
rugged beauty of a cliff that has been battered by the wind but
refuses to crumble.

Angelou has chronicled her adventures through four volumes of
autobiography—a fifth is forthcoming—that stand out among her
poetry and plays as candid self-examination and a tribute to a
survivor's spirit.

Readers of *I Know Why the Caged Bird Sings* will remember the
cruel details. She was raped at 8, bore an illegitimate son at 15, ran a
small brothel (and worked briefly in one), saw her brother imprisoned
and her friends mistreated. Her grandmother and uncle raised her;
her parents, who were separated and searched widely for love, became affectionate shadows who dwelt on the outskirts of her
adolescence.

Her later books chronicle her triumphs: a European tour as a
principal dancer in *Porgy and Bess,* a leading role in the acclaimed
off-Broadway production of Jean Genet's *The Blacks,* groundbreak-
ing forays into American civil rights (as northern head of the SCLC),
film (as the first black female director, with *Georgia, Georgia* in 1972)
and African independence (she traveled with Vusumzi Make, a South
African freedom fighter).

Yet no preparatory reading can prepare you for the woman who owns this two-story brick home.

You expect the direct stares, the firm, fleeting handshake, the weary but courteous voice. You cannot adequately anticipate her presence: the big-boned body, still carried formally at 55, the polite but forbidding glances, the lips that curve unexpectedly into the smile that precedes a throbbing laugh.

We spoke on a rainy Monday. She sat in her library downstairs, stretched out in half-light among volumes ranging from Ovid to James Baldwin. The various shades of brown she wore blended with the orange sofa and set off the white strand of pearls at her long neck. She sipped white wine and smoked cigarettes, not nervously or with apparent pleasure but as an afterthought.

She had agreed to speak about the world premiere of her new play, *On A Southern Journey,* which GM Productions will do next weekend at Spirit Square. But her conversation, like her writing, led her from the event to the intriguing woman behind it.

This is an edited version of that morning's interview.

Does the act of writing get easier the more you do it?
No. Each morning, when I turn over that yellow pad—I write longhand—I doubt. Will I be able to do it? Is it worth it? As you get older and become more recognized, you feel no more secure. You can put all of yourself on the paper, yet it's no good.

As a free-lancer, the writer has to be the creative person and the person who stands aside and says, "Watch that." One of the worst things that happened in the '60s was the idea of letting it all hang out. A generation grew up without discipline, without saying, "I am obliged to go between this pole and that pole." So you saw this stream-of-consciousness-dig-where-I'm-comin'-from; the message was in there, but by the time you had waded through all that stuff . . . Hawthorne said, "Easy reading is damned hard writing." A wonderful thought.

It's hard with a play, which is not finished until it's spoken.
And directed. And other people bring themselves to it.

Your poetry is like that. It seems to require reading aloud.

The verb is well-chosen. You know, from the time I was 7½ until I was almost 13, I didn't talk. I was persuaded to talk by a woman who knew I loved and memorized poetry. She said, "Poetry is music written for the human voice. Until you read it (aloud), you will never love it."

Now, poetry was my friend, the thing I would call up when I was lonely or scared—Poe or Dunbar or Countee Cullen or Langston Hughes or Kipling—and she was taking my friend away. So when I was about 12, I went under the house and started to speak poetry. Until I felt it over my tongue, through my teeth and across my lips, I would never love it. That has influenced the way I hear poetry when I'm writing it; I write for the voice, not the eye.

Do you regret not performing? You do read your own work, but do you miss the stage?

Not at all. Any time I've acted, I've been twisted into it. I did Kunta Kinte's grandmother in "Roots" because I wanted to direct two segments. I did *Look Away* with Geraldine Page on Broadway (and got a Tony nomination) because I wanted Gerry to perform in a play of mine.

Everything costs. My mom told me when I was young, "You may not always get what you pay for, but you will definitely pay for what you get." Knowing that, you prepare your payments in time, commitment, or whatever.

Acting is too temporary, anyway. I don't like getting my stuff together and standing in front of an audience, and then it's over. I want to be able to touch (the work). If my short story is rejected, at least it's in my files. If it's published, it gives me something I can lay my hand on. I have a closet full of my books in French and Spanish and Japanese and Russian. I open it when I'm really depressed and the books are not coming, and I can get away.

How can a Russian get inside the story of a black girl from Stamps?

I write about the black experience, because it's what I know. But I'm always talking about the human condition, what human beings feel and how we feel. Given these circumstances, a human being will react this way: he'll be happy, will weep, will celebrate, will fall. So my books are popular in Asia, in Africa, in Europe.

Why would I, a black girl in the South, fall in love with Tolstoy or Dickens? I was Danton and Madame Defarge and all those people in *A Tale of Two Cities.* I was Daphne du Maurier and the Bronte sisters in a town where blacks were not allowed to cross the street. I was educated by those writers. Not about themselves and their people, but about me, what I could hope for.

Does the South still fascinate you the way it once did?
I'm caught by it, and this is a curious thing. The black Southerner and white Southerner are locked to the land and to history, a painful history of guilt and cruelty and ignorance. It clings to us like the moss on the trees.

That's what my play is about. Two women who have gone north— one black, one white—have done very well and think they're terribly sophisticated. But once back South, they revert to old ways and stereotypes.

Is there anything of value to be preserved in the culture?
Oh, yes. Strangely enough, there's a great love that few people want to discuss, a love of people for people. And black people love the land. The history we have lived and died for over 350 years is our history, whether we like it or not. We have to say, "This is what happened. Are we courageous and serious enough to try to make some changes?"

The hope of the human species is that every generation will be a little bit better. That's how we climbed out of the trees. You have to see where we've come from in the last few thousand years.

Religion has meant a lot to you, hasn't it?
I have a great attachment—that's such a weak word—a gratitude for the presence of God. (When) we're praying, we are celebrating our existence with God. I grew up in the Baptist church, so I prefer and understand the Baptist ritual, but all roads lead to Rome.

If you know that, you don't put value judgments on (religions). You use the wisdom of all of them. We are a community of children of God, whether we admit it or not, whether we call it God or the Creator or the Source or Nature. We're a community.

So much of your life has been spent in intimacy with lovers and

*friends and family. Would you be able to function with the security
and confidence you have if you were left totally alone?*

In North Carolina, I have a 12-room house and live alone. Mom's
at the other end of the phone, and I call my son, Guy. But we're all
alone. We are born alone, and when we take that last breath that
won't come, we're absolutely alone.

I have what black Americans call "play family." I have a play
mother and father in California who are older than mine; I have a
play sister here at Wake Forest and one in Chicago, a couple in
Africa, one in Oakland. We shook hands and said, "I'll be your
sister." But if I had none of that, there would be no life for me.

Living is so difficult at best. Even if you have a good job and a
family, it's difficult to stand up and oppose gravity and go about the
business of your responsibilities.

*You've written that young people grow up like or unlike their
parents, depending upon how well they understand them. Do you
see yourself in Guy?*

Oh, yes. I see myself, and I see somebody totally different. I was
blessed with a revelation when I was very young. He was born to me
at 15, and I saw him as a person at 20. Till then, he'd been like an
appendage, something attached to my hip that I carried around and
loved and fed and tickled. But the absolute greatest thing that
happened to me was my son, because I had to grow and learn not to
smother him.

I'm very strong. And somebody 6 feet tall . . . looking up at that
mountain could have been terribly intimidating. I grew up with my
grandmother, who was 6-2, and I thought maybe she was God, with
her mental repose, her serenity, her deep voice and great love.

Guy's teenage years were frustrating for me; I didn't know how to
guide him without controlling him. In a country run by white males,
who for the most part have said, "Black males, get back," I wanted
to help him count. I didn't want him to hate whites; I didn't want him
to fear them. So I prayed a lot and used my intelligence.

He became Western Airlines' first black executive. They said they
hired him because he speaks Arabic and French, but he said, "They
hired me for threshold effect. I understand that. But I want to see
who I am. I want to have a man's job in my hand, have him call me a

racial slur, and not take his job. I want to see if I'm all right inside."
And that happened.

We've both wept a lot, because I made mistakes. I'm human. But
he's a good person, and you can't ask for more than that. You can
ask for beauty, money, power, but there's nothing greater than the
moral sense of rightness.

*If circumstances had been different, and you hadn't become a
writer on the advice of your friends, what would have been a
satisfying career?*

I've always written. Over at Wake Forest, in the Rare Books Room,
they have journals from when I was 9 years old. When I was asked to
write *Caged Bird*, I had already written poetry, plays, 10 hours for
TV.

Nothing so frightens me as writing, but nothing so satisfies me. It's
like a swimmer in the (English) Channel: you face the stingrays and
waves and cold and grease, and finally you reach that other shore,
and you put your foot on the ground—Aaaaahhhhh! (She laughs.)
That's what I feel. But I have to get right back in the water.

What else do you want to achieve as a writer?

It's said that a good speaker has four or five different topics but
one theme, whether it's furniture building or thermonuclear propul-
sion. My theme is that human beings are more alike than un-alike.
That is in my music, my poetry, my films, my plays, my books: To
remind us that we are more alike, especially since I've grown up in
racial turbulence and unfairness. That's why I pray to become a great
writer.

How will you know?

Just by writing. I won't know it by awards or by anything anybody
tells me. When I die, I hope I will still be trying to achieve that. It's not
something you reach, you see. But it's like becoming a good Jew or
Christian or Buddhist or lover. Finally, you think, "*Now*, I'm cool."
But you just start the next morning, trying all over again.

Maya Angelou
Claudia Tate/1983

From *Black Women Writers at Work,* edited by Claudia Tate (New York: Continuum, 1983), 1-11. Copyright © 1983 by Continuum. Reprinted by permission.

Maya Angelou, author, poet, playwright, stage and screen performer, director, and former nightclub singer, was born Marguerite Johnson in 1928 in St. Louis, Missouri. She attended public schools in Arkansas and California, later studied dance with Martha Graham and drama with Frank Silvera.

She began her literary career as a poet. Her published collections include *Just Give Me a Cool Drink of Water 'Fore I Diiie* (1971); *Oh Pray My Wings Are Gonna Fit Me Well* (1975); and *And Still I Rise* (1978). These are characterized by a spontaneous joyfulness and an indomitable spirit to survive and succeed.

Angelou's four autobiographical works depict sequential periods of her early life. *I Know Why the Caged Bird Sings* (1970) is about Marguerite Johnson and her brother Bailey, growing up in Arkansas, Missouri and California. It is the story of a black girl stumbling about in a society that devalues her beauty and her ambition. *Gather Together In My Name* (1974) covers the period after the birth of Marguerite's son Guy and her courageous struggle as a single parent to provide for him. *Singin' and Swingin' and Gettin' Merry Like Christmas* (1976) describes Maya's stage debut, concluding with her return from the international tour of *Porgy and Bess. The Heart of a Woman* (1981) has a more mature Maya becoming more comfortable with her creativity and her success.

Maya Angelou: Image making is very important for every human being. It is especially important for black American women in that we are, by being black, a minority in the United States, and by being female, the less powerful of the genders. So, we have two areas we must address. If we look out of our eyes at the immediate world around us, we see whites and males in dominant roles. We need to see our mothers, aunts, our sisters, and grandmothers. We need to see Frances Harper, Sojourner Truth, Fannie Lou Hamer, women of our heritage. We need to have these women preserved. We need them all: . . . Constance Motley, Etta Motten. . . . All of these women are important as role models. Depending on our profession, some may be even more important. Zora Neale Hurston means a great deal to me as a writer. So does Josephine Baker, but not in the same way because her profession is not directly related to mine. Yet I would imagine for someone like Diahann Carroll or Diana Ross, Miss Baker must mean a great deal. I would imagine that Bessie Smith and Mammie Smith, though they are important to me, would be even more so to Aretha Franklin.

If I were a black male writer, I would think of Frederick Douglass, who was not just a politician, but as a writer was stunning. In the nineteenth century I would think of William Wells Brown, Martin Delaney, and certainly David Walker, who showed not only purpose but method. In the twentieth century I would think of Richard Wright, Jean Toomer, and so on. They mean a great deal to me. I'm black, and they experienced America as blacks. These particular writers may mean more to the black male writer, just as I imagine Jack Johnson would mean a great deal to Jesse Owens, and Jesse Owens a great deal to Arthur Ashe.

Claudia Tate: When you write, are you particularly conscious of preserving certain kinds of images of black people?

Angelou: Well, I am some time, though I can't actually say when this happens in the creation of the work. I make writing as much a part of my life as I do eating or listening to music. Once I left church, and as I walked down the street, three young black women stopped me and asked if I would have a glass of wine with them. I said, "Yes." One is a painter; one is an actress, and one a singer. We talked, and when I started to leave, I tried to tell them what it means to me to see young black women. I tried to tell them, but I could hardly explain it. My eyes filled with tears. In one way, it means all the work, all the loneliness and discipline my work exacts, demands, is not in vain. It also means, in a more atavistic, absolutely internal way, that I can never die. It's like living through children. So when I approach a piece of work, *that* is in my approach, whether it's a poem that might appear frivolous or is a serious piece. In my approach I take as fact that my work will be carried on.

C.T.: Did you envision young Maya as a symbolic character for every black girl growing up in America?

Angelou: Yes, after a while I did. It's a strange condition, being an autobiographer and a poet. I have to be so internal, and yet while writing, I have to be apart from the story so that I don't fall into indulgence. Whenever I speak about the books, I always think in terms of the Maya character. When I wrote the telcplay of *I Know Why the Caged Bird Sings,* I would refer to the Maya character so as not to mean me. It's damned difficult for me to preserve this distancing. But it's very necessary.

C.T.: What has been the effect of the women's movement on black women?

Angelou: Black women and white women are in strange positions in our separate communities. In the social gatherings of black people, black women have always been predominant. That is to say, in the church it's always Sister Hudson, Sister Thomas and Sister Witheringay who keep the church alive. In lay gatherings it's always Lottie who cooks, and Mary who's going over to Bonita's where there is a good party going on. Also, black women are the nurturers of children in our community. White women are in a different position in their social institutions. White men, who are in effect their fathers, husbands, brothers, their sons, nephews and uncles, say to white women, or imply in any case: "I don't really need you to run my institutions. I need you in certain places and in those places you must be kept—in the bedroom, in the kitchen, in the nursery, and on the pedestal." Black women have never been told this. Black women have not historically stood in the pulpit, but that doesn't undermine the fact that they built the churches and maintain the pulpits. The people who have historically been heads of institutions in black communities have never said to black women—and they, too, are their fathers, husbands, brothers, their sons, nephews and uncles— "We don't need you in our institutions." So there is a fundamental difference.

One of the problems I see that faces black women in the eighties, just as it has in the past two decades, has been dealt with quite well in Michele Wallace's *Black Macho and the Myth of the Superwoman*. A number of black men in the sixties fell for a terrible, terrible ploy. They felt that in order to be total and free and independent and powerful, they had to be like white men to their women. So there was a terrible time when black men told their women that if you really love me, you must walk three steps behind me.

I try to live what I consider a "poetic existence." That means I take responsibility for the air I breathe and the space I take up. I try to be immediate, to be totally present for all my work. *I try.* This interview with you is a prime example of this. I am withdrawing from the grief that awaits me over the death of someone dear so that I can be present for you, for myself, for your work and for the people who will read it, so I can tell you exactly how I feel and what I think and try to answer your questions cheerfully—if I feel cheerful—as I can. That to me is poetic. I try for concentrated consciousness which I miss by more than half, but I'm trying.

C.T.: How do you fit writing into your life?

Angelou: Writing is a part of my life; cooking is a part of my life. Making love is a part of my life; walking down the street is a part of it. Writing demands more time, but it takes from all of these other activities. They all feed into the writing. I think it's dangerous to concern oneself too damned much with "being an artist." It's more important to get the work done. You don't have to concern yourself with it, just get it done. The pondering pose—the back of the hand glued against the forehead—is baloney. People spend more time posing than getting the work done. The work is all there is. And when it's done, then you can laugh, have a pot of beans, stroke some child's head, or skip down the street.

C.T.: What is your responsibility as a writer?

Angelou: My responsibility as a writer is to be as good as I can be at my craft. So I study my craft. I don't simply write what I feel, let it all hang out. That's baloney. That's no craft at all. Learning the craft, understanding what language can do, gaining control of the language, enables one to make people weep, make them laugh, even make them go to war. You can do this by learning how to harness the power of the word. So studying my craft is one of my responsibilities. The other is to be as good a human being as I possibly can be so that once I have achieved control of the language, I don't force my weaknesses on a public who might then pick them up and abuse themselves.

During the sixties some lecturers went to universities and took thoughtless liberties with young people. They told them "to turn on, tune in and drop out." People still do that. They go to universities and students will ask them, "Mr. So-and-So, Ms./Miss./Mrs./Brother/ Sister So-and-So, these teachers here at this institution aren't happening, like what should we do?" Many lecturers have said, "Don't take it! Walk out! Let your protest be seen." That lecturer then gets on a plane, first-class, with a double scotch on-the-rocks, jets off to San Juan, Puerto Rico for a few days' rest, then travels to some other place where he or she is being paid two to three thousand dollars to speak. Those young people risk and sometimes lose their scholastic lives on that zoom because somebody's been irresponsible. I loathe that. I will not do it. I *am* responsible. I *am* trying to be responsible.

So first, I'm always trying to be a better human being, and second, I continue to learn my craft. Then, when I have something positive to say, I can say it beautifully. That's my responsibility.

C.T.: Do you see any distinctions in the ways black male and female writers dramatize their themes and select significant events? This is a general question, but perhaps there is some basis for analysis. Gayl Jones responded to this question by saying she thought women tended to deal with events concerning the family, the community, personal events, that were not generally thought to be important by male writers. She said that male writers tended to select "representative" events for the significant events in their works. Toni Bambara said she thought women writers were concerned with developing a circumscribed place from which the story would unfold. Have you observed such patterns in your reading?

Angelou: I find those observations interesting. In fact, the question is very interesting. I think black male writers do deal with the particular, but we are so conditioned by a sexist society that we tend to think when they do so that they mean it representationally; and when black females deal with the particular they only mean it as such. Whether we look at works by Richard Wright, James Baldwin, or John Killens—I'm thinking of novelists—we immediately say this is a generalization; this is meant as an overview, a microcosmic view of the world at large. Yet, if we look at works by Toni Morrison or Toni Bambara, if we look at Alice Walker's work or Hurston's, Rosa Guy's, Louise Meriwether's, or Paule Marshall's, we must say that these works are meant as general statements, universal statements. If *Daddy Was a Numbers Runner* [by Louise Meriwether] is not a microcosm of a macrocosm, I don't know what it is. If Paule Marshall's *Chosen Place and Timeless People* is not a microcosm, I don't know what it is. I don't know what *Ruby* [by Rosa Guy] is if it is not a microcosm of a larger world. I see everybody's work as an example of the particular, which is indicative of the general. I don't see any difference really. Whether it's Claude Brown's or Gayl Jones's. I can look at *Manchild in the Promised Land* and at *Corregidora* and see that these writers are talking about particular situations and yet about the general human condition. They are instructive for the generalities of our lives. Therefore, I won't indulge inherent distinctions between men and women writers.

C.T.: Do you consider your quartet to be autobiographical novels or autobiographies?

Angelou: They are autobiographies. When I wrote *I Know Why the Caged Bird Sings,* I wasn't thinking so much about my own life or identity. I was thinking about a particular time in which I lived and the influences of that time on a number of people. I kept thinking, what about that time? What were the people around young Maya doing? I used the central figure—myself—as a focus to show how one person can make it through those times.

I really got roped into writing *The Caged Bird.* At that time I was really only concerned with poetry, though I'd written a television series. Anyway, James Baldwin took me to a party at Jules Feiffer's house. It was just the four of us: Jimmy Baldwin and me, Jules Feiffer and his wife, at that time Judy Feiffer. We sat up until three or four o'clock in the morning, drinking scotch and telling tales. The next morning Judy Feiffer called a friend of hers at Random House and said, "You know the poet, Maya Angelou? If you can get her to write a book . . . '" Then Robert Loomis at Random House phoned, and I said, "No, I'm not interested." I went out to California and produced my series for WNET. Loomis called two or three times, and I said, "No, I'm not interested. Thank you so much." Then, I'm sure he talked to Baldwin because he used a ploy which I'm not proud to say

I haven't gained control of yet. He called and said, "Miss Angelou, it's been nice talking to you. I'm rather glad you decided not to write an autobiography because to write an autobiography as literature is the most difficult thing anyone could do." I said, "I'll do it." Now that's an area I don't have control of yet at this age. The minute someone says I can't, all my energy goes up and I say, what? What? I'm still unable to say that you may be wrong and walk away. I'm not pleased with that. I want to get beyond that.

C.T.: How did you select the events to present in the autobiographies?

Angelou: Some events stood out in my mind more than others. Some, though, were never recorded because they either were so bad or so painful, that there was no way to write about them honestly and artistically without making them melodramatic. They would have taken the book off its course. All my work, my life, everything is about survival. All my work is meant to say, "You may encounter many defeats, but you must not be defeated." In fact, the encountering may be the very experience which creates the vitality and the power to endure.

C.T.: You are a writer, poet, director, composer, lyricist, dancer, singer, journalist, teacher and lecturer. Can you say what the source of such creative diversity is?

Angelou: I don't do the dancing anymore. The rest I try. I believe talent is like electricity. We don't understand electricity. We use it. Electricity makes no judgment. You can plug into it and light up a lamp, keep a heart pump going, light a cathedral, or you can electrocute a person with it. Electricity will do all that. It makes no judgment. I think talent is like that. I believe every person is born with talent. I believe anyone can learn the craft of painting and paint.

I believe all things are possible for a human being, and I don't think there's anything in the world I can't do. Of course, I can't be five feet four because I'm six feet tall. I can't be a man because I'm a woman. The physical gifts are given to me, just like having two arms is a gift. In my creative source, whatever that is, I don't see why I can't sculpt. Why shouldn't I? Human beings sculpt. I'm a human being. I refuse to indulge any man-made differences between myself and another human being. I will not do it. I'm not going to live very long. If I live another fifty years, it's not very long. So I should indulge

somebody else's prejudice at their whim and not for my own convenience! Never happen! Not me!

C.T.: How do you integrate protest in your work?

Angelou: Protest is an inherent part of my work. You can't just not
write about protest themes or not sing about them. It's a part of life. If
I don't agree with a part of life, then my work has to address it.

I remember in the early fifties I read a book, *Dom Casmurro*. It
was written by Machado De Assis, a nineteenth-century Brazilian. I
thought it was very good. A month later I thought about the book
and went back and reread it. Two months later I read the book again,
and six months later I realized the sensation that I had had while
reading the book was as if I had walked down to a beach to watch a
sunset. I had watched the sunset and turned around, only to find that
while I had been standing there the tide had come in over my head. I
decided to write like that. I would never get on a soapbox; instead, I
would pull in the reader. My work is intended to be slowly absorbed
into the system on deeper and deeper levels.

C.T.: Would you describe your writing process?

Angelou: I usually get up at about 5:30, and I'm ready to have
coffee by 6, usually with my husband. He goes off to his work
around 6:30, and I go off to mine. I keep a hotel room in which I do
my work—a tiny, mean room with just a bed, and sometimes, if I can
find it, a face basin. I keep a dictionary, a Bible, a deck of cards and a
bottle of sherry in the room. I try to get there around 7, and I work
until 2 in the afternoon. If the work is going badly, I stay until 12:30.
If it's going well, I'll stay as long as it's going well. It's lonely, and it's
marvelous. I edit while I'm working. When I come home at 2, I read
over what I've written that day, and then try to put it out of my mind.
I shower, prepare dinner, so that when my husband comes home, I'm
not totally absorbed in my work. We have a semblance of a normal
life. We have a drink together and have dinner. Maybe after dinner I'll
read to him what I've written that day. He doesn't comment. I don't
invite comments from anyone but my editor, but hearing it aloud is
good. Sometimes I hear the dissonance; then I'll try to straighten it
out in the morning. When I've finished the creative work and the
editing and have six hundred handwritten pages, I send it to my
editor. Then we both begin to work. I've kept the same editor
through six books. We have a relationship that's kind of famous

among publishers, since oftentimes writers shift from one publisher to
another for larger advances. I just stay with my own editor, and we'll
be together as long as he and I are alive. He understands my work
rhythm, and I understand his. We respect each other, but the nit-
picking does come. He'll say, "This bothers me—on page twelve, line
three, why do you have a comma there? Do you mean to break the
flow?"

C.T.: How do you feel about your past works?

Angelou: Generally, I forget them. I'm totally free of them. They
have their own life. I've done well by them, or I did the best I could,
which is all I can say. I'm not cavalier about work anymore than I am
about sitting here with you, or cooking a meal, or cleaning my house.
I've tried to be totally present, so that when I'm finished with a piece
of work, I'm finished. I remember one occasion when we were in
New York City at the Waldorf Astoria some years ago. I think I was
with my sister friends—Rosa [Guy], Paule [Marshall] and Louise
[Meriwether]. We were sitting at a table near the bandstand during
some tribute for someone, and I felt people staring at me. Someone
was singing, say, stage left, and some people were performing a
dance. It was very nice, but I felt people staring; so I turned around,
and they were. My sister friends were all smiling. I wondered what
was happening. I had been following the performance. Well, it turned
out that the singer was doing a piece of mine, and they had choreographed a dance to it. I had forgotten the work altogether. The work,
once completed, does not need me. The work I'm working on needs
my total concentration. The one that's finished doesn't belong to me
anymore. It belongs to itself.

C.T.: Would you comment on your title selections?

Angelou: As you probably know, the title *I Know Why the Caged
Bird Sings* is from [Paul Lawrence] Dunbar's "Sympathy." *Gather
Together in My Name,* though it does have a biblical origin, comes
from the fact I saw so many adults lying to so many young people,
lying in their teeth, saying, "You know, when I was young, I never
would have done . . . Why I couldn't . . . I shouldn't . . ." Lying.
Young people know when you're lying; so I thought for all those
parents and non-parents alike who have lied about their past, I will
tell it.

Singin' and Swingin' and Gettin' Merry Like Christmas comes
from a time in the twenties and thirties when black people used to

have rent parties. On Saturday night from around nine when they'd give these parties, through the next morning when they would go to church and have the Sunday meal, until early Sunday evening was the time when everyone was encouraged to sing and swing and get merry like Christmas so one would have some fuel with which to live the rest of the week.

Just Give Me a Cool Drink of Water 'Fore I Diiie refers to my belief that we as individuals in a species are still so innocent that we think we could ask our murderer just before he puts the final wrench upon the throat, "Would you please give me a cool drink of water?" and he would do so. That's innocence. It's lovely.

The tune of *Oh, Pray My Wings Are Gonna Fit Me Well* originally comes from a slave holler, and the words from a nineteenth-century spiritual:

> Oh, pray my wings are gonna fit me well.
> I'm a lay down this heavy load.
> I tried them on at the gates of hell.
> I'm a lay down this heavy load.

I planned to put all the things bothering me—my heavy load—in that book, and let them pass.

The title poem of *And Still I Rise* refers to the indomitable spirit of black people. Here's a bit of it:

> You may write me down in history
> With your bitter, twisted lies,
> You may trod me in the very dirt
> But still, like dust, I'll rise.

C.T.: Can black women writers help clarify or help to resolve the black sexist debate that was rekindled by Ntozake Shange's *For Colored Girls Who Have Considered Suicide When the Rainbow Is Enuf* and Michele Wallace's *Black Macho and the Myth of the Superwoman?*

Angelou: Neither Miss Shange nor Miss Wallace started the dialogue, so I wouldn't suggest any black woman is going to stop it. If anything could have clarified the dialogue, Toni Morrison's *The Song of Solomon* should have been the work to do that. I don't know if that is a chore or a goal black women writers should assume. If someone feels so inclined, then she should go on and do it.

Everything good tends to clarify. By good I mean well written and well researched. There is nothing so strong as an idea whose time has come. The writer—male or female—who is meant to clarify this issue will do so. I, myself, have no encouragement in that direction. There's a lot that hasn't been said. It may be necessary to hear the male view of *For Colored Girls* in a book or spoken upon the stage. It may be necessary, and I know it will be very painful.

C.T.: What writers have influenced your work?

Angelou: There were two men who probably formed my writing ambition more than any others. They were Paul Lawrence Dunbar and William Shakespeare. I love them. I love the rhythm and sweetness of Dunbar's dialect verse. I love "Candle Lighting Time" and "Little Brown Baby." I also love James Weldon Johnson's "Creation."

I am also impressed by living writers. I'm impressed with James Baldwin. I continue to see not only his craftsmanship but his courage. That means a lot to me. Courage may be the most important of all the virtues because without it one cannot practice any other virtue with consistency. I'm impressed by Toni Morrison a great deal. I long for her new works. I'm impressed by the growth of Rosa Guy. I'm impressed by Ann Petry. I'm impressed by the work of Joan Didion. Her first collection, *Slouching Toward Jerusalem,* contains short pieces, which are absolutely stunning. I would walk fifty blocks in high heels to buy the works of any of these writers. I'm a country girl, so that means a lot.

C.T.: Have any of your works been misunderstood?

Angelou: A number of people have asked me why I wrote about the rape in *I Know Why the Caged Bird Sings*. They wanted to know why I had to tell that rape happens in the black community. I wanted people to see that the man was not totally an ogre. The hard thing about writing or directing or producing is to make sure one doesn't make the negative person totally negative. I try to tell the truth and preserve it in all artistic forms.

The West Interview: Maya Angelou

Sal Manna/1986

San Jose Mercury News, 22 June 1986, 4-5. Copyright © 1986 by Sal Manna. Reprinted by permission.

Maya Angelou's life has been a tribute to the indomitability of the human spirit. Her childhood in rural Arkansas was full of hardships, but she has become a celebrated dancer, actress, singer, civil rights activist, writer and poet. Her autobiographical *I Know Why the Caged Bird Sings* was a 1970 best seller and four succeeding volumes, including the recent *All God's Children Need Traveling Shoes,* have garnered critical acclaim. She is a professor of American studies at Wake Forest University in Winston-Salem, N.C.

Q. This latest installment of your autobiography is about your return to Africa, specifically Ghana, in the early '60s. Why write a book now about that period?

A. I have a feeling that beneath lots of our despair and hurt is the search, the need, to find a home. We're so peripatetic in this society. West Africans have a saying that if you go to hell, you'll find some Americans there. We're always leaving our beautiful homes and families and friends to search for something. I wanted to look at that portion of the human breast which longs to belong.

Q. Did Africa fulfill your expectations?

A. It's like the Russian Jews who go to Israel and expect the red carpet. "She's here at last!" We fictionalize a place first and call it home and its allegiances make us take it to our hearts, but it's never what you think it'll be. In Ghana, black Americans were looked on differently. They were suspicious of us.

Q. What was your biggest mistake in going there?

A. Mistake is a harsh word. One of my errors in judgment was the idea that if I learned an African language, wore the native clothing and ate the African food that I would become an African. I found that you can fool some of the people some of the time, but you can't fool yourself.

Q. Can you go home again?

A. Thomas Wolfe was right—and he was wrong. You see, you can never *leave* home. It's under your fingernails, in the bend of your hair. It sings out of your mouth. What I found is that I had to come home to America to write about coming home to Africa. As I write in the book, "Many of us had only begun to realize in Africa that the Stars and Stripes was our flag and our only flag, and that knowledge was almost too painful to bear."

Q. You were once Martin Luther King's northern coordinator for the Southern Christian Leadership Conference, and you've been a friend of so many black leaders. Who are today's black heroes?

A. Jesse Jackson is one. And any person who's really intent on making this a better country for all the people. Not a divisive person.

Q. What is your opinion of Louis Farrakhan?

A. I think Rev. Farrakhan is to be considered by followers of his movement.

Q. That's diplomatic.

A. He is dangerous. Allow me to restate that. I think when he considers more the possibility of being a great leader, he will know that his charisma and personality and energy can encourage love and unity, rather than hate and division. He will see that black Americans have been here since the year 1619, and this is as much our country as anyone else's, save the Native Americans. We will all live together or not at all.

Q. How are you looked upon by the more radical elements of the black movement?

A. My people love me. My people including my people who are not black. It's more than respect. And I am grateful for that. Yes, I speak to the black experience, but am always talking about the human condition—about what we can endure, dream, fail at and still survive. They love me because I tell the truth—and I tell it gently.

Q. There has been a strong trend toward Islam among black Americans. You are a very steadfast Christian. How does that fit in politically?

A. I'm religious. A real religious person is respectful of other religious persons. So a *true* Buddhist or Jew or Muslim does not deny another's belief. All roads lead to God. If I had been born in Japan, I would have been a religious Shinto. It's in my nature to be religious. I try to be a good Christian. That does not come at anyone else's expense. True religion says we are all one. I'm not talking about the fanatics in any religion. I think when you see those people you should run like hell, praying all the time.

Q. You're so much more accommodating and soothing than your earlier days. You once wrote in a poem that "I'll believe in Liberal's aid for us/When I see a white man load a Black man's gun." What brought about the change?

A. Yeah, I was hot when I was 22, wasn't I? I'll tell you: I think it's that as I've grown older, I realize that now I don't have that long to live. It is much more useful being constructive than destructive.

Don't get me wrong. I still feel you should rock the boat. And if you're not in it, you should turn it over. But not unthinkingly. Protest without serious consideration is dangerous. You have to back up what you say. But once you find the truth, you ought to be prepared to stand on the street corner and use all your gifts to right the wrong.

Q. What did you think of *The Color Purple?*

A. I loved the book. The movie disappointed me because so many people I do love were bowled over by it. I felt it was a romantic treatment that perhaps could have been dealt with more honestly. The filmmakers are terribly adept. They can push certain buttons— like having a little dog who is lost and then comes back—and make you weep. But it doesn't mean anything.

Q. The controversy over the film's depiction of black life has divided the black community. Where do you stand?

A. I recently gave the keynote speech at the National Black Writers convention. The theme was the social responsibility of the black writer to the community. But I knew what it was really about. It was a euphemism for talking about *The Color Purple.* I suggested that we not fall prey to the Machiavellian dictum of separate and rule, divide and conquer. Attacks on the movie are providing a delicious delectation for white racists.

Q. There's a feeling in Hollywood that if there's so much hassle over a well-intentioned effort, that Hollywood just shouldn't bother with black subject matter, period.

A. I don't think it would have made any difference if the film had been made or not made. The situation for blacks in Hollywood is terrible. Listen, after *Roots,* you would have thought the exposure of this cadre of great black actors would usher in a new age. It did not. I played Kunta Kinte's grandmother, I should know.

Q. Is racism still a major issue in America?

A. Racism is still a major issue because it is a habit. It is a devastating disease. But it took us 370 years to get to this place and 200 years to establish racism. It won't be obliterated by the passing of a law or the charismatic presence of a Malcolm X or Martin Luther King, Jr. It will be a tedious process and a long one. We will have to have people with strong and big hearts working for a few generations to obliterate the ugliness of it. There's something little spoken of. In the early 1800's, Thomas Jefferson wrote a letter to a friend saying that we should send the slaves home to Africa. Why? Because, he said, it will take us five generations for them to forgive us.

Q. Has life significantly improved for blacks in America since your childhood?

A. Life has changed for the better for the majority of blacks. It would be irresponsible not to say so. Twenty years ago the idea that Los Angeles, Detroit, Chicago and Atlanta would have black mayors—brought in by a constituency of blacks and whites—would have been unthinkable. Or that a black woman would win a Pulitzer prize as Alice Walker did [for *The Color Purple*] or that a black woman would be nominated for a National Book Award as I was.

Q. How do you feel about the situation in South Africa?

A. That, too, will change. There is nothing so powerful as an idea whose time has come. Nothing can stop it. But South Africa will be freed by South Africans.

Q. Should the United States work to bring about the end of apartheid?

A. We should be involved in protesting the treatment of blacks there as we should about anyone anywhere who is subjugated. But we should do it for the sake of our own morality, for ourselves. Our moral health as a nation is what is at stake.

Q. Aren't intellectuals supposed to be cynical? You are so full of hope.

A. I believe love is what links those molecules in DNA. It can't be photographed. It's love that holds us together as human beings.

Kicking Ass

Aminatta Forna/1986

Girl About Town Magazine, 13 October 1986, 22. Copyright ©
1986 by Girl About Town Magazine. Reprinted by permission.

"I love," said Maya Angelou, "to see a young girl go out and grab the
world by the lapels. Life's a bitch. You've got to go out and kick ass."
We were sitting drinking coffee in the discreet opulence of Knights-
bridge's Basil Street Hotel. I was ostensibly interviewing her about the
fourth and latest volume of her autobiography *The Heart Of A
Woman.* In reality she was simply chatting at her own pace and I was
listening. Maya Angelou is like that. She is a woman who has kicked
a lot of ass in her time and taken more than a few blows herself.

"I always knew that I needed to have money," she confides. "I am
black, I'm a woman, I'm also six feet tall. I've got to keep the sons of
bitches off my back somehow."

In the 1960s when Ms. Angelou visited London she used to visit
her bank and draw out £100 in 10 shilling notes. "Then," she says, "I
would go to a restaurant and call over the maitre d'. They didn't like
blacks and they didn't like women on their own, but I would give him
a folded 10s note, and ask him to get me a table. It worked every
time. I would sit eating my food and I would look at him thinking, 'I
just bought your ass for ten shillings.' "

Born in 1928 in the deep South of America, she grew up with her
grandmother and brother Bailey in a society where lynchings and
racial hatred were a part of everyday life. At five she went to live with
her glamorous mother in California where she was abused and raped
by her mother's lover. In the courtroom the lawyers ripped her to
pieces and set her assailant free. He was found beaten to death hours
later, but Maya remained mute for five years.

At 16, she gave birth to her son Guy. Since then, in her attempts to
survive and provide for her son, she has worked as a nightclub
singer, actress and waitress, toured Europe as a dancer with the black
opera *Porgy and Bess,* slept rough for weeks, turned to prostitution
and drugs, and become a magazine editor, poet and writer.

161

Whilst working for the Black struggle under Martin Luther King in the 1960s, she met and married the South African freedom fighter Vusumzi Make after a week long courtship. When the marriage broke up in Egypt she emigrated to Ghana where she edited the *African Review*.

Now she holds the Reynolds Professorship at Wake Forest University in North Carolina, where she teaches "whatever comes to mind," usually linked in some way to race, but encompassing politics, theatre and literature. She has returned to the South as the triumphant and conquering heroine, holding one of the most coveted academic posts. A far cry from the frightened little black girl who left when the future could hold nothing for a black woman.

But she is surprisingly unaffected by her own success. Talking of her teaching post she says: "I just mumble around. I don't treat it as if it's any different from any other job in life. I have neither the interest nor the inclination to live in or create an ivory tower." Her face splits into a wide and toothy grin, her trademark, as she continues. "I love to teach, though. My students are bright and daring. Even if they weren't it wouldn't matter. All I ask of them, of anyone, is that they be courageous."

Maya Angelou has never lacked courage and doubtless never will. But her convictions in other matters are relatively recent. In *The Heart of a Woman*, she writes at length about her determination to be a "good African wife" to Vusumzi Make. I found this infuriating, and since the fifth volume *All God's Children Need Traveling Shoes* won't be published until 1987, I was curious to know whether she deserved her brilliant reputation.

Ms. Angelou, I asked her, do you now consider yourself a feminist? Her eyes almost gave off sparks. "What do you mean, do I consider myself a feminist? I am a feminist. I've been female for a long time now. I'd be stupid not to be on my own side."

In self-defence, I replied that this did not always seem to have been the case. Her eyes softened. One thing about Maya Angelou is that she speaks with the same depth of emotion and intensity of feeling with which she writes. Some authors are sterile, empty vessels who seem to have put everything they ever had to offer onto the paper already. Maya Angelou still has a lot to offer. When she talks of her

mistakes, you feel like crying for her. And yet seconds later she is full
of guts and laughter, swearing and delighting her company.

"When I was young," she explained, "I tried hard. I thought, as
many women do, that if I fitted within the confines, I would lead a
pretty little life. But it never works. Not for anyone. And I learnt that. I
have changed, at least I hope I have. We are all in the process. I hope
I am continuing to learn."

Was she disappointed to find that her husband, a man who de-
voted his life to the fight for black equality, did not want to give his
wife, or any other woman, a slice of the cake? "I am always disappointed," she answered, slowly and rather sadly, "in the narrowness
of anyone. That a person can actually figure out how to chew gum
and brush their teeth, and yet cannot see that human beings are
more alike than unalike."

"It is wrong, however, to think that black men ought to be less
sexist. They want the same things as any other man. Black men in
the U.S. love my work and feel that I haven't romanticised or
stereotyped them. Some men are really asses, and some men are
really wonderful."

"Suffering of itself does not necessarily sensitise. Look at Israel.
They know what it is to suffer and yet they don't feel that for the
Palestinians.

"I'll tell you the truth, my dear," she said leaning back and lighting
a cigarette. "Sometimes people say they want change, but they really
want exchange. They don't want to change the system, they just
want to control the existing system."

Maya Angelou wants to change the system. Her books are read all
over the world and translated into many different languages. One,
the first, has been turned into a television film. But does she think
that women and men of different colours and cultures could relate to
the experiences of a black American woman?

"They seem to," she answers, "but it's difficult to say. I get a lot of
letters from West Indian and working class women, and some English
men. People do relate. I think of English novels of the 19th century.
People in China somehow manage to relate to Oliver Twist."

Could we then expect the fifth volume of her autobiography? She
looked doubtful, but there was a gleam in her eyes. "Possibly," was

all she would give away. We discussed her plans for the immediate future and in the space of several minutes she had mentioned: a book of poetry to be released in January entitled *Now Sheba Sings the Song*; "it's a play on the Song of Solomon. We never heard Sheba's song." A novel, "I'd like to try fiction, but it might try me." As well as a Broadway musical based on the story of two African kings.

"I like a challenge," she says cheerfully and rather unnecessarily. The fact is, she only sat down to write her autobiography in the first place because someone bet her she couldn't.

Now, looking forward to her 60th birthday, which she describes as the beginning of "real life" and with an almost legendary career and life behind her, would she have done anything differently if she had her life all over again? She looked thoughtful, wistful even. "Probably not. Only because all the mistakes I've made and all the unkindness I've faced and displayed have taught me something. If things had been different I might still not be trying to be a better person.

"I've blown it so many times," she admits, becoming serious. Then brightening: "But like I said before, life's a bitch. Now it's your turn," she turns to me, "to go out and show those asses what you're made of."

Zelo Interviews Maya Angelou

Russell Harris/1986

Zelo, Fall 1986, 64-67. Copyright © 1986 by Zelo Publishing, Inc. Reprinted by permission.

Shadows formed by overhanging pines encase her three-story colonial house in Winston-Salem, North Carolina. Inside, one's senses are treated to paintings by John Biggers, Phoebe, and other leading Black artists. African music reverberates throughout the house, complementing the carvings and sculptures lining the walls and covering the table tops. There are rooms designed for work and there are rooms designed for refuge. But in every corner of every room is the heart of a brilliant, elegant and indomitable woman: Maya Angelou.

Her name alone is indicative of the many struggles and triumphs she has experienced. Maya, originally "my sister," is the name given to her by her brother during their childhood upbringing in the rural town of Stamps, Arkansas. While connoting the love they shared, it also binds her to a past filled with hardship and oppression. Such was the cornerstone of her success. Angelou marks her professional debut in San Francisco as a Calypso singer. From there, with only a high school education and an unbreakable spirit, Maya Angelou has spanned the globe with her multi-faceted talents. She was a member of the European touring company of *Porgy and Bess* and the associate editor of the *Arab Observer* in Cairo. An early childhood incident left her speechless for many years, but now she is fluent in a half dozen languages.

Maya Angelou currently holds the Reynolds Chair at Wake Forest University. It is a lifetime endowment that affords her the chance to teach any subject of her choosing in the field of humanities. But she is far more renowned for her remarkable literary achievements. Beginning with *I Know Why the Caged Bird Sings,* she retraces her steps from childhood to womanhood in a style that has won her national and international acclaim. The latest of her five-part autobiographical series, *All God's Children Need*

Traveling Shoes, chronicles her flight to freedom in Africa.
She tells of her struggles as a single parent, a freedom
fighter, and a displaced soul in search of a homeland.

It was early Saturday morning when we invaded her
home with camera and audio equipment. She greeted us
with homemade pastries, coffee and joy. With a lit cigarette
in hand and her shoes tossed to the side, Maya Angelou
proceeded to give hope to all displaced souls.

Russell Harris: I'd like to discuss your latest novel *(All God's
Children Need Traveling Shoes).* It left me with a haunting feeling.
You and the other Black Americans about whom you write left this
country and journeyed to Africa because of the sense of displacement
you experienced living in a staunchly racist society. And now, some
twenty years later after integration, after the initiation of civil rights, I
find there is still a strong feeling of displacement among the new
generation of Black Americans. This generation is not as radical or as
adamant about seeking change as yours, which I think is due largely
in part to an overwhelming sense of confusion.

Maya Angelou: There is a wonderful old saying which I hope I
can remember: "There is so much good in the worst of us and so
much bad in the best of us that it doesn't behoove any of us to scorn
the rest of us." That's close. For every action there is inaction. That is
one of the laws of physics, one of the laws of life-balance. For the
positive of integration there is a concomitant negative of integration.
And for the negative of segregation there is a concomitant positive; it
follows.

During segregation, Black students ofttimes were taught out of
passé books because those were the books that were handed to
them—sometimes passé ideas, old fashioned methods. With those
negatives there were the positives. They were often taught by
teachers who were committed to teaching and committed to teaching
black children. Those teachers took the student who would have
been considered backwards or slow or uneducable—took him or her
by the hand, figuratively and literally, and walked them through the
primers and through the grades—leading up to the ninth and
possibly tenth. Now there were those good things. Quite often,

however, the teachers were themselves only educated to the tenth grade.

I think that it is dangerous to see only one side of anything. It is erroneous. You cannot come up with any sort of Stafolic logic if you see only one side. Young people today, young Black people today, have a sense of dislocation for a number of reasons, one historic. Their fathers did; their grandmothers did. We have always had this sense of dislocation and it is inevitable that the young people have inherited it. They have simultaneously inherited something called the American dream. And with the urgency of the '50's, '60's and '70's— with the promise nearly kept during those years or a promise that it would be kept, there is an inevitable contradiction.

There is an inevitable burden on young Black people today. They have burdens I know nothing of. That is to say I didn't grow up with them. I did not believe when I was twenty that the promise would be kept. I knew that I had to work at least ten times harder than my white counterpart. I knew it. And even then when I worked and I was successful at my work I also knew that I would never be white; and that's not in color but "white" meaning automatically privileged. Now enough young Black people are visited at once by this sense of dislocation which they have inherited and simultaneously with the belief that they can be privileged. There is no such possibility, and if it ever happens that we are all considered a people, a nation indivisible and undivided, then it will be hundreds of years from now. It will be when racism itself has disappeared, has melted, thrown off into the ether. But that is not likely in the forseeable future. It is not likely because as a species we are still all so crushingly ignorant . . . blitheringly ignorant.

RH: Do you believe the present generation of Black Americans has grown so blinded by this "promise" that they, we, have become apathetic? Are we perhaps conceding?

MA: I don't know. I don't see apathy. I mean I just don't see it. I see a moment that may appear to be inertia, but inertia is an exacting word. It at once means movement . . . reaching a point of explosion. It also is used commonly to mean no movement. I don't see apathy. I see confusion. I think, too, that since another rule of life or law of nature is that there is always movement . . . nothing ceases . . . no

thing . . . nothing . . . no thing . . . not this paper . . . not stone . . .
nothing is dead. Fascinating!

RH: It gives hope.

MA: As the old song goes, as long as there is life there is hope.
Everything is in movement. So what appears to be apathy or inertia
is the common sense of the word. It is simply a stasis. It is a movement before the next movement. It's impossible to say what the next
movement will be. I mean utterly impossible.

RH: Speaking of movement . . . I don't recall Malcolm X being as
prominent a figure in your first four novels as Dr. Martin Luther King.
Yet, Malcolm X is mentioned quite extensively in your latest work.
The views held by these two men were radically opposed, to say the
least. What prompted you to revise your outlook?

MA: I really left Dr. King because I married a revolutionary. Then
too, I was young and I had seen all the work of Dr. King. All that
heart and passion and courage; especially courage. Love and
courage . . . they seem to come to no avail. I couldn't see beyond it. I
thought, well I agree with Malcolm. I had only met him once before
in the United States so I hadn't had a chance to make a friend. In
Ghana we became friends. I didn't realize at the time that Martin and
Malcolm were a pair, like peaches and cream. Much like my grandmother and Mrs. Flowers (from *I Know Why the Caged Bird Sings*).
Mrs. Flowers was highly educated and my grandmother wasn't. But
they were a pair, like coffee and cake . . . absolutely. One needs time
and needs the activity of mental exercise to make such connections.
One needs courage first to do it; admitting what one deduces to
finally see. And I'm sure now, at my age, in twenty years (if it is my
fortune to live that long) I will think of things that I said and did at my
age and think, damn, (laughter) is that only as far as I got? I had the
nerve to stand up in front of people and say that? One learns a little
bit.

RH: Your latest book seemed a bit more pedantic than the
previous ones. I didn't sense as much of a story being told as I did a
strictly factual account of your efforts to return to Africa to find home.

MA: I think you might need another reading, because there are
other stories in this book. There is the story of a single mother raising
a male child and trying to learn when to let go and how not to
smother, how not to abandon either . . . bring him too close or push

him too far away. And that is one of the central stories. The story of the Black Americans trying to return home is the central story. It is central in that all human beings look for home. It is given to us. And maybe all living things for all I know. For as soon as the flower, vegetable or tree grows it gives forth so that it can return home to the source of life. That African at home who has never been sent abroad is a story in that book. The sense of belonging, irremovable like a tree; that's a story in that book. So there are many and I think you might want to read it again.

RH: Is this home now?

MA: This is a home. My paintings and books are here. I have friends and loves in North Carolina. I think of it as my home. I didn't come here to stay. I didn't come anywhere to stay. Not on this earth or anywhere else. So I plan to be here. Life offers us tickets to places which we have not knowingly asked for. (Then it makes us pay the fare.) I expect to be here, but I know life and anything can happen.

RH: The news program, "Nightline," did an episode on literacy in America. One of the guests on the program said that language should be used in a way to entertain the listener. Another gentleman said something to the effect that if all you want to say in life is "pass the salt" or "fix the carburetor" then you don't really need the elegance or refinement of speech, but if you want to say "stop racial injustice" then it is imperative that you have a strong command of the language.

MA: A vocabulary is imperative. Imperative! Just for the enjoyment of life. Because as a thinking species as opposed to an innate or an instinctive species we must cogitate. In order to understand anything one needs to run it through the cogitation.

RH: There was at one time a short-lived movement that advocated the practice of teaching Black children from the less educated, more impoverished backgrounds in the vernacular of their environment. Do you view that as a viable solution to the problems of literacy?

MA: If one looks at history as we are told it and as it is written, there have been times of great plagues in human history. That was a plague. That kind of concept is a plague because it does not encourage cogitation. Every person whether he or she lives in the United States, in Ghana, in Morocco, in Beijing, every person needs the language of the marketplace; the language of the heart and the language of the marketplace. The language of the heart allows us intimacy. It is the conveyance of the tenderest of emotions, of the most delicate, the most fragile, the most vulnerable. And usually that language is learned at the mother's knee if one is lucky enough to have a mother who gives that language out of love to the child. That is one language. Everybody speaks two languages, at least two. Now, to use that intimate, personal and private language in the marketplace is to be vulnerable to every vulture. To use it because that's all you have is to be like a turtle without a shell. One needs both languages and they are both easily obtainable.

RH: There is a section in the opening part of the book when you express your fear and helplessness over your son's automobile accident. In it you state: "Had I been less timid, I would have cursed God. Had I come from a different background, I would have gone further and denied His very existence. Having neither the courage nor the historical precedent, I raged inside myself like a blinded bull in a metal stall." In keeping with our earlier discussion about the pervasive feeling of dislocation among Black Americans today, I think there also is a feeling of being trapped in our heritage, in "historical precedent," as you call it. The feeling of entrapment is due in part to an innate desire to remember and hopefully pass on our heritage, but I also think it is due largely to the pressure exuded by Black parents. It's a form of protection intended to prevent their children from getting too caught up in the "promise" or the notion that they too are privileged.

MA: Now let's just wait, just hold one minute. Let us look and see if that has always been so. First, we have a cultural carryover from slavery. Let us see that. The Black family (when it could be a family), like all other people and like all species save probably reptiles, do their best to keep their young alive, thereby keeping themselves alive . . . having some chance of immortality. Slavery exacerbated that condition so that people became really protective of their young. "Don't go . . . don't sit . . . watch ya mouth . . . shut up! . . . sit down . . . hush . . . be quiet . . . stay in the back!" That is also true in many other cultures. In some cultures if a mother or father is told that their child is beautiful, they say: "No, no, no, he's not!" hoping then that the angels would not come and take him. We see that in Edgar Allen Poe's "Annabelle Lee." Annabelle Lee was so beautiful that the angels came by night and took her. So we see that love sometimes suffocates, sometimes smothers in an attempt to keep the beloved.

Now let us look too at Benjamin Banneker. Look at his correspondence with Thomas Jefferson. Here's a man, some end part in the absolute center of slavery who laid out the plans for Washington, D.C. Here was a man who had been a slave, and his parents were slaves. One must perceive this and see that he was not caught up by that same system which will smother in an attempt to protect. And one walks down the same century and sees the list of thousands of Black people who said "I've got to break away. Thank you for your caring but I must break away." You cannot blame the family for its attempts to say, "Stay, I can hold you. As long as I can touch you I feel more secure." No matter how it says it. The family may say "You'll never make it." Whatever it says it means stay with me so I can keep my eyes on you. The family is not to be blamed for that. That is innate. It's like blinking when someone throws pepper in your eyes. The family, on the other hand, does not always win in what it thinks is its way. By holding on, it doesn't always win. It sometimes smothers that very young one. And they can't be blamed for that either.

RH: You've been a singer, dancer, poet, teacher and writer without benefit of a formal education. Is there one field that you cherish?

MA: Well, first I am a writer. But I find that I love to teach. I'm a very good teacher. And it may be that had I had an ordinary education rather than the extraordinary education, I might have become an exceedingly successful real estate broker (laughter). It's true. I had a dream when I was about eighteen that that's what I was going to do. I was going to have my own briefcase and I was going to be a hot-diggity-dog big property manager.

RH: Do you feel that today it is best to combine education plus experience?

MA: One needs both. I was very fortunate. I was curious and handicapped as a young person. And so I read everything I could get my hands on and I have a good memory. And I have a lot of energy. It's a blessing. So I continued to learn. I'm hungry for knowledge still. Not every young person is blessed or visited with that combination. So he or she desperately needs to go to a university and be introduced to some of the great ideas of humankind. One needs to worry over the question of "Why am I here, what am I doing here of all things in this place, this life?" One needs to know Aristotle and Plato. One needs it desperately. One must have Leopold and Pascal. Must! I mean desperately, if one is to be at ease anywhere. One should have read the African folk tale to see what the West African calls deep thinking. One must worry over ideas that if I come forward how far do we have to go before we meet? And when we meet will I go through you and you go through me and continue until we meet someone else? This is an African concept. Do we stay once we meet or do I actually go right through you and pass through you and continue on that road. Is that what life is? All this knowledge is available at universities and one is more likely to run into a great teacher at a university than one is at a pool hall. It just follows.

Out of thirty teachers a person has in a period of three years at a university, he or she might run into two who bring stimulation to that mental machine and then one is encouraged to go to the literature . . . go to it. The teacher doesn't teach, not really. The teacher offers stimulation and ways in which the person can educate himself or herself. At best the teacher wakes up, shakes up that person and makes a person hungry. That's when you really hit it—when you make them hungry. There is nothing more exciting in teaching.

What I really teach is one thing; that is I am a human being. Nothing human can be alien to me. That's all I teach. There is nothing alien that you can think that I can't think. And the worst, the most vile thing you can think, I have the capability of thinking. And the most glorious, the most ecstatic, generous, kind thing any human being can think, I have the machinery to think it. What about a glass of wine now?

Maya Angelou

Tricia Crane/1987

Los Angeles Herald Examiner, 25 May 1987, sec. B, 1, 5. Copyright © 1987 by the Los Angeles Herald Examiner. Reprinted by permission.

Maya Angelou's husky voice fills the red restaurant booth. The woman who calls herself the most-read black woman writer in America is talking about being a woman in this country.

"We are much more sensual than we agree to be," she says. "It's from that whole Calvinistic business that if it feels good it must be evil. Women in other cultures seem more relaxed, seem to love themselves more."

Angelou, the author of many books, including *All God's Children Need Traveling Shoes*, is in Los Angeles to promote her latest work, a book called *Now Sheba Sings the Song*. She has also just finished writing the lyrics for a new Roberta Flack album and is in the midst of writing a screenplay for a TV movie about black fathers. And next month, when an anthology called *American Childhoods* is published, it will contain the story of Angelou's rape as she told it in her autobiography, *I Know Why The Caged Bird Sings*.

But of all these projects, it is the book of drawings—*Sheba Sings the Blues*—that is most on Angelou's mind. The work was the product of a collaboration between Angelou and artist Tom Feelings. He contributed dozens of elegant sepia drawings of black women. She wrote the text, an illustrative poem that celebrates the spirit of black women that reads in part:

> My impertinent buttocks
> (High, redolent, tight as dark drums)
> Send the wind to shake tall grasses
> Introduce frenzy into the hearts of small men.

Of this tribute to the strength, dignity, sexuality and beauty of black women, Angelou says, "It's a book that says something that needs to be said. And to say it through the black experience, as all my books do, is something that is needed, too."

173

From the columns of my thighs
I take the strength to hold the world aloft
Standing, too often, with a cloud of loneliness
Forming halos for my head.

Born Marguerite Johnson in St. Louis in 1928, Angelou took the name Maya from the nickname her younger brother Bailey gave her when they were kids. "Maya" was his way of pronouncing "mine." At the age of 4, Angelou was uprooted after her parents separated. She and Bailey went to live with their grandmother in rural Arkansas. At the age of 7, Angelou was uprooted again, traveling back to St. Louis to live with her mother and her mother's lover, a man Angelou refers to in *I Know Why the Caged Bird Sings* as "Mr. Freeman." It was Mr. Freeman who on one cruel day brought Angelou's childhood to a brutal and premature end. Tried and found guilty of rape, the man never had a chance to serve jail time. He was freed only to die at the hands of a lynch mob.

That experience left Angelou mute for five years. Of that time she later observed: "I discovered that to achieve perfect personal silence, all I had to do was to attach myself leechlike to sound. I began to listen to everything. I gave up some youth for knowledge, but my gain was more valuable than the loss."

That gain had to do with learning to live life joyfully in the midst of tremendous pain.

"Bitterness is very dangerous," she says. "It's like cancer; it eats upon the host. It doesn't do a damned thing to the object of the bitterness. Retention and exclusivity and isolation and distance do nothing to anyone but the person who set them up and indulged in them. That person lives a life of meanness and narrowness."

During the five years of silence that followed the rape, Angelou became a voracious reader and observer of the world.

When she started speaking and ever since, it was with great eloquence.

"At best we live a hundred years, and if we are lucky, we live it reasonably safe from the predation of age and trying our best to be open. But those who live out of timidity and fear narrow their tunnel down even more and are wasting the experience of life. All of that is to say that I consciously decide not to have my life narrowed by fear or timidity or narrowed by someone else for their convenience. It's something that has to be decided all the time. It's not a decision you make and then say to yourself, 'I've got it made now.' It's like trying to be a Christian or a Jew or a Buddhist. It's every day and I don't know how many times a day and with what ferocity the decision has to be made and be clung to to be open."

Angelou describes the all-important process by which she was able to forgive the man who raped her. It had to do, she says, with "seeing the man. I don't mean physically seeing him. But trying to understand how really sick and alone that man was. I don't mean that I condone at all. But to try to understand is always healing.

"Still, there's not been a day since the rape 50 years ago during which I have not thought of it."

Especially when Angelou was with a lover.

"It was very complicated, very confusing. But I had to get beyond distrust. That, again, is like making the decision to be existential. You get beyond the distrust every other day, every other hour. I still don't feel as comfortable with huge men. I just don't."

Despite her emotional scar, Angelou exudes a sense of spiritual peace that has been hard-won. As a young woman she tried to escape the pain. Before she was 20, Angelou drove racing cars in Mexico, worked as a streetcar conductor in San Francisco and acted as an amateur madam for two aging prostitutes. But gradually Angelou stopped and confronted the pain and found herself.

She became an actress and singer, touring Europe with a company that performed *Porgy and Bess*. She started publishing her poems and taught for a time at the University of Ghana. The lore she had lost herself in as a young girl had left a profound impression.

"Yesterday I was talking to someone who said that young people and poor people no longer read," she says. "He told me that, if you go to a sharecropper's hut, you will find that they don't know any poetry. I don't believe that. If you went to a white sharecropper's hut in the South and even if it's only Joyce Kilmer's 'Trees,' somebody knows it. And if you go to a black sharecropper's, you would find that people know 'Little brown baby with sparkling eyes' and 'I've Known Rivers' by Langston Hughes. Maybe they don't have shelves of books, but they know the words, the stories, by heart."

And Angelou also does not believe that black men are as callous with their women and children as is often portrayed in the media. In particular, she does not believe the grim portrait of irresponsible and uncaring black teen-age fathers presented in the Bill Moyers TV special aired last year, "The Vanishing Family—Crisis in Black America," on CBS. Blaming black men for feeling hopeless when the society they live in offers them no opportunities is unfair, she argues. And perpetuating the image of callous black men as she says the Moyers special did is irresponsible.

"A teen-age boy watches that thing, and before you know it, he says, 'Oh, that's the way we are, that's the way we're supposed to be.' I think it does more harm than good."

It was by sheer serendipity that Angelou got a chance to respond to the program she so disliked.

"I got a call from a producer at CBS who asked me if I would like to write about teen-age parenting and I said no. Then she asked me if I would like to do it from the boy's point of view and I said, 'Yes, indeed!' "

Researching the script took Angelou on a tour of homes for unwed mothers in a number of urban centers. What she found was a great number of teen fathers who are not uncaring but are simply paralyzed by hopelessness that they sometimes cover with the pretense of detachment.

Angelou is hopeful that her own special will "make us all aware that those are our children, that they belong to all of us and we must educate them so that we don't have repetitions of this."

If Angelou has removed herself for the most part from women's organizations that are not specifically for black women it is because, she says, she has observed that these groups tend to discount black women, suffering from what she calls "a paucity of courtesy and a paucity of humor.

"Who wants to live in a world without courtesy and humor?" she asks.

To illustrate the reason she has taken such a dislike to white feminists, she tells the following story:

"I remember being in London at a cocktail party some years ago, and a woman standing nearby was speaking in a very affected British accent to anyone who cared to listen. 'If women ruled the world,' she

said, 'we wouldn't have had the cruelties, the famines, the wars.'
Then she turned to me where I was standing drinking and she asked,
'Don't you agree, my dear?'

"I looked at her and said, 'Not at all, my dear. I don't agree. I remember the Medicis. Oh, no. I remember the empress of China. I
remember the women who spat on the little black children who were
trying to go to school. And I *know* that somebody washes the sheets
for the Ku Klux Klan. Do you think those macho men wash their own
sheets? Make no mistake. Women do it.' And I said, 'Anyway, I don't
come to cocktail parties to speak about issues of such pith and
moment. I come to drink. So excuse me.

"After I walked away, this man came up to me and said, 'Let me
take you to dinner.' And we got married. I found out after that he
had been married to Germaine Greer.' "

Angelou makes her home now in North Carolina, where she lives
alone. "I'm not married now," she offers, "sorry to say."

How many husbands have there been?

"I don't number them," Angelou retorts. "I don't number them
because multiple marriages tend to imply that a person is not
serious."

And Angelou is anything but "not serious," especially about
love.

"If you have enough courage to love someone, and also if you
have the unmitigated gall to accept love in return, then you are an
inspiration to the species. And if you have again the courage to back
up a private emotion with a public declaration and you bring all of
your energies, all your love and laughter and everything—good
cooking and bad cooking, good sex or bad sex, and all that to your
relationship and having said in public 'I have committed myself to
doing this with this person,' then you should be an inspiration.
Unfortunately, because we tend to be deepdown shallow, we find
things to laugh at, to ridicule, to laugh at that particular demonstration. We've become so sadly shallow and callous that 'mother' is the
first two syllables of one of the worst curse words in our language.
God is a part of cursing, part of our profanity. Love is something for
afternoon television. It's shallow and it's shabby. So I no longer say
I've been married X amount of times because I know it will not be
understood.

"I've been separated six years now, sadly, because it was a great marriage, though we wore it out, we just used it up."

Having said that, Angelou sighs a great sigh and then looks a bit mischievous.

"But I have noticed just lately that I have a twinkle in my eye again."

And she breaks into a huge radiant smile.

A Journey through Life

Valerie Webster/1987

Yorkshire Post, 27 July 1987. Reprinted by courtesy of the Yorkshire Post.

Meeting Black American writer Maya Angelou is a daunting prospect. What do you say, after you have said "Hello" to a woman whose work experience has run the gamut from prostitution to professorship, a sexually-abused child of the Depression-era Deep South whose autobiography is now required reading for schoolchildren Black and White throughout America?

In the event, after a warm greeting on the doorstep, I did not have to say anything. Domesticity, that shared icebreaker of women worldwide intervened. The caterer engaged by Maya's publishers to feed us had brought genteel portions of cold curried chicken and an overstated green salad. "You can't invite people to lunch and only give them that" roared Maya, vanishing stovewards.

Only when the dining table groaned under a massive bowl of spicey golden rice, a vast platter of lamb barbequed Southern-style in a Kentish Town back garden and the green salad transformed into abundance with the eggs, avocado, green beans and dressing she had added, did she light a cigarette and come to rest.

While she was in London she rented TV reporter Jon Snow's Victorian cottage. "It's always hard cooking in other people's kitchens. Especially when they obviously aren't cooks" she explained, clearly deeply concerned for her temporary landlord's gastronomic well-being.

In addition to being a Black activist, author, poet, actress, dancer and academic, Maya Angelou emphatically *is* a cook. She learned from watching her grandmother in Arkansas and her mother in St. Louis. Now she misses no opportunity to prepare banquets for her friends and only total exhaustion will reduce her to entering a restaurant.

Her enjoyment of good food, like her enjoyment of good

company, good music, good sex and good looks in others, permeates her books. Her writing is a unique blend of sensuousness and sensitivity. And if even that cannot make bad times of the kind she has encountered seem good, reading her autobiography, like meeting its author is essentially an upbeat experience.

Unbelievably she will be 60 next year but she still has the enthusiasm for life and the open-minded receptiveness to what it has to offer a girl. "Retire? People keep telling me I should cut back on what I do but I don't know how to." And if at times she tells herself she should behave like the grandmother and Professor of American Studies she has become, at others the old madcap Maya spirit takes over.

"I was partying the other night at the celebration given for the four black MPs. I got so emotional. I sat at a table with some people I didn't know and they turned out to be Bernie Grant's family. I was so happy for them. They came here 30 or 40 years ago with expectations that they would make a better life and, thank God, it's worked out. But at what a cost!

"Then in her speech Diane Abbott quoted from one of my poems 'And Still I Rise.' After that I danced like I was 17. And I flirted quite blatantly with men young enough to be my sons."

Already an annual visitor to Britain before 1984, when Virago published the first volume of her American bestseller autobiography, I Know Why the Caged Bird Sings, here, she is here this year for the publication of her fifth volume, All God's Children Need Traveling Shoes, on August 10, and to give her live one woman show, reading poetry and possibly singing, at Liverpool Philharmonic Hall on August 8.

The latest book brings her chequered career up to the Sixties when, like many Black Americans, she went to West Africa in search of her roots. Those which went before told how she grew up with her storekeeper grandmother, was raped by her mother's lover at the age of eight, became a one-parent family at 16 and earned her living by prostitution before becoming an actress and dancer and subsequently a writer and journalist.

When the man who raped her was subsequently violently killed she stopped talking for five years and she believes that period as a silent observer fuelled the powers of observation and recall that now enables her to recreate her past life without ever having kept any kind of diary.

As *Traveling Shoes* tells, it came as a shock to her to find that Mother Africa was relatively uninterested in her returning children. The Ghanaians took scant notice and were even at times suspicious of the newcomers who had sought spiritual refuge among them. But once Maya had accepted this indifference, encounters like a chance meeting with an old woman who bore a striking physical resemblance to her in a village which generations before had been pillaged for slaves gave her a new sense of herself and her people's past.

She will write one more volume of autobiography, bringing us up to the publication of *Caged Bird* then go no further. "After that it would just be writing about writing which is something I don't want to do."

A former worker for Dr. Martin Luther King's Southern Christian Leadership Conference, Maya eventually rejected the concept of non-violence as a means of ending segregation in the United States. Now, 20 years on, she admits a great deal has been achieved without recourse to large scale organised violence. "In many ways it's much better—though in some much worse—that I'd have believed it could be when I was growing up in Arkansas. In every sphere of American life from the highest to the lowest you'll today find Black people. There's a danger, I suppose, that the sons of Black upper-middle class families going to Harvard might forget the struggle that's made it possible. But they'll still find, even if they graduate top of their class in Harvard, that when it comes to getting the top jobs they're fourth in line and then maybe they'll remember."

Maya views the present situation of Britain's Black population with a mixture of hope and despair. Young Blacks born here, have, she feels, the same sense of lack of roots which drove her and many fellow Americans to Africa in the Sixties. "The people who came here to work in the Fifties and Sixties have always looked on Jamaica and Trinidad and Barbados as home and felt they could, if the worst came to the worst, go back there. For that reason they never seemed very interested in Black history. But I find a new interest among Blacks who have been born in Britain and known no other home. In the Fifties I was optimistic about Britain's racial future. Suddenly all these people from Asia and the Caribbean were coming to the country that was the Mother of the Commonwealth. It could have been a model of integration not only for the United States, but for the whole world. But it wasn't to be."

However she senses hope in the election of four Black MPs. Pressure for change, she feels, must come from within the Black community. Whites can support but not lead. "But nothing" she declares "is more powerful than an idea when its time has come."

Though herself a strong and confident woman, Maya Angelou calls herself a "womanist" rather than a "feminist." Feminists, she believes, lack humour. And even after two short-lived marriages, far from regarding men as the enemy, she relishes their company. Blatant sexist attitudes such as she encountered in West Africa she tolerates on the grounds of "cultural differences."

But tolerance is a strong element in her character and one in which she has schooled herself over the years. In her progress from childhood in the segregated South to international literary fame and a professorship at a 95 per-cent-White North Carolina private university her attitude to Whites has inevitably changed. "When I was a child I didn't think they were human. No members of the human race could behave as they did. Now I share the view of Terence, the Roman playwright who was himself a freed African slave, and who wrote "I am a human being therefore nothing human can be foreign to me."

Actually Terence said "I am a man" but Maya Angelou would forgive him that, on the grounds of cultural differences.

The New Black Man's Burden

John Cunningham/1987

The Guardian, 13 August 1987. Copyright © 1987 by *The Guardian.* Reprinted by permission.

Mute misery for them began so early—raped in childhood, pregnant in early teens, hardened in their twenties to husbands walking out—the wonder is that black women in America still have strength to put their sorrows into novels, poems and biographies. But they do and their success has been so spectacular over the last 20 years that all the best-known black authors in the United States now are women.

And it is the cruelty, deception and fickleness of men—who often get themselves killed as an ironic escape from responsibility for their wrong doings—that has most aroused sisterly instincts from white readers. And attracted the marketing instincts of publishers and film-makers; as a theme, suffering sells.

The actual and fictional profile of the disadvantaged black US male is in part a shaming one; from Maya Angelou, raped as an eight-year-old by her mother's boyfriend, through the string of no-good sugar daddies in Ntozake Shange's work, to the demonic cruelty of Mister, in Alice Walker's *The Color Purple.* But now a debate is starting; asserting that what some men call "the revenge of the women" has gone far enough.

The tip of the complaint is that women so dominate the "black section" of the literary scene that publishers (who insist they know what their readers want) are now biased against manuscripts submitted by black male authors. It does seem odd that editors haven't discovered a serious writer as successor to the aging James Baldwin, or a popular writer to repeat the mass success of Alex Haley's *Roots.* Black women writers, by contrast, have made the covers of *Newsweek* and the *New York Sunday Times Magazine,* as a measure of their fame.

The burden of the complaint goes deeper and wider. It affects not only the 40 million blacks but the way American society treats them.

It is that, by harping on the shortcomings of the brothers, women writers are doing down a section of the population so nobbled by disadvantage that its survival is a cause for concern. In addition, such accounts, whether in biography or fiction, reinforce racial stereotyping by whites and divide the black community against itself.

"What you have now is an unholy alliance between neo-conservatives, feminists and the traditional blue collar man and they're dumping all the problems of the United States on black men," says novelist Ishmael Reed. "There is a minority of black women writers who are getting all the publicity and reaping all the dividends that come about as a result of bashing black men," he says in the magazine *Ebony Man*. "They'll have to answer to history and to their consciences."

Whatever the impact of blacks being portrayed as burdening, brutalising and abandoning their women, there is a real social problem underlying the books. The life-chances for a male born into a low income family are not good. Compared with a white male in similar family circumstances, a black is more likely to be brought up by a single parent, to need welfare support, to flunk his grades at school, to be unemployed, to be in trouble with the police; more likely to do drugs. And, up to the age of 35, he's far more likely to die a violent death than a white man.

All this is true, in spite of there being a prosperous, well-rooted professional black middle class; the literary debate is particularly crucial; as some black males see it, women writers are endangering the self-image and solidarity by exposing the community's weaknesses to US society at large.

In the thick of this and well-placed to untangle some of the strands, is Maya Angelou. She is in the best-seller league, with volumes of her autobiography stretching from *I Know Why the Caged Bird Sings*, to the latest, *All God's Children Need Traveling Shoes*. No denying the harsh treatment she received from men and recounted in her books: they are biography, not fiction. Yet she is not a feminist, out to seek a man-hating revenge; she is, as she carefully says, a womanist.

Angelou has a cagey preface before weighing in: "I'm always quite leery of this theme because I'm reminded of the Machiavellian theory, separate and rule, divide and conquer and I refuse to be a gladiator for the express delectation of people who won't give a damn about my life—about our life."

On the publishing front, it's true, she says, that some houses—
"because of the vividness of the street riots and the social and political
upsets" of the Sixties—did bring out books by black writers. "In some
cases, they published crap, so they were able to say later, in defence,
we won't publish books which don't sell." There's also a racism in
the United States, she argues, which dictates, in publishing as in any
other activity, how far up the ladder a few blacks are allowed to go.

Inasmuch as these factors have worked recently against male
authors, she understands. "I'm afraid that a number of men—I
understand their frustration, but not the absence of really intelligent
observation—feel jealousy about the situation. But at the same time,
to take arms against women, there is a sadness about that. Some of
the men who were so angry with Alice Walker admitted later that
they hadn't read the book.

"This ninny [referring to one particularly hostile black author]
implied that *The Color Purple* would absolutely destroy black
Americans. But it's interesting that we've survived rapes, slavery,
ridicule, abuse, discrimination and you tell us we are so weak that a
book is going to destroy us. Please!"

There was a time when black men and women writers shared the
laurels, along with musicians and artists, in the Harlem Renaissance
of the 1920s and 1930s; but in the decades since then, it is black
male authors who have been dominant. That was true, right up to the
Black Power period of the 1960s, and some of the Black Panthers
were harsh with the sisters. "When Eldridge Cleaver said (in *Soul On
Ice*) 'I regard black women as a rehearsal so that I can rape white
women,' black women didn't jump all over him," says Angelou.
Maybe they should have.

And black writers who might be envying Maya Angelou's mega-
success are not jumping all over her, if only because they see more to
complain about in the writings of other women. "If black men are
such brutes, such beasts and treat their women as terrible as Alice
Walker and Toni Morrison say they do," biographer Addison Gayle is
quoted in *Ebony* magazine as saying, "how can you blame society
for not granting integration to them, for not making it possible for
black men to achieve."

"There are brutes in Angelou's experience, too, of course, but she
has this to say: "I suppose I'm about the only female writer not to be
attacked because the theme of my work is that, it can be rough, it can

be tough but someone dares to love somebody and so we survive. If you have the courage to love, you survive."

And just as she doesn't go along with the notion of a literary conspiracy involving feminists welcoming their black sisters on board because of their terrible experiences of lovers-turned-rapist, husbands-turned-exploiters, Angelou reckons a bit of social history is needed to straighten out some misunderstandings about black male/female roles and relationships.

"A number of black men will say they prefer to be with white women because they concede, surrender to their demands for total control. Black women don't do that." And she describes an historical equality, rooted in a mutuality of suffering, generated in slavery: "We (men and women) were sold together, we were brought from the African coast together. We were brought, spoon-fashion over here together; we stood on the auction-block together. We were sold together. And we survived together." Equal work-value implied an equal partnership in marriage.

What's more, in spite of the desolation of a broken partnership, "It must be said in many relationships, it's not that the black men themselves are so ready to leave; it's that black women ask them to leave because they are aware of what they will not accept." This attitude pre-dates ideas in white societies in the west of sexual equality.

What does worry Maya Angelou—who acknowledges the gravity of the problems facing U.S. blacks thus: "We are in a situation now where we might not survive; we are in a situation more dangerous than slavery"—is the lack of a strategy and the polarisation of the community.

"We are becoming polarised again, so that there is a middle class, and a professional class and a working class, an under class, a literate class and a drug class and an illiterate class. We have almost a steel floor between the middle and the under classes, so strong that only a few can puncture it.

"The young boy in the ghetto will rarely believe he can escape, unless he can sing or dance—boxing is gone. There is a hopelessness there; a despair; a self-loathing which comes out of so many things and which causes the person to loathe anyone who looks like him. We we have the plethora of black-on-black crime and sexual violence you hear so much about."

To any outsider, the scale of the problem which holds a substantial part of America's blacks in its clutches is immense: almost every statistic is dismal, from the numbers of unmarried teenage mothers, to the proportion of black families below the national income, to the saddest update of all: blacks comprise 12 per cent of the population but account for 25 per cent of AIDS virus carriers, largely because of drug-users sharing needles.

It might not be surprising if women writers of two generations, from Maya Angelou, who is 59, down to younger practitioners, hone in on the fractured heart of the family. And because Maya Angelou is an optimist, a survivor, she stresses the strengths: the national political leaders, Andrew Young and Jesse Jackson; the strong black mayors of major cities and the mass membership of black churches and women's organisations. They are all having a part to play in putting together a national strategy so that blacks themselves collectively would think out for their future.

And there is this virtue, too. What sustained, collective deprivation has forged is a sort of black matriarchy. It is, after all, women who are the life-enhancing characters in so many recent books. They are the social reality as well. It is common, with babies born to young mothers, for the parenting to be done by grandmothers, who are the constant factor, emotional, religious and economic in many black families.

Maya Angelou herself was brought up in this way and says being shipped off to her grandmother's care as a young girl "was the best thing that ever happened to me." Later, bonds with her own mother were forged. Now, after five slices of her own autobiography, the book she really wants to write is about her own mother: small and frail but enduring.

Singing, Swinging, and Still Living Life to the Full

Devinia Sookia/1987

Caribbean Times, 21 August 1987. Reprinted by courtesy of the Caribbean Times and Devinia Sookia.

I was a little nervous before meeting this writer—a university lecturer-mother-singer-dancer-actress-black activist. But as soon as she rose to greet me, all my apprehension disappeared. She was so friendly and displayed such warmth that it seemed like we had known each other for years. At 6 ft., she looked very handsome with her dark hair, smooth complexion and round face.

The remarkable insight she showed into human nature was very appealing. She fitted my image of a writer and woman perfectly. At any rate she was willing to listen as we talked of women, marriage, literature, politics and just about every other subject.

Maya Angelou, born Marguerite Johnson, has seen her books become rapid bestsellers in Britain. Born in 1928 in St. Louis, Missouri, Maya has had many careers which are recorded in her volumes.

In *I Know Why the Caged Bird Sings* (1970) Maya writes about her childhood. It is a very poignant and moving story of a little girl, aged 3, who, together with her 4-year-old brother, goes to live with her grandmother, Annie Henderson, in the small southern town of Stamps in Arkansas.

They were sent there from California, after their parents' broken marriage. Annie Henderson, "Momma," owned property and the only black store in town. She even owned land on which whites lived.

Annie was a stern and very religious person. Then Maya and her brother were sent to their mother in St. Louis, came back to Stamps and then went again to live with their mother in San Francisco.

At the age of 8 she was raped by her mother's boyfriend. For five years she took refuge in silence and spoke only to her brother. At 16 she got pregnant and gave birth to her son Guy.

In her second book, *Gather Together in My Name* (1974), Maya recalls her struggle as an unemployed and single parent, briefly forced through circumstances to turn to prostitution and drugs.

Maya's third book, *Singin' and Swingin' and Gettin' Merry Like Christmas* (1976), describes her stage debut and her return from the international tour of *Porgy and Bess* in which she was featured as a dancer.

Her fourth book, *The Heart of a Woman,* is set in the turbulent 1960s of black power, segregation and Martin Luther King's dreams. Maya relates an important period of her life. We read about how she began writing and how restlessness made her move to New York where she survived her baptism into the Harlem Writer's Group, her struggle to bring up her son Guy as a single mother and to earn a living as a singer.

After hearing Martin Luther King speak she organised a fund-raising cabaret for freedom for the Southern Christian Leadership Conference and was invited to become their coordinator.

She met her husband Vusumzi Make (Vus), a smooth talking, highly motivated person. Married life created many tensions and frustrations for an intelligent woman like Maya, not happy only to play housewife. Refusing such insularity, she accepted a part in Genet's *The Blacks*. This period in her life seems to have been very important as she becomes aware of her own desires, needs and limitations.

It can be said that she truly came of age at this time, though she was already 30. She talks a lot of her husband in the book, though the marriage failed. She takes a job as editor of the *Arab Observer.*

The marriage disintegrates slowly and she goes to Ghana to place her son in the university there. The book ends with the moving parting of Maya from Guy.

In the fifth and latest volume of her brilliant autobiography, *All God's Children Need Traveling Shoes,* Maya relates her emigration to Ghana. At first she felt like being at home and even better. Then she discovered that "you can't go home again." On a sexual and social level she was made aware of why black Americans behave the way they do when they are in Africa.

She writes about black solidarity and distrust of black Americans. Encountering the country on its own terms, she comes to a new

awareness of herself, slavery and black betrayal, civil rights and
mothering.

Woman's File: Maya, what sort of woman do you regard yourself as?

Maya: I am an artist and I would rather be known as an intelligent
woman than an intellectual one.

Woman's File: Which one of your five-volume autobiographies do
you consider to be your most significant accomplishment and why?

Maya: Well, this is like asking which one of your five children do
you like best. However, the last one is always the dearest one as he is
the youngest. So my last book is the newest one and closer to me.
For every writer the newest work is the closest one as it has not had
its own life yet. It is still a child and not a grown-up yet.

Woman's File: Your new book of poetry, *Now Sheba Sings the
Song*, is dedicated to all your sisters. Why is that?

Maya: My dedication is to all my brown, black, beige, yellow, red
and white sisters. The book is an attempt to herald the various kinds
of beauty of women, some plain, some young, and of all colours.

Woman's File: At what time in your life did you first realise that
you had the gift of writing?

Maya: I started writing when I was very young. I love language
and I love English. In the university there are little copies of poetry
and prose which I wrote when I was 9. This is the time when I
realised that I liked writing.

Woman's File: Your first two books relate the most unhappy time
of your life, whereas the third one, *Singin' and Swingin' and Gettin'
Merry Like Christmas*, has happier moments, though there are some
bad things in it. How did you feel when writing the third one?

Maya: Well, happiness is like your hair: only one out of ten million
people has the traumatic experience of turning grey overnight. It is
gradual. You get two grey hairs and then dozens, and then before you
know it you have a beautiful streak like salt and pepper in there.

Well, happiness does not come immediately but I became more in
control of my life and that's when I almost stopped being at the
sufferance of fate.

Woman's File: So *Singin' and Swingin'* relates a time when you
were more experienced in life and could bear a crisis more?

Maya: Yes. I could bear more and even learn ways to get out of a crisis. That happens to all of us as we grow up, take more responsibilities ourselves, and stop being buffeted by every wind that comes.

Woman's File: What advice have you got for young black women writers who want to achieve success?

Maya: I would advise them to read everything, I mean all the black writers, all the white writers, all the Asian writers, the Russian writers and if possible, read the translations. They should read the works of somebody as diverse as Rabindranath Tagore. A young, black, female writer needs to know everybody. She must know the works of Shakespeare.

Woman's File: Why did you refuse to write your autobiography when asked by Robert Loomis at Random House?

Maya: Well, I thought then I really was a playwright and a poet. But then when he said that it would be impossible for me to write an autobiography, I had to prove to him that he was wrong.

Woman's File: Why do you think black women writers like Alice Walker, Andre Lorde and yourself have been more successful than Phyllis Wheatley, Zora Neale Hurston and Nella Larsen?

Maya: Well, Phyllis Wheatley wrote 217 years ago when she was a slave. Zora Neale and Nella Larsen wrote long ago. To be a woman writer and be accepted 40 years ago was not possible because of the social restrictions on black women, whereas it was not very difficult for black women writers in my time to be accepted.

My first book was a best seller. Alice Walker had written poetry and a novel before *Color Purple*, so her work had been heard of before *Color Purple*. Audre Lord has been writing great poetry for 20 years and was respected before she became internationally famous.

Woman's File: When you worked with Martin Luther King, you believed in non-violence. Do you still do so?

Maya: I believed that non-violent marches and protests would really change the political structure of the United States. Now I believe that it is wise to have some sort of protest but young militants themselves should make the decision.

Woman's File: Do you think that married women can have careers and play an important part in society, as well as being housewives?

Maya: Absolutely. I think they are the first teachers that children know. They have an important impact on them. The housewife should not think that she has stopped learning just because she is a wife.

She should continue to read and encourage her husband, family and friends to enter into important political and social conversations.

If I was living today as a young housewife or a Caribbean woman working outside the house, I would make every effort to read everything Chris James and Braithwaite wrote so that I would know not only where I am today but how I got here and why in so many cases our children are running crazy on the streets.

The housewife needs to be able to talk to the kids but if she thinks that once she is married she does not have to read any more, then that is really bad.

Woman's File: What do you think of black people in Britain?

Maya: I imagine that this generation of young blacks in Britain is as different from the generation which preceded them as chalk is from cheese.

Woman's File: From your own experience in life, can you tell us any valuable lesson that you have learned?

Maya: I think that one of the things I have learned is that as human beings we may encounter many defeats but we must not be defeated.

In fact it may even be imperative that we encounter the defeats so that we can see who we are. Each time you overcome a burden or barrier, you feel better about yourself. You become stronger.

It is like being at school. Once you pass, you feel okay. You may not attain the level you wanted but you passed.

The next time you encounter a test you feel a little stronger. You keep overcoming. Then finally you walk with more assertiveness, more pride and more confidence.

Woman's File: Do you think that the black community has achieved something in Britain?

Maya: Well, first the achievement of four black MPs at the same time is amazing and exciting. We must remember that each of these four black officials has got some hard work to accomplish.

I cannot say to the black community in Britain but I can say to myself that when I read about the actions of these four people, I must remember to have patience, as they are pathfinders and the people who come along after them are only road makers.

Another thing we must remember is to step aside and let young people take over because they are impatient. If they were not impatient as a species we would all still be in the trees.

It is important for the elders to be willing to give wisdom and not to try to direct everything. Young people see themselves living in this world and it is their life yet to be lived.

Woman's File: Maya, you are a lady with a considerable load on your shoulders. Yet you are always relaxed. How do you do that?

Maya: Life is all I have got—not money, not fame, not a lover, not a son or a grandson. Things which a telephone call tell you that you no longer have at any time. They can go, whether it is a position, a title, a house, a family or money. All ahead is this life. This is all I have.

So in this life I want to love, laugh, weep, see human beings, be a responsible person, and I'm never bored.

On this Maya told me a short story about life: My grandmother used to have a store in a little village in Arkansas and people used to come to the store in summer and say, "Miss Henderson, you know, I just hate this heat. It's killing me."

My grandmother would just nod her head. In winter they would say: "Miss Henderson, I just hate this cold." Grandmother would nod her head again. As soon as the person would leave she would call me. She was 6 ft 2 ins and was like a giant to me.

She would say: "Sister, did you hear what Brother Thomas, or Sister Joan said?" I would not utter a word because I knew if I did she would have knocked me to the ground.

She would then say: "Sister, all over the world, white and black and others went to sleep last night when that man went to sleep and they were never to wake again.

Rich or poor, their beds had become their cooling boards and their blankets had become their winding sheets and they would give anything for five minutes of what that man is complaining about."

Our interview ended on these words of hers: "Then I realized that every day is a gift. So I enjoy every moment of life. I try to be always pleasant. When any person tries to pay me attention, I think that he does not have to do that for me. Life is a gift, and I try to respond with grace and courtesy. So I would be foolish not to be open and enjoy this moment."

The Maya Character

Jackie Kay/1987

Marxism Today, September 1987, 18, 21. Reprinted by courtesy of *Marxism Today*.

I Know Why the Caged Bird Sings *was first published in the States by Random House; it wasn't published again here until 15 years later. I would be very interested to know exactly what was the response when it was first published in 1970?*

Well, within a week it was on the bestseller list, the national bestseller list, and it stayed there for some time.

Why do you think it took Britain so long to bring out a British edition?

British publishers, in fact established publishers, said in effect that my work would be of no interest to the British reading public, although it had been offered from the very first, and my publisher, Random House, was consistently told every year at the International Bookmart, unfortunately no.

So I used to come to Britain, to England—I like London, and I have London friends—and in the pub or at parties people would ask me: 'What do you do?' And I'd say: 'I'm a writer,' and they'd answer: 'Are you going to get anything published?' Books of mine sell hundreds of thousands in Europe, and so I'd say: 'Actually I'm a bit famous,' and they'd say: 'Oh go on, you're not published in Britain . . .'

When did you start writing?

Almost immediately. I mean my papers are at Wake Forrest University in North Carolina, letters from folks and important papers. Now I have papers, poems and prose I wrote at nine years old, which have been sent to Wake Forest. Admittedly it may have been the worst poetry west of the Rockies, but there is something, you know.

I was interested to read that you refer to the Maya in your autobiographies as the 'Maya character,' is that right? You think of her as a 'Maya character,' not exactly the same as yourself? How difficult is it to maintain this distance?

I didn't read that in any article. I don't believe anyone has ever asked me that. The person I was yesterday is not exactly the same as the person I am today, understandably. So if that is so, then the person I wrote about 20 years ago knew only *that* much. Now, writing today, about somebody 20 years ago, one has to impose a kind of distance, otherwise I will imbue that person with the wisdom I have today.

That is the difficulty in writing autobiography as literature. You have to keep that distance and not imply that this person knew what she was doing from the vantage point of 1987. No one in the world has ever asked me that. That difficulty is probably the horn, the unicorny horn of the dilemma from which I spin, to try to keep that distance. And what is lovely, and I've never thought about this before, is that in writing poetry I can write from today. I can admit that I have now got wrinkles and now got this, and I now know better than I knew 20 years ago.

I think I am the only serious writer who has chosen the autobiographical form as the main form to carry my work, my expression. I pray that in each book I am getting closer to finding the mystery of really manipulating and being manipulated by this medium, to pulling it open, stretching it.

Memory is a fascinating thing, memory and time. You must be constantly thinking about how we edit memory, and that whole subject.

Well, it's fascinating. In truth, when I set out to write, I choose some sort of 'every-human-being' emotions, themes. So I will choose generosity, meanness of spirit, romantic love, loss of love, familiar love, ambition, greed, hate. And then I will set myself back in that time and try to see what incidents contained that particular theme. I may find seven. Some of them are too dramatic, I can't write them without being melodramatic you understand, so I say no, I won't write that one. Some are too weak. But I find one and I think, aha, this one. Now let me enchant myself back to that day or that month, or those months, so I can remember everything about that one incident. In that way the work is episodic, you see, but if I'm lucky and work hard it should flow so that it looks like just a story being told.

Protest is integral to your work and your life. Can you tell us what first politicized you? Or do you believe that black Americans have no other choice than to be fighters?

Well, there is no choice if you want to stay alive, otherwise you ally yourself with death and the end of action. Nothing in life stops, nothing. I don't know. I think we're all politicized and I couldn't say what was the first incident. It starts so early and it's so consistent.

So when you say you don't tolerate fools, that applies to you when you were young as well, doesn't it?

You see, what will happen, unfortunately, if we tolerate the fool, a person who really acts foolishly, will be that we ally ourselves with them. Sometimes a person will insult you, and if you respond he says: 'Oh I was just teasing.' Now quite often the person really wants you dead, maybe just for four minutes, and then he would resuscitate you. But what he means by those vicious remarks is *die*. Well, as soon as I hear it from anybody anywhere I say: 'Stop it, not me, this is my life, this is all I've got.'

In the 1960s, you worked alongside Dr. Martin Luther King as a civil rights campaigner. I'd just like to hear more about that period from your point of view.

The period was absolutely intoxicating. The streets were filled with people who were on their toes, figuratively, with alertness. There was a promise in the air, like a delicious aroma of a wonderful soup being cooked in the kitchen on a cold day when you are hungry. It really appeared as if we were going to overcome racism, sexism, violence, hate.

So while it was strident, it was hopeful and it was as if there was a heaven in the air. It was a wonderful time.

And what has happened to the civil rights movement?

Well, it was derailed, understandably, by those, to quote Miss Margaret Walker: 'who tower over us omnisciently and laugh.'

Angela Davis was recently here in London, invited over by the ANC. What do you remember of the time when she was on America's Ten Most Wanted People's List?

Well naturally a number of people were involved in keeping her secure, because we knew it was a put-up job, just one more way to kill one of the leaders. After she was apprehended, Margaret Burnam, who is now a black judge, but was then a young lawyer and a sister friend of Angela's, got me in to see her. The way I could go in person was to be credited as a legal adviser. She was in a 'facility' which was designed by Frank Lloyd Wright—pink and blue nestled in the hills—what artistry! So I asked her once: 'Here you are, in this pretty palace, and what do you think?' She said: 'Girl, the joint is the joint.' And when she finally won her freedom, I interviewed her.

There was a popular television series in the States; the host gave it up for a year and six of us took it over. I could interview anyone I wanted for those six. So I interviewed Angela in her sister's kitchen. We just sat over coffee and biscuits and it was really sweet.

In August there was a rally in London to commemorate the 1956 South African women's march to Pretoria. That was just a year after Rosa Parks refused to go to the back of that bus in 1955. Do you feel you have a responsibility as an artist to record our heroes and heroines, our Rosa Parks and Ruby Doris figures?

Well, let me come back before I answer that please. One of the challenges for any radical (and I use the word to mean revolutionary, reformer) is to remain human and not to take on the trappings of the opposition and become dehumanised. That's very important. That's one of the gifts that black American women have, and try to share; always the humanity, the sweetness. And under oppression, kicking butt and taking names, they are still laughing sometimes and hugging. Very important.

Everything we do, I mean I don't know how broad that landscape is, is an action of recording. The impetus to record, I don't know whether that comes from the artists or whether artists are the recorder. That's two different things and yet they serve the same end. If I set out with the idea that I ought to record, then maybe my artistry suffers; if I set out with . . . I don't know. It's a very complex question. I do know that people live in direct relation to the heroes and she-roes they have.

In Caged Bird, *you tell us that as a young girl you took responsibility for your rapist's death—which was the reason you became mute. Child abuse is now talked about more than it was then. Do you think this changes anything?*

Well, more often than not the victim, especially if you are a member of a depressed class or gender or sex, is loaded with the guilt for that action against herself or himself. It is always so. The young girl today is no less made to feel guilty or feels no less guilty than I did 40 years ago. And I know, I know too well, that the girls feel as much involved in the crime as the criminal.

When you were younger you never thought of white people as being real people; you thought that if you put your finger through them it would come out the other end. I find that fascinating and funny because it had such a strong spark of survival in it.

Well, they didn't act like people in my little town in the South, they were so mean, you know. People laughed and people cried and people hugged each other and people got mad at each other and people rocked on the back porch or the front porch and sang and people loved children and they'd say, 'Come here girl' and hug you all the time. Well, *they* didn't do anything like that, so I thought *they* weren't people.

In a recent article, which you wrote for the Independent, *you describe a celebration you attended for the four black British MPs. You said the solidarity between black and white people gave you an incredible high. How important do you feel alliances with white people are?*

We will survive together or we will die together; it is imperative that we make alliances, sincere alliances. But you see the difficulty is only equals make friends; any other relationship is out of bounds, so if the white thinks that he is better than the black or the Asian, then the relationship can never be peer, then there can never be any friendship. If the black woman thinks she s better than the white woman there can never be any serious meeting point.

In the early 70s, Amiri Baraka wrote such things as the woman's role was to be feminine and submissive. How far do you think black male attitudes have changed since then, since the Black Panther movement?

That was an aberration which took place and black women for a while said: 'Okay, we'll see what you do with this,' and it didn't happen. Black women said: 'No babe we don't take it like that,' and we don't, we haven't. We were sold together, bought together on the African continent, lay spoon fashion in the filthy hatchets of slave ships together, got up on the auction block together, stood together, sold again together, got up before sunrise, got up after sunset, together, worked those cane fields and cotton fields and the mines and all that together. Please, we are equal.

In your latest book, All God's Children Need Traveling Shoes, *you describe being in Ghana at the age of 33. You say: 'We had come home, and if home was not what we had expected, never mind, our need for belonging allowed us to ignore the obvious and to create real places or even illusory places, befitting our imagination.' This reminds me of a VS Naipaul story, where the narrator says: 'All landscapes are in the end only in the imagination; to be faced with the reality is to start again.'*

You can never go home again, but the truth is you can never leave home, so it's all right. And yet it is innate in human nature to try to go home again, and it may in fact be what life is all about: getting back to home, back to death, and then out of death and back to life.

Many black British people today possess a kind of myth of return. They think that by returning to Africa, once they set foot on African soil, they will suddenly become whole again.

Everything will be all right!

Don't you think that's dangerous?

I think it's important, though it's good to have that, and it's good to go back. A part of that is true: you find that mores, customs, attitudes, melodies, rhythms which you thought came from Jamaica, or even from Britain, actually had their origins on that continent. And somehow you are made more strong. But you also find out, ah, I really am an American, I really am an African as well. But I am a new type of African, I am also an American, or I am also British, or I'm also Jamaican . . . I've found the source of so many things that I had not known to be other than black American, or even that I thought had originated due to slavery, you see, and that is encouraging and uplifting.

At the beginning of this interview, you said it is important to maintain the distance between who you are now and who you were then. Does the language you use in Gather Together *to describe an encounter with two lesbians ('lecherous old hags,' and 'dirty things') relate to how you felt then? Has your attitude towards lesbians changed over the years?*

Oh, yes, of course, but I mean I was 18 and they were old! They were 28. To me, I thought, well, at 18 you think anybody over 23 is a crone. I think I wouldn't have thought that, I wouldn't have been so mean, had I not sensed that they wanted to take advantage of me. And I felt that about anybody, anybody who wanted to take advantage of me. That has not changed; it has polished a bit. Had they been two men, or two anybodys, who wanted to outwit me, I would have been the same. Even then I had an aunt who was gay, who was a lesbian, and who I loved, and who helped me raise my son, Guy.

When you were young, you had a fear of being a lesbian yourself, didn't you?

Yes, I thought if I was going to be a lesbian, I was going to live this sad life that was written about in *The Well of Loneliness.*

Loneliness and more loneliness!

I told my mum when I thought I was going to be a lesbian; I sat on the side of her bed and told her my vulva was growing. My mum said: 'What no, get the dictionary,' and she said: 'This is very natural.' And so I was quite relieved. But about 10 years later, my son Guy came to me, he was about 10, and he said: 'Mum I want to ask you something. What do you think about lesbians.' I said: 'Lesbians, Jesus, I don't.' He says: 'Well, I'm going to tell you something: Aunt Lottie is a lesbian but if you don't change the way you treat her I'll never speak to you again!' Obviously, I support any group which means to survive and make a better world.

How Maya Angelou Overcame All the Odds

Bev Gilligan/1987

From *Woman Magazine*, 3 October 1987, 1. Copyright © 1987 by Woman Magazine, London, England. Reprinted by permission.

American author Maya Angelou strolls into her favourite London restaurant, "The Old Poodle Dog in Sloane Square," sporting a black sequinned skull cap and a grey frilly frock, her fingers festooned with exotic rings.

She sips a glass of champagne, orders a double scotch and lights the first of several cigarettes.

With two new books recently published—*All God's Children Need Traveling Shoes* and *Now Sheba Sings the Song*—and her 60th birthday next April, she declares in her slow, rich-as-molasses Southern drawl: "I feel as if my life's just starting. I have no idea what's next. I may end up drowning in my morning oatmeal." And her eyes sparkle with suppressed humor.

Her wit and warmth are legendary. Yet in her 59 years, Maya Angelou has undergone almost every crisis known to womankind. She was raped by her mother's lover at eight, became a single parent at 16, worked as a prostitute, waitress and singer and recently separated acrimoniously from the man she considered her last and best love.

But in spite of all the heartache, her face remains unlined, her appetite for experience undiminished. And, although she says it would be "simpler" if her next romantic interest were a black American like herself, she isn't narrowing the search.

"If the next man who makes me laugh is bright, mostly cheerful and just happens to be four foot tall and a four hundred pound Japanese Sumo wrestler, I will have him and make no apologies to anyone," she announces. "I will cherish him and be grateful.

"I very rarely see what people look like," she admits. "When I introduced my last husband to my housekeeper, she took me to one side and said, 'He's *fat*, honey, ain't he?' Fat? Somehow that had not been the essence of the man."

Maya feels that after the failure of her last marriage she will, in the future, relegate relationships to loving friendships. But that doesn't exclude close bodily contact. "We are all in need of some physical attention, male and female," she maintains. "It takes some of the strain off and allows you to go on and do open heart surgery or play an East Indian nose flute with the left nostril.

"It doesn't mean being in *love,* but being in *like . . .* "

But she can't see herself marrying again. "I just do not feel there is anybody who would not be threatened by my success," she confesses. "No matter how strong a man is, I have seen them gradually become insecure, sorry, sad.

"I can pretend to be ditsy and silly—I *am* frivolous—but there is an intellect, a deepness, that I can not pretend doesn't exist. And who would I serve if I pretended not to know what I know? I would be lying not only to him—which never works—but to myself, which is the worst part.

"I cannot be less than the most I can be, otherwise, I would be spitting at God. If I've been given this much talent and this much intelligence, then I'm obliged to use it."

And she had such high hopes of her last husband, a British builder. "He has so much pzazz," she says softly. "He courted me in London, before I was published here. We were in a wine bar in the King's Road and an American who knew me came up and said to him, 'Do you realise this is one of the heaviest women in America . . . how are you going to cope?'

"And the man turned and said, 'I am a weight lifter.' And I thought, oooooooh . . . " And she rolls her eyes as she relishes the memory.

"But as the fame and the success increased and the books were best sellers, and I became the first black woman producer in Hollywood, he couldn't stand it.

"I brought all my energy and laughter and frivolity and seriousness to the marriage and it failed. It wore out. So I don't think *I* failed—*it* failed."

Maya believes it's her faith that's kept her going. "The black church in America is like another world," she says. "It's full of hilarity, ecstasy, despair, poignancy, sadness and human warmth.

"We go to church not for duty's sake, but for the joy of it, the music, the excitement."

Her only son Guy has also brought her immense happiness. "If I have a monument in this world, it is my son," she says proudly. "He is a joy, a sheer delight. A good human being who belongs to himself. He's 42 now, with a son of his own.

"I really love human beings. I really am so amused by the human condition," she smiles. "I can't believe that a creature meant to crawl through slimy swamps stands erect; decides not to eat his brother and sister who are probably delicious and creates incredible figures like Christ, Buddha and Moses.

"It's so thrilling to be here on this tiny blob of spit and sand, reading our own meaning into the stars. I'm grateful to be alive and intelligent. And I'm glad I'll live only a short time. I have no dreams to be kept alive for 400 years with the help of chemical research.

"But immortality? Yes, I dream of immortality. Not in this body but in my ideas and spirit."

Maya credits her own concern and compassion for the human race to the five years she was mute, after she was raped at the age of eight. Her mother's lover was lynched the next day and the shock robbed Maya of speech.

"I can't segregate all my sense but I do think my respect for human beings comes from that period of muteness when I learned how to concentrate. I imagined my whole body as an ear and as a result I've been able to learn languages"—she speaks seven fluently—"by just giving myself over to the sound."

Maya's mother couldn't get through to her daughter after the ordeal. "She used all her resources . . . she sang, she danced," Maya recalls. But to no avail. Maya and her brother Bailey were sent to the grandmother's.

And it was there, in the deep south, that she first became aware of racism. It was one of the reasons she went to work for the American civil rights leader, Martin Luther King. "Martin had all the frailty and ferocity, the tenderness and passion of you and I. Which means of course, he often stumbled over his own feet. However, he had the incredible talent of being able to forgive himself. To say, 'I have fallen, I will get up.' And that itself is not only admirable, inspirational."

Courage is the quality she admires the most. "It doesn't mean not being afraid," she explains. "It means being afraid but facing it."

One of her favorite quotations is, "I shall die, but that is all I will do for death."

And—hallelujah—she has no intention of doing it just yet . . .

Maya Angelou

Greg Hitt/1987

Winston-Salem Journal, 6 December 1987, sec. A, 13, 16.
Copyright © 1987 by the *Winston-Salem Journal.* Reprinted by
permission.

It is an Easter Sunday crowd on a late November afternoon.

Cars line both sides of the street behind Mount Zion Baptist
Church. The sanctuary is full, its balcony bulging, as more than
1,000 people squeeze in for a Sunday night shout with Maya
Angelou and the Inspirational Choir.

"We're not a small church," says the Rev. Serenus T. Churn. "But I
don't mind telling you, we don't push the walls back like that every
Sunday."

Miss Angelou is a poet and writer whose works have won
international acclaim as testaments to black life in America.

She lives in Winston-Salem, teaches at Wake Forest University, and
attends church at Mount Zion on Martin Luther King Jr. Blvd., where
once a year she gives the congregation what she spends the rest of
the year giving the world: a reading.

This night she breathes life into works of Langston Hughes, June
Jordan, Richard Wright and Paul Laurence Dunbar, as well as poems
of her own. But it is her voice, as much as the words, that engages
the crowd. Burnished and full, the voice is a theatrical blend of city
sass and back-country molasses.

"I have known rivers," Miss Angelou says, casting sadness over the
crowd with the opening line to Hughes' *The Negro Speaks of Rivers.*

"I have known rivers ancient and older than the flow of human
blood in human veins—and my soul has grown deep like the river."

She draws out the word "deep" as if using it to measure the water,
and here and there members of the audience say "Amen."

"I bathed in the Euphrates when dawns were young," she
continues. "I built my hut along the Congo and it lulled me to sleep. I
lived along the Nile and I built those tremendous pyramids high
above it.

"I saw the Mississippi when Abe Lincoln went all the way down to New Orleans," she says, adding sweetness to her voice, "and I have watched its muddy bosom grow all golden in the sunset. I say I have known rivers—and my *soouuul* is as deep as all the rivers."

A baby's cry breaks the silence as Miss Angelou yields the altar to the choir, which after a short piano introduction, launches as one voice into "God Is Still Moving," a gospel song that is more march than hymn.

Miss Angelou stands to the side, her hand tapping out the slow beat of the song.

"My God," the choir sings, "He moves me!"

Over lunch and a bottle of white wine at her home in Old Town a few days later, Miss Angelou offered a prayer to God, and after giving thanks for the meat loaf and rice, she gave thanks for something else.

"The Lord has a marvelous wit," she said after unfolding her hands. "How can we not see it in ourselves? In who we are and how we act?"

Her self-criticism was to the point. Miss Angelou, 59, has made a name for herself by examining her life—by exploring the Lord's wit, if you will, and its work within her.

Her life has been well-chronicled in her five sequential volumes of autobiography. Her works have been translated into 10 languages and have made best-seller lists in New York and London.

The most famous, *I Know Why the Caged Bird Sings,* was made into a television movie in 1979.

The book describes a troubled childhood that led her from the segregation of Stamps, Ark., to California and the harsh realities of being an unwed mother.

Miss Angelou was born in St. Louis and lived for a short while in California before her parents split up and after her father sent her and her brother, Bailey Johnson Jr., to live with their grandmother in Stamps. Miss Angelou was 3, her brother 4, and they made the train trip by themselves, with a "To Whom It May Concern" note tied to their wrists telling who they were and where they were bound.

Under her grandmother's watchful eye, she learned to be mindful of Stamps' racial division and respectful of the church, although it did little to help her cope with the trauma of being raped when she was

8. The experience left her broken, and by choice she became a mute, retreating into herself.

"I read every book in the black school, because there was nothing else to do," she said.

"I didn't talk, so I read and memorized."

She discovered Edgar Allan Poe, Rudyard Kipling, Langston Hughes, W.E.B. Du Bois and William Shakespeare. Shakespeare, she said, captured the emotions of her youth in his 28th Sonnet.

The sonnet rolls off her tongue with little prompting:

"When in disgrace with fortune and men's eyes,
I all alone bemoan my outcast state.
And trouble a deaf heaven with my bootless cries,
And look upon myself and curse my fate . . . "

"That was me—absolutely me—wishing to be anything rather than to be black and poor and a girl in the dirt roads of Arkansas," she said.

"Can you imagine if somebody told him in the 16th century, 'Listen, you're going to inspire a black girl in the 20th century in Arkansas, who will be a mute'?"

In 1941, when she was 13, she and her brother left Stamps for California again to live with their mother. There, she said, she came into adulthood, working as a Creole cook, a bordello madam, and eventually a dancer and singer.

Her stage work won her a role in a tour of *Porgy and Bess* that took her to 22 countries in Europe and Africa in 1954 and 1955. Upon her return, she found her talent in steady demand.

In 1959, she moved to New York City, drawn like a moth to the light of its exploding black culture. The scene was sparking her friend, the late James Baldwin, and other black writers, who became poets in the struggle for civil rights.

Miss Angelou began writing and joined the Harlem Writers Guild, although she had to sing to support herself.

She was also drawn into politics and produced a revue, *Cabaret for Freedom,* to help raise money for the Southern Christian Leadership Conference and the Rev. Martin Luther King, Jr.

For her efforts, King appointed Miss Angelou the northern coordinator for SCLC.

But she was eventually led to a man calling for more direct action—Malcolm X, the militant black Muslim leader.

She worked on a committee that scheduled events for Malcolm X and rated a mention in his autobiography.

Author Alex Haley helped to compile that book, although Haley didn't recall Miss Angelou's work on the committee until reminded of it recently.

"That's been so long ago," he said, "and so much has happened since then."

Haley first met Miss Angelou more than 20 years ago and counts her among his close friends, so much so that he is planning a weekend next March at his home in Tennessee to honor her.

"She has become, now a legend," he said. "When I'm traveling and giving talks I continually meet people who want to know about her, who say they just want to touch her or be with her."

Dolly McPherson speaks with reverence about Miss Angelou. Ms. McPherson, a professor of English at Wake Forest, wrote her doctoral dissertation on Miss Angelou, examining her work and place in American cultural history.

"She has grown in her artistry," said Ms. McPherson, who was working at the Institute of International Education 25 years ago when she met Miss Angelou.

"I have seen profound changes in her since her days of acting, performing and singing."

In the early 1960s, Miss Angelou married a South African exile, who opposed that country's white-controlled government, and accompanied him to Africa. The marriage did not last, but her encounter with Africa changed her.

She realized then, Ms. McPherson said, that though she was black, she was not totally African.

She often wears African-style dresses and headwraps, but she sees herself as an American, as well as a Southerner.

"The South and I are inextricably bound by recent history," she said. "The last 300 years, and the history of slavery, have made me a Southerner."

The singers of the Inspirational Choir have Mount Zion clapping and singing along with a foot-stomper of a song, "Where Shall I Be."

"Where shall I be when it shines," they sing. "Where shall I be when it shines?"

The song has an a cappella feel, despite the backdrop of piano, organ and bass. Voices rise and fall in unison.

Above them, a soloist shouts "Hey now" and "Oh, Lawd," letting his voice come down on the bluesy, syncopated offbeats.

"Where shall I be when it shines, oh, yeah," they sing. "Where shall I be when it shines?"

The choir finishes to a roadhouse round of applause.

The moment has a joyful intimacy, and Miss Angelou shows it on her face as she steps back into the spotlight.

She is tall, six feet in her bare feet, and sure enough of herself to bring off the floor-length purple and pink outfit and matching spangled cap she wears.

Miss Angelou has a presence that commands attention. Haley called it "Hollywood energy."

"When she walks into the room, you know she's there," Haley said. "It's a palpable thing."

Thomas Mullen agrees. He saw Miss Angelou take a campus audience hostage when she first spoke at Wake Forest in 1971.

"She had the audience so caught up that by the end of the evening they were standing up and firing questions at her right and left," said Mullen, the dean of the college at Wake Forest. "Usually you have to pry questions out of kids. She opened them up. She made them feel something."

She does the same at Mount Zion, walking around with her hand on her hip and talking to the crowd in a loose, gossipy tone.

"Some people enjoy gospel music," she said, "and some people are just a little *too* pretentious."

She begins a reading of "Weekend Glory," a poem she wrote about a working woman who tried to fit a party and church into the same weekend.

"City folks, who don't know the facts, posing and preenin' and putting on acts, are stretchin' their necks and strainin' their backs," she says.

"They move into condos, up over their ranks. They lend their souls to the local banks. Buying big cars they can't afford, then ride around town actin' bored."

It is poetry—at least it was published as such—but coming out of Miss Angelou's mouth it sounds more prosaic, more like she's giving somebody a piece of her mind.

"My life ain't heaven, but it sure ain't hell," she finishes. "I'm not on top, but I call it swell if I'm able to work, and get paid right, and have the luck to go to church on Sunday, enjoy myself, and be black on Saturday night."

Miss Angelou held up a glass of wine, considering it in the sunlight that fell through her dining room window.

"I like it for its savor," she said, exploring what wine means to her. "I respect it for its Biblical importance, despite what the fundamentalists say. You know, the other day I heard some fundamentalist say, 'Yes, Jesus made wine, but it was non-alcoholic.' Now can you believe that?"

She shook her head, laughed, and took another swallow.

Wine, she said, is an elixir—good for the palate as well as the heart. It is not a wellspring of inspiration, however. That comes from some more mysterious place.

"God knows," she mused. "Or maybe I should say just God."

Miss Angelou gazed outside, her eyes settling on the naked trees, which had dropped leaves onto the basketball court below.

Neighborhood children are allowed to play on the court, if they knock first to make sure that Miss Angelou is not working.

"The thump, thump, thump," she said, bouncing an imaginary ball on the carpet, "just would not do."

Writing rarely comes easy, she said, but it is not a task she shrinks from.

In addition to the autobiographies, she has published four books of poetry and has written for television.

She wrote and produced *Sisters, Sisters,* a critically acclaimed full-length film that was broadcast on NBC in 1982.

Last spring, she published a book of poetry with artist Tom Feelings. Her next book, she said, will be about her mother.

But it is the autobiographies that have put butter on her bread. When working on one, she rents a hotel room, and every day for five or six months she goes there to hammer out the words.

It was publisher Robert Loomis, the vice president and executive editor of Random House, who first persuaded her to try *Caged Bird*. He did so at the suggestion of Judith Feiffer, the former wife of editorial cartoonist Jules Feiffer.

"They had had a dinner party and Maya and James Baldwin and Jules Feiffer and Judy all ended up trading stories," Loomis recalled. "Now that's a crowd with good storytellers—raconteurs every one— and Maya held her own. Judy called me up and told me that she was really something."

Loomis made Miss Angelou two or three offers, but she didn't warm to the idea until he expressed it as a challenge.

"He called me again," Miss Angelou said, "and said that to write an autobiography—as literature—is almost impossible. I said right then I'd do it."

Miss Angelou's books are not so much about what has happened to her, as they are about what she has learned.

One theme comes up repeatedly: the devotion to growth, to self-evaluation, whether she's writing about prejudice or politics or poetry. Loomis remembered reading *Caged Bird* and wondering at its openness and honesty.

"It was different than anything I'd ever read," he said.

"It was special and unique. She wrote with such anger and disgust at the prejudice, but did not have any of that bitterness, which ruins a lot of writers."

What comes out in the books is a sense of someone sick of stagnation—someone searching for change.

That search brought her to Winston-Salem in 1981, when she accepted a lifetime position as a Reynolds Professor of American Studies.

She teaches courses in black literature and cultural history.

She is no different as a teacher, she said, than she is as a friend, lover or writer.

Her goal is always the same.

"My aspiration is not achievable, which may be all right if I accept that the process is more important than the result," she said.

"I want to know more—not intellectually—to know more so I can be a better human being, to be an honest, courageous, funny and loving human being. That's what I want to be—and I blow it about 86 times a day. My hope is to cut that to 70."

She laughed, but her voice carried an edge of sarcasm. She sipped from her glass and, after swallowing, took a deep breath.

"Our greatest urge is to be loved," she said.

"The most hateful person, the most actively cruel person, acts out of a need to be loved. The need to be loved is fundamental. The moment we exit that womb, we start crying for human touch.

"Touch me! Care for me!" She threw up her arms, a baby grabbing at air.

"Take me. Hold me! Tell me I'm important—to you. That's right. That's it . . . so naturally, I want to be loved. I also want to have the unmitigated courage to love in return."

The air is muggy at Mount Zion, despite the chill that settled outside after sundown.

Paper programs have been enlisted as fans and handkerchiefs have appeared in the audience to dab sweat from brows.

The Inspirational Choir has brought the crowd down with "Hidden Place," a moody ballad about salvation.

"I've found Jesus," a young woman sings, wringing her voice as she takes the lead. "Ohhh, I've found a hiding place in Jesus. In Jesus!"

Miss Angelou, too, mirrors the moment.

When the song winds down, she talks for a few minutes, painting unsettling images of nighttime and tears, before moving into *Still I Rise,* her historical indictment of racism.

"You may write me down in history, with your bitter twisted lies," she says.

"You may trod me in the very dirt, but still, like dust, I'll rise. Does my sassiness upset you? Why are you beset with gloom, because I walk like I've got oil wells pumping in my living room."

She delivers the last line with an unexpected sense of hope, laughing and strutting and pumping her arms to give life to the image.

The crowd responds with laughter and applause.

The moment is intimate, and it stands in sharp contrast to a dinner Miss Angelou attended two nights earlier in Raleigh.

About 600 people attended, only six of them black, to see her presented with the North Carolina Award for Literature.

That evening, Miss Angelou said, smacked of a society celebrating itself.

This evening at the church is different—spiritual and loving.

She speaks of rebirth and renewal. As earlier, in the heat of delivery her poems become prose.

"Does my sassiness upset you?" she asks, ending the question with a single haughty laugh.

"Ha! Don't take it so hard, just 'cause I laugh—Ha! Ha!—as if I have gold mines diggin' in my own back yard.

"You can shoot me with your words. You may cut me with your lies. You can kill me with your hatefulness, but just like light, I'll rise."

Her voice floats with those last two words, then falls hard as she begins the next paragraph.

"Out of the huts of history's shame, I rise. Up from a past that's rooted in pain, I rise. A black ocean, leaping and wide, welling and swelling, bearing in the tide.

"Leaving behind nights of terror, centuries of fear, I rise. Into a daybreak miraculously clear, I rise. Bringing the gifts that my ancestors gave, I am the hope—and the dream—of the slave.

"And so," she says, smacking her hands together and pointing with a finger to a far corner of the sanctuary, "there I go!"

A Life in the Day of Maya Angelou

Carol Sarler/1987

The Sunday Times Magazine, 27 December 1987, 50. Copyright © 1987 by the *Times.* Reprinted by permission.

I wake usually about six and get immediately out of bed. Then I begin to wonder why. I have a fiendish attachment to something called Rose Geranium from Floris so I take a shower with a cloth which is green with the stuff—it's so aromatic that people down the street know that I've taken a shower and somehow I feel I've been pretty good to myself. I make very strong coffee and sit in the sunroom with the newspaper, the *Winston-Salem Journal,* the only paper in town.

I love to read the letters to the editor. I like to see what angers people; only one in a hundred says 'I love what you're doing,' the other 99 say they hate the paper or this is nonsense or that is absolutely wrong. I feel as if I've just met eight people, little human vignettes. And I look outside, I live in a wooded area and I don't think, I just look.

At about 8:30 I start looking at the house because the housekeeper arrives at nine and I'm still too well brought-up to offer Mrs. Cunningham a house in too much disarray so I straighten up before she comes in. She has been my housekeeper for six years now—my sister has suggested that in another life she was a staff-sergeant. I give to her and she gives to me and we live together with a lot of laughter. My secretary, Mrs. Garris, also comes at nine and that's when real life begins. Mrs. Garris is a lovely southern black lady with efficiency and grace vying for dominance in her spirit. She says, 'Ms. Angelou, you've got to sign this, send that, agree to that, deny this . . . ' and I say, 'Mrs. Garris, I will talk to you in an hour.'

At ten I deal with my correspondence; I get about 300 letters a week. People send me all sorts of things, especially manuscripts. It's not fair, everybody's work deserves the attention of a qualified editor and I'm not that, so Mrs. Garris writes back to explain that and to say that I don't read unsolicited manuscripts. Then she goes off to lunch and I usually invite friends over. I'm a very serious cook and I prepare what to me is a fabulous lunch for two or three people like breadcrumbed turkey-breast cooked in butter, wine and lemon, served with rice and zucchini and there's my home-made bread. I offer good wine and we laugh and talk. I cook in competitions around the United States to raise money for Cancer Research, the American Jewish Association, Sickle Cell Anemia—we have these events where celebrities get together and people pay up to $250 to eat the food.

In the afternoon I read—if I'm teaching I read works coming out of the theme of my class and I put on the music to complement the reading. For instance, if I'm doing a course on African culture's impact on the world I will read Basil Davidson's *Last Kingdoms of Africa* and I'll put on tapes of African music, Odetta singing 19th-century slave songs, Mahalia Jackson singing anything—and I turn it up very loud, it's all over my house, that insistence of the music which helps to entrench me into the era. Unless I'm involved in something really important, Mrs. Garris and Mrs. Cunningham come up to say goodbye at five—really sweet—and then I have my house back.

At the time I suppose its tea-time for other people, I help myself to a very nice drink—Dewar's White Label whiskey—and I look at my paintings. I'm a collector of black American art and I have paintings throughout my house, wonderful paintings that sing. It's a big house and I keep extending it. I always use the same builder and he says he's waiting for me to stretch down to the next street just to give me more walls for the paintings.

I'm convinced that black American art, while it is graphic, is rooted in music. Romaine Beardon, who is the most expensive but is considered the leading living black artist in the United States, also writes about blues. I collect Beardon and I collect John Biggers as well and he is an *aficionado* of African music—when you see the work you can hear the music. Some paintings I pass right by and two weeks later they will stop me and say, 'haven't you been listening to me lately?'

About seven I start to prepare dinner for myself; I drink more than I eat, but I prepare a proper dinner and put on candles and pretty music—all for me. If I'm not good to myself, how can I expect anyone else to be good to me? Then I read again, unless there's something on the television. Often something meaningless—sometimes I just don't want to be informed, increased, elevated, developed, I want something like an old Hollywood musical. Now that's really precious when the world is exploding in South Africa and Northern Ireland and the Middle East, but I know that the next morning the phone will ring and I will be asked to be involved and within hours I could be in jail or on a picket line, so I have to stop when I can.

If I do go out I like to go to friends—however, unless there is an issue which calls for immediate discussion, I don't like cocktail chit-chat over Israel, or the Arabs. I think everyone young should do that with lots of cheap wine, sitting on the floor and shouting and arguing, but I don't do it now.

The issues have too much importance to be minimalised by someone saying, 'Now where is Syria?' I love good stories, funny stories, told by the person against him or herself. That's what I want of an evening, then I go home to bed by 12. If my gentleman friend is there, that's different. My gentleman friend visits every two or three months for four or five days from Ohio. I don't worry what he does when he's not there, I hope he has a good time. If he ever didn't come back, then he wasn't for me.

When I'm writing, none of anything I've said applies. When I'm writing, everything shuts down. I get up about five, take a shower and don't use the Floris—I don't want that sensual gratification. I get in my car and drive off to a hotel room: I can't write in my house, I take a hotel room and ask them to take everything off the walls so there's me, the Bible, Roget's Thesaurus and some good, dry sherry and I'm at work by 6:30. I write on the bed lying down—one elbow is darker than the other, really black from leaning on it—and I write in longhand on yellow pads. Once into it, all disbelief is suspended, it's beautiful. I hate to go, but I've set for myself 12:30 as the time to leave, because after that it's an indulgence, it becomes stuff I'm going to edit out anyway.

Then back home, shower, fresh clothes, and I go shopping for nice food and pretend to be sane. I don't see Mrs. Cunningham or Mrs. Garris or my gentleman friend, nobody. I play a lot of solitaire—in a month when I'm writing I use two or three decks of cards. After dinner I re-read what I've written . . . if April is the cruellest month, then eight o'clock at night is the cruellest hour because that's when I start to edit and all that pretty stuff I've written gets axed out. So if I've written 10 or 12 pages in six hours, it'll end up as three or four if I'm lucky.

But writing really is my life. Thinking about it when I'm not doing it is terribly painful but when I'm doing it . . . it's a lot like if I was a long-distance swimmer and had to jump into a pool covered with ice: it sounds terrible, but once in it and two or three laps done, I'm home and free . . .

A Conversation between Rosa Guy and Maya Angelou

Rosa Guy/1988

From *Writing Lives: Conversations Between Women Writers,* edited by Mary Chamberlain (London: Virago, 1988), 1-23. Copyright © 1988 by Virago. Reprinted by permission.

MAYA ANGELOU and ROSA GUY stand apart in this anthology. Close friends for over twenty-five years, they chose not to present an interview but allow us a glimpse, through conversation, at the intellectual, political and emotional depth of their relationship.

Rosa Guy, though born in Trinidad, grew up in Harlem. She started factory work at fourteen. Realizing that she got the worst jobs because she was Black, she became involved first with unions at her workplaces and then in the larger struggle for Black freedom. She also started to write, for the stage, and then novels. She was a founding member of the Harlem Writers' Guild and is the author of *A Measure of Time* (Virago 1984) and a number of novels for young adults including *Friends, Ruby* and *My Love, My Love* (Virago 1987). She lives in New York.

Maya Angelou was born in 1928 in St. Louis, Missouri but grew up in Stamps, Arkansas and California. She has been a waitress, singer, dancer, Black activist, editor and mother. In her twenties she toured Europe and Africa with *Porgy and Bess.* Moving to New York she joined the Harlem Writers' Guild and continued to earn her living as a night club singer and performer in Genet's *The Blacks.* She became involved in Black struggles in the 1960s and then spent several years in Ghana as editor of *African Review.* Maya Angelou has published several volumes of poetry including *And Still I Rise* (Virago 1987) and her five volume autobiography, published by Virago, has been widely acclaimed. She is now Reynolds Professor of American Studies at Wake Forest University in North Carolina.

M.A. How did you decide to become a writer? You're Black, female and a Trinidadian . . .

R.G. I wanted to be an actress. But I didn't look exactly like Hilda Simms and that was the type they liked, very pale and very pretty hair . . .

M.A. Pretty hair? You mean hair like white folks?

R.G. Yeah. Like white folks. I decided to write my own play and put myself into it. I had my first play done off Broadway. From then on I considered myself a playwright. But the canvas proved too restrictive. I decided to try the short story. And then that too was restricted . . .

M.A. I want to go back to 'pretty hair.' It's of particular interest that you, whom I know personally to have been engaged in the projection of the concept of Black beauty long before the phrase 'black is beautiful' became popular, would use the phrase 'pretty hair' meaning straight hair, white folks' hair. That shows the profound power of the self destructive-image—

R.G. —that we are burdened with, even in the West Indies where I was born. We were taught that you didn't go round with a person who was 'pickey headed.' We have to fight through a lot of things, and the first is the self image that was given to us. We've had to struggle through a lot of things that other people generally don't. It's particularly true in the Western hemisphere. Isn't that why we both straighten our hair?

M.A. There is that contradiction in knowing that one is gorgeous and lovely, in good health and about the size one wants to be, and feels sexy and sensual, that one is attractive. There is that and at the same time there is the contradiction of it. And then to be Black and female as opposed to being white and male is a total contradiction. A double contradiction.

R.G. We were demeaned yet always had to aspire to freedom— the heights. Our ambition was nurtured by the Western society—the same society which said that you're female. You're Black. You can't climb here. That probably made us strong.

M.A. Using the canvas of contradiction, I'd like us to talk about deciding to be literary, a part of the literature which, in Western society, has been, and probably will be, dominated by white men.

When people talk about American literature, they really mean Hemingway, Faulkner and Poe and when they do include women it's Emily Dickinson and Edna St. Vincent Millay. To decide to take that on and say, 'I will speak and will be heard'—that takes a lot of guts.

R.G. Historically the Black American woman has been forced into this position. There had to be a certain period in the history of Black folks when the woman had to say, 'Look, this is what's happening.' Literature is an emotional history of what is happening at a specific time, at a specific place. And so our literature is as meaningful as any. Perhaps even more because of a changing world. The world is so small . . . We are the tools of the progression of people's understanding. We're saying we are here, and we are . . .

The courage that it takes to break through so many different barriers is always intriguing. It takes a lot to decide you're not going to live a certain type of life. For instance, when you were a prostitute and you decided to make this break because of your son. I could understand that. What always impresses me is how did you come to the point where you decided?

M.A. The only two things I've ever loved in my life are dancing and writing. I have a belief that if you don't love something, you'll never be great at it. I made my living as a singer, but I never loved it. But I loved to dance as much as I loved writing, but by twenty-two my knees were gone and so there was no chance of ever achieving the best I had to give in that, and I never loved anything else but writing. To love it and have that sense of achievement when you almost got the sentence right.

R.G. Didn't you feel that sometimes you had to prove yourself? Feeling rejected by your mother, having to go through the traumas of being rejected and not being able to reach her, feeling that cold core that you couldn't reach. Did you feel bitter?

M.A. Bitterness is a different word. Anger. Bitterness is like cancer. It eats upon the host. But anger is like fire. It burns it all clean. I was very angry. I haven't stopped being angry at a number of things. I saw my mother once between the time I was three and thirteen. As far as I know, I got one letter, one package from her in those ten years with a little white doll. The very idea! I was young and all that, but I knew that this was an insult and I convinced myself that she was

dead and somebody else who couldn't have been my mother had
sent me this doll.

R.G. But those are the angers that people rarely live through.
Children have a tendency to hold more against their parents than
anybody else. Even when they feel that it's all been worked out, they
remember.

M.A. You remember, you don't forget. But I think the reason I've
been able to be successful, not just as a writer, but as a woman and
as a person is that at about twenty-two—Guy, my son, was already
seven or six—for some incredible reason, I saw my mother separate
from me. Absolutely separate. And I thought, I see, you're not really
my mother, the mother I wanted and needed; you're a character. And
I began to see her like a character I would have read about. Now that
didn't mean that in lonely or bitter or painful moments I didn't still
want her to be that big-bosomed, open-armed, steady, consistent
person. But I'd say that 60 percent of the time I saw her as a
character. Then it grew to be 70 per cent. Then 80. And then my
own resistance allowed me to accept her as the character.

R.G. I still go back to that resentment against people who have
rejected us at a particular time. Somewhere in the mind it sticks . . .

M.A. We all bring almost unnameable information from childhood.
We are unable to shuffle all that particular mortal coil. If we are lucky,
we make transitions, and don't live in that time of pain and rejection
and loneliness and desolation. But there will understandably be bits
of it which adhere to us and will not be pulled off by love nor money.
You know? And when you speak of my youth and aloneness, I'm
obliged also to think of yours. Being a pre-teen, eight or nine years
old, and coming to the United States from the security and awe and
beauty and warmth of Trinidad. One of the most poignant pictures I
have in my mind is you and your sister in summer dresses coming to
New York on a boat—

R.G. On the coldest day, January, of the year, and freezing on the
deck—

M.A. —and having less than the couple of years with your Mom
before she died . . .

R.G. Coming to a new country, losing one's mother, and living
with an intolerant father, made the first years of my life even more

precious; I have relived my youngest years in the West Indies as
much as I lived my actual growing years in the United States. Then I
got into my rebellious teens. When my father died, I was fourteen
and alone—my sister and I were alone, in the United States. It's not
easy to be alone even when you're a rebellious teen. If you get angry,
there's no one to be angry with. You can't stay angry with someone
who died—except to blame them for their own death . . . which I did
. . . The struggle just to survive in New York had its telling effect on
my sister (and I want to write about her) as well as on me. My sister
had such a terrible time taking care of me. In later years she was
really bitter against me. I had robbed her of her youth—through no
fault of my own. It's strange that when one rebels, one copes much
better than someone who gives. My sister gave her youth to protect
me and the rest of her life she was vulnerable. She never had a
rebellious spirit. She didn't rebel against religion, against society,
against anything. She was always begging. She begged me to be
good. She begged others to love me, to understand me, to love her.
That begging quality followed her into adulthood.

   M.A. I don't know, because I look at my brother and myself. I was
the one giving and I gave to him although he's older . . .

   R.G. But you were angry with your mother. You had anger. My
sister never had anger. She had sorrow. She felt abused. She was the
orphan. It puts one in a special category; it has its moulding qualities.

   M.A. I felt as an orphan—

   R.G. —but you had parents. That's where your anger grows. You
could get angry with them. When you have no one to get angry with,
to react against, you fall in upon yourself . . . I think here is where we
may have similarities. We both wanted love, and our lives were so
unrestricted, we didn't have our families to say do this and do that,
nor support through tragic experiences. A lot of anguish that I live
with today come from those tragedies I experienced as a teenager.
The pain is so brutal when you're hurt, just asking to be loved . . .

   M.A. I know, you're really up for grabs. I know that in my case I
was grabbed, and so were you.

   R.G. I love deeply. I couldn't ever have a romance without falling
madly in love. And each time the young man turned from me, I
would suffer intolerably. I went through this process endlessly.

M.A. I know it is endless. We carry that love of the man into our adulthood and into our work.

R.G. There are different levels of love . . . But I always have to say 'I love you' because I have to love.

M.A. That's right. Those I love, my friends; I am in love with my friends. Now, that does not mean that we have sex. But the moment I begin to identify myself with someone . . . and I have the vulnerability of being physically attached I consider myself in danger. That is, there is the possibility that someone can control me. Now no sister friend or brother friend can control me because I'm not vulnerable to that extent.

R.G. To a certain extent all my friends control me—as long as they don't interfere with my work. Then I have a battle within myself. I have a tendency to fall in love. I always hope that once that feeling goes, then a friendship can stay and it's very important.

M.A. I have been in love many times with men with whom I was sexually involved. And they became essential to my life. A break-up of a friendship is terrible. Devastating. But a break-up of a friendship with sex in it is absolutely obliterating. It tears me up—that absolute tearing apart of my body and my mind and my heart and my thoughts and I and romance have been thrown on the floor. I hang over the chairs. I weep . . . I'm very cautious, very, about sexual love . . . I remember your insistence upon your space to work and remember years ago you might have a gentleman friend at your house and you and your friend, lover, would go to bed and in the morning when I'd get up about six you would already have been working. We'd have coffee and I'd ask, 'What happened to your friend?' And you'd say, 'He had to go.' And the first year or so I used to say, 'Damn. All Rosa's lovers are surely early risers.' And finally it was revealed to me that they were awakened and told, 'I'm sorry, but you have to go. I have to work.' And sometimes there would be snow outside . . .

R.G. That's not quite fair! I do get a restlessness in the morning when I get up and I'm working. Anyone around or very near to me can compute my restlessness. I become another person. I have to work . . .

M.A. When I was married—I've kept the habit now—at five

o'clock in the morning there's no sleeping, there's no being with me. I cannot bear it. I don't have to see anybody, I don't have to talk, but try and stay in that ambiance of investigation.

R.G. Sometimes people think that you're selfish or self centred. But it isn't that at all. I don't feel selfish.

M.A. Or is it that? And so what?

I want us to look at the question of need. I would like us to look at our own involvement with the immediate past, that is in our lifetime, and then the greater past out of which we came. The writers you read and I read as we were living—

R.G. Most of the writers with whom I was most impressed were the French and Russian writers of another period. The one American writer who stood out to me was Richard Wright—and Dreiser. I took to their naturalism. I was able to understand so much of the country through them. Certainly I understood Black America because of Richard Wright. But then, I had come up through the slums of Harlem and had seen so much of what he wrote about. My writing evolved like that, pulling into me everything in terms of what is happening, particularly to young people in the United States and in the hemisphere. I developed a hemispheric consciousness. I feel particularly well equipped to write about the hemisphere having been born in the West Indies and having suffered the injustices of the North American continent and travelled extremely in that region. When we formed the Harlem Writers' Guild together, John Killens used to say—something I thought very important—you must write as though you are God. I was! Pooling my experiences, my understanding, I was creating my world. My creation which I projected, to give more understanding to the world.

M.A. I started writing when I was mute. I always thought I could write because I loved to read so much. I loved the melody of Poe and I loved Paul Laurence Dunbar. I had memorized so much of Dunbar, Poe, Shakespeare, James Weldon Johnson, Longfellow. When my son was able to be quiet enough to listen, I taught him those poets. A few years ago he gave a reading of his poetry and he started the reading by saying 'First, let me recite to you some of the poets my mother raised me on . . . ' In the contemporary world, I confess to having been impressed by Ann Petry. I had *The Street* in my hand, I used to carry it around . . .

In the early 1950s—the Garvey movement—I went to Harlem and saw Black Ethiopia. These were my people and they didn't have accents, but they were Ethiopians. I mean, they didn't have African accents. Those that I listened to spoke just like everybody else and that broadened my light a great deal, my own understanding of our oneness.

R.G. Yes, this oneness, I believe I bring to the literary scene. I was a little girl when I went to my first Garvey parade. My shoes were tight. I had walked for miles before anyone noticed my torment. I was in pain—crawling. Then someone picked me up and put me in a truck. Around that time I was in the midst of a political upheaval, not really understanding a thing about it. I just knew that we West Indians were all for Garvey. I thought we were the only ones conscious of Africa.

Years later when Alpheus Hunton, Lou Burnham and Lorraine Hansberry started *Freedom,* the newspaper in which Paul Robeson wrote, they portrayed Africa—a big black giant, in shackles, ready to break loose. I realized then that there was a large segment of Black America caught up in the African movement, in African history. Before that . . . I remember having a fight in grammar school. I had been talking to a friend . . . an American girl . . . I had ended my remark by saying, 'Anyhow, we all come from Africa!' She answered, 'Oh no, I don't come from Africa.' Whereupon I informed her, 'Your ancestors did.' No, my ancestors did not, she said. 'My ancestors live in New York. Right on 118th Street.' 'No,' I insisted, 'they all came from Africa.' She socked me. We ended by pulling each other's hair out in the street . . . There was such a division then. Most Americans didn't want—

M.A. —an African connection. But it must be remembered that in Garvey's heyday, there were not that many West Indians anywhere in the United States. His existence was used as a focal point for the West Indian community and they were able to stay together, but the Black American, without his charisma and his presence, went on into other things. But the tales of the Black American who didn't want to be connected with Africa can be recounted as the West Indians who didn't want to be connected either, who would say, 'I'm a British citizen' . . . The self loathing which is always part of oppression had its way with all of us.

R.G. At the Harlem Writers' Guild we were trying to teach African history in some of the schools to young people . . . and these Black kids would just fall on the floor and laugh. John Henrik Clarke would get furious and he'd have to tell them about themselves.

M.A. Well, all they had seen was Tarzan. I noticed it in Africa too. There were so many people I encountered who really thought of us all as Rochester. That's who they'd seen. Eddie Rochester, Mantan Moreland, Willie Best, Dorothy Dandridge's aunt, Hattie Daniels. Just the people who were in the movies. Who else did they have? So a hundred people met Dr. Du Bois, five hundred met Leo Hansberry. But the majority of people, their only connection with us were those movies . . . Then, as one gets a little wiser, a little more erudite, we begin to see the oneness of our struggle. And I think that view influenced both you and me, and those friends we had with whom we became involved in New York.

R.G. Because we were artists struggling to be known and having a fight against the stigma of being Black in the United States. What a struggle! Everything was a struggle.

M.A. Everything. I meant for the political. I'd rather for us to get up and try to lead demonstrations against the horrors that were taking place in Africa, and were taking place in the U.S. . . . We became the radii which came in finally to touch that circle which was our oneness and our responsibility to everybody. We reached the point where we thought we were one with all oppressed people.

R.G. . . . a historical development, really. There was also the whole question of activity on the Left. It was all broadening, reaching, and touching each other and broadening. And finally understanding the horrible oppression—

M.A. —in the world. You see, I had gone to a Communist school in the 1940s and had read Marx as an intellectual exercise, not knowing how much had actually gotten down into the old brain. I had had so little real connection with the Left that I must say that in 1956 I met Oscar Brown Jr., Frank London Brown, Big Clyde, Daddy O'Daley in Chicago. There were about eight Black men in Chicago who were political—clear, severe, funny. They knew how to laugh and they influenced both Abby Lincoln and me. We used to sit and talk as you and I talk. And we found no Black men to talk this political, with what was happening in the world and what was happening with Blacks, and shouldn't we call ourselves Black as opposed to Negro. Abby and I had decided in California that we were Black. That is what we were and wanted to be called. Black. They put into words for me and for Abby thoughts we had had, but we had never heard articulated by live human beings and live Black men. So by the time in 1957 I got to New York again as a singer, I was singing folk songs, calypso and Black American blues. And I would have for my march-in music 'Lift Every Voice and Sing' in these swank places. I had a decent shape and wore very tight clothes, but I would sing these horrible folk songs about their killing me. My political horizon had been enlarged by so many things so that by the time I met John Killens I became socially politicized. All the people who I admired were thinking as well as I, and better. And articulating as well as I and much better.

R.G. I had been in the American Negro Theatre before. There was Sidney Poitier and Ruby Dee and Alice Childress and Clarice Taylor and Maxwell Glanville, Harry Belafonte, Isabelle Sanford. Just a group of people who really were interested in acting, not politics. They were all for drama. I went to Connecticut, to rescue my marriage. When I came back ANT was no longer in existence. I had no place to go. I kept looking around. I wanted to write. Someone told me about the Jefferson school and I went there. I met Phillip Bonosky there. He had a workshop. I started writing. But I wanted to be in Harlem so I left, and went to join a group called The Committee for the Negro in the Arts. I also met Paul Robeson and Alpheus Hunton. Absolute giants. One could not help but be impressed. Minds were pried open by their keen insight, the manner in which they explained things. One had to join the struggle for the oppressed . . .

M.A. Speaking of giants, let us touch on Malcolm X and how we met him.

R.G. That was an exciting day! That was an exciting time. We had then made our views felt to the world. We had stopped Adlai Stevenson from speaking at the United Nations while protesting about the death of Lumumba. New York was seething. Everyone who had any consciousness was out in the streets. And we were a little upset that Brother Malcolm had not joined, and Madame Maya Angelou decided, well, we have to get this brother to join with us.

M.A. It was so exciting. When neither Malcolm X nor any of the Nation of Islam came to be with us, we were terribly put out and didn't understand. And so, you and I called him and asked for a meeting. And he told us to come to the restaurant the next day; so we went that morning and Malcolm X came in his dark suit and white shirt and tie. Very impressive and very gentlemanly to us—holding our seats while we sat down at the table. Of course, there were the three or four bodyguards who were in the background, and he said to us, 'You're wondering why . . . ' I mean, he took over the meeting immediately and said, 'You're wondering why our people did not participate in the demonstration at the United Nations.' And we both said yes. I mean, we were, one would have to see us in those days because we were pretty bold and—

R.G. —very dedicated. As I remember it, although he sympathized with us, their struggle was an entirely different struggle.

M.A. He said the Nation of Islam does not demonstrate. "We do not have anything to do with asking whites, the blue-eyed devils, for anything,' and so forth. Now, he was really, I thought at the time, talking at cross purposes. I didn't see why he didn't think it was one struggle, but what he did say was so amazing to me because he said he had been called by the *New York Times* and all these different magazines to ask what did he think. That since the Nation of Islam didn't participate, didn't he condemn us? And he said no, he didn't condemn any Black person who did anything, but the Nation of Islam wouldn't. Then he said, 'But I tell you this'—it was like Jesus speaking to Peter and the Disciples—he said, 'Before this time tomorrow, every Black leader they can find will condemn you.' We couldn't believe it. We had met him like mid-morning. It was a bright day and by the time the evening paper came out there was a statement from Roy Wilkins, and almost everybody except A. Philip Randolph. Everybody said that there was implication that these were Communists, these were outsiders who had come in . . .

R.G. And even some of our very close friends were condemning—

M.A. —us as outsiders who are trouble-makers. And that wasn't the way to do it.

R.G. It was really a fantastic demonstration. Also it was a turning point, I feel, even though Malcolm X did not come with us. Malcolm was a fantastic person, I believe, because he was in the process of growth.

M.A. Yes, exactly.

R.G. And he just kept on growing and growing and he never stopped growing. And he changed.

M.A. He certainly changed. And it was wonderful to see it and to be a part of the time in which one could see that kind of growth, and to know it is possible, is encouraging as well. I look at some of the men of the time and think of how they grew . . .

R.G. Would you say they grew because of us? We sort of forced it on them. Because everyone was sitting back . . .

M.A. Yes, us, but us in a very large way because while we happened to be in New York and close to media, there were young men and women at the time who were doing some pretty brave things in other parts of the country.

R.G. Not at that time. Not at that particular time. After. Because one of the things that we saw very clearly at that point: everybody was upset by the death of Patrice Lumumba. Young people in Central America were protesting. Students in Africa, in Europe, in China, but not one in the U.S. After our demonstrations there was a ground swell of students in the United States coming out in support.

M.A. That's true. I hadn't thought about that. The Civil Rights Movement in this country was very active and very inspirational, but was really focused on American civil rights.

R.G. After we demonstrated a group of young students came in from Boston. I remember that particularly. *Freedomways* was being launched. Its reception was given at the home of Du Bois. I met the Boston group outside and they said 'You are Rosa Guy!' To them I was a heroine. Really. I mean, they could have put me on their shoulders.

M.A. They almost did that with us in Harlem everytime we'd go.

R.G. Do you remember this fellow who always had this little cap? He'd say 'You two. You should never be separated. You should never be separated.' And there we were on the street corner shouting and carrying on and drawing a crowd.

M.A. And, really, always talking about Africa. Always . . . There was a qualitative growth in Martin Luther King. To me, having just to see him grow from the American Civil Rights Movement, the passive resistance, the non-violent resistance, and to see him grow into one going to Africa, meeting with Nkrumah, returning, broadening his sight to include all oppressed people (which is why he was killed, of course), so that his Poor People's March said, 'I want Black people, poor white, Native American, Mexican American, Asian American; I want everybody who is poor, downtrodden and oppressed, come. We will sit in Washington.' I believe this is why Malcolm was killed. When Malcolm said, 'I no longer believe that by nature a person is born evil. I have seen blue-eyed, blond-haired men who I can call brother with a straight face and an open heart.' The minute he said that, he had to be done. If he had kept narrow, he would have remained, you know?

R.G. It was all right to be a Black nationalist and to talk about the blue-eyed devils. It was all right to talk about the establishment, and what should be done to it, or about aspects of life that dealt with Black/white hatred. But the moment that Blacks and whites seemed united, they were always condemned, called Communist or some vicious anti-Americans and were not allowed to parade. They were not granted permits. I've known groups of Blacks and whites at that time trying to obtain permission, license to parade. They were refused. But the Black nationalists who were violent against whites, for whatever reason, or those who were trying to exploit the newly emerging African nations, were never refused. That was when I realized the establishment feared unity between Blacks and whites. So long as we fought alone, we were ineffective.

M.A. It's fascinating. But these are the things we have seen.

R.G. After that period we were into the Vietnam War. Fantastic whites were joining anti-war movements, anti-oppression movements. But the Kent State massacre. Suddenly it changed and there was once again a complete separation. The whites really didn't believe that they would be killed like we were being trampled on, had been trampled on. And the minute they realized that, they became a little bit more fearful. And the movements all sort of started diminishing.

M.A. I think that the movements also became more and more particular, more and more exclusive. They began to involve other aspects of the American society with which they didn't agree. So one already got ecology and the struggle for better air, and better earth preservations. And this is coming out of the Civil Rights Movement. There's the anti-war movement which seemed to a number of non-Blacks to be a safer struggle. I'm sorry to say, the women's movement seemed to be a safer struggle. The free student movement seemed to be a safer struggle. If they were all white, if they were not involved with the Blacks, they thought they wouldn't be killed. And they were right.

R.G. They had to have lost interest in Blacks.

M.A. They were all right as long as they were not engaged with Blacks . . .

Some of the most distressing subjects which I encounter on university campuses are one, the subject of the schism between Black men and Black women and two, that Black young people have no commitment, no awareness of the struggle and their places in the struggle, and the inheritance which is theirs naturally of triumph, of defeat, of the glory of struggling for equality and fairness which they have inherited by right from the people who went before them. And I wonder, let us take the last subject first, what do you think of young people, young Black people in particular, of today?

R.G. This generation of young is a generation cut off from the past. They have no role models, no direction and are taking their cues from the movies, the television—that dream world. They to a great extent reject their past history, believing that they have arrived. That is not true, of course. But today there seems a lack of leadership on just about every level—black and white. Strange ideas and ideologies abound. One doesn't know what is going to happen. I'm concerned . . .

M.A. I find it of effective use to repeat to young people a story which has been in our lore since the nineteenth century, about the Black person who decided because he had a job and a title and a wife who looked like he wanted her to look, and a house with a two-car garage, and all that, that he was beyond the long reach of prejudice and discrimination.Only to find, of course, that if you are Black, you are still, to so many people, that ex-slave, no matter what you wear, no matter what job you have, no matter how clearly you speak or how profoundly you think. And, when I tell that to young Blacks, more often than not, they look at each other disbelievingly.

And it's so heartbreaking to me that I also see a generation who will live out that bitter statement, 'He who does not learn from his history is doomed to repeat it.' And I think that, oh, if you could just learn you might not have to repeat *all* the experiences. But I'm afraid that many will.

There are some young Black women, however, that I particularly want to talk about, younger than I in any case, young Black women who are writing, who are inspirational to me. For example, a group of young women in Atlanta have a magazine called *Sage*. I'm impressed with Gloria Naylor's continuing to work. I'm impressed certainly with Alice Walker. I was hopeful and am still hopeful of Alyse Sutherland who wrote a book many years ago called *Let the Lion Eat Straw*. A wonderful book. Lucille Clifton and Carolyn Rogers and those younger Black women who have not become well known. That they continue to struggle and write is inspirational. Do you think so?

R.G. Yes. There is something that disturbs me, and that is the thinking of the middle class. One of the phenomena in this country is the widening, the deepening, gulf between the haves and have-nots which I find in the devastation of innercities throughout the country. There is no concern about the struggle—or lack of it—going on in the inner cities throughout the country. Yet this is where the majority of our next generation of Blacks is emerging. With the progressive use of drugs in the inner cities there is a new, live-for-the-moment, don't-give-a-damn-about-dying, attitude that is being concretized in the streets and being exploited by the drug barons. It's an attitude which needs concern.

When Sonny Bonds, the drug dealer and murderer, was jailed, young Blacks looked up to him as a modern-day Robin Hood. A hero. Making it big. The inner cities might have some of the best-dressed people in the world. The biggest cars. They are single-minded about let's make it. That's what society is about. The American dream as expressed in "Dallas," "The Colbys," etc. Too many children are coming into the world and being exposed to only this environment—drugs and the American dream. Crimes are committed in its name. And the middle-class Blacks also condemn them. We are all victimized by the excesses, which is rapidly becoming the norm. But what happens when the Black middle class forget the historical roots of this development? Who then can readjust the imbalances? It's frightening. Young writers coming up must address themselves to this problem. There must be a way to turn the rapid deterioration around. Billions are being spent in world destruction while our Black communities are dying. We need our middle class, our young writers to understand, to raise a hue and cry over this. To at least start a dialogue. There are many good, sincere young writers coming up. Many well-meaning. Gloria Naylor I find to be one of the most fascinating, Lucille Clifton. But the cries and screams from the inner cities must be louder. Must be heard. We can no longer allow ourselves introspection about the days that were, we have to ready ourselves for the battle of days that are coming which are so . . .

M.A. Absolutely new!

R.G. New and terrible, and it needs young minds to address themselves to it. To face the problems.

M.A. I know that many of us of another generation, established writers and so, are looked at almost as if we are relics. But if a near contemporary of theirs . . .

R.G. They do need someone who will speak to them. Shout at them.

M.A. I mean of their type to speak to them. I'm thinking of somebody about twenty-five who is angry, has a burning need to speak for that group.

R.G. Yes, and for everything that it represents and what it will represent because I think that the tragedy is too imminent.

M.A. Now, I'll tell you what is happening. A number of young people are being satisfied with 'rapping.' And so they take this cheapest way out of saying something about the street. And quite often I'm asked, is this poetry? And I say no. That is rapping. There may be poetic lyric, that kind of rhyme structure, AB, AB, ABC; AB, AB, ABC. But most of it, of 100 per cent, 15 per cent may be considered to have poetic imagery in it. Too many young Blacks, as far as I can see it, and young whites for that matter, have been told that if you just tell what you think, that is great writing. Well, that is not so, as we know. Some, in fact, very established Black writers were frigging irresponsible in the 1960s when they told any Black person that if you're Black you can write poetry. Now that is such a lie. The truth is that if you're Black in the U.S., or any country for that matter, you are living in a poetic existence. In that there is struggle and loss and pain and tears and humiliation and all that. But writing poetry is a different matter. And so a number of young people, I think, today have inherited some of that casual indifference. And so instead of going on to sit down and really tell it—

R.G. —they become hero-worshippers. They are willing to opt for trying to become big names, and they're not concerned with the quality of struggle, of craftsmanship and struggle. And as we were talking about a while ago, where we have joined the struggle of the world, they have become so fully American. They have no concern, no understanding in actual terms of how their future, or our future is linked with—

M.A. —Nicaragua—

R.G. —And South Africa—

M.A. —the Middle East—

I want to go back to the world of Black women, the world of Black women writers. I think first I'd like us to talk about the propensity to build friendship and the need for friendship among Black women. I want us to talk about it because I'm serious about encouraging young Black women not to lose this thing we have had historically, and might be the singular most important aspect of our survival.

R.G. Do you see a pulling away or a changing from the patterns?

M.A. I did see it in the Sixties. And it frightened me a great deal because a number of men told a number of women that in order to prove how really loyal and supportive they were they should be like servants to them. They should walk three steps behind them. They couldn't have these binding relationships, these friendships which we have had during slavery, since slavery. During and after slavery, Black women who would have children would always have auntie so-and-so, or cousin so-and-so, or sister so-and-so with whom they could leave the children and go to work. And that was always those friendships which were not only supportive but, I believe, helped us together so that we could be as good mothers as we could be, and as good lovers, and as good wives as we could be. And so, in the Sixties when I saw that waning I became very concerned about where we were going. Now, what I seem to see is a coming back together, a re-establishment of those bonds. But it's not healthy. Quite often young Black women come together to—not to support themselves, but to bemoan their outcast state and to attack Black men, to say Black men are nothing. And to reinforce their own loneliness and aloneness. Not to get joy out of being with a woman friend or sister friend. And it worries me.

R.G. I don't know what to say about that, I really don't. I look at the young women I meet in Europe, in the U.S. and educated women in the West Indies. Many of them are alone. Many are involved in professions. Some because this is what they have. It is not because they are not looking for a relationship with Black men, but they seem not to be able to establish the relationship with Black men. I suppose that there are not quite as many, never have been as many men as there are women. There are, of course, more women getting educated and men hate that. Wars take men away. Drugs take the men away—

M.A. —and prison takes the men away.

R.G. Women find themselves alone. That's the reason that in the inner cities, particularly, there are so many single women, single parents, mothers. In the middle class, many hard working young women are without men. Now, I don't find that they are pulling apart from other women. Rather they have women as friends. Groups of women meet, talk, plan strategy in terms of work. They are very healthy in that respect, which doesn't prevent them from being lonely. What do I say to them? I say, well, if there is a possibility, if loneliness is there and you need a male companion, then I don't think one necessarily has to stay with Black men. Just broaden yourself out and meet white men, or Asian men—

M.A. —Hispanic—

R.G. —or Hispanic, and have a real international or inter-racial sort of relationship.

M.A. I agree with that, but I think the need we have for friendship is so deep, it is part of race memory, if you will, and yet, in a temporary world with sit-coms where everything is resolved in twenty-seven minutes, a number of young women, I think, satisfy themselves with superficial acquaintances, and I think of you and me talking together, having lived through twenty-five plus years of friendship—loss on both parts, and gainings, and love affairs that we've had, and marriages and children threatened and children found—and all these things that we have lived through, speaks of the power of a profound friendship. Not just that superficial 'we work together, let's stop off at a bar and have a drink.' I really want young women to develop those kinds of bonds which allow people to know that they can count on somebody who will give them the best advice, the best shoulder to lean on, and somebody who expects the most from her.

R.G. One person goes out and gives of herself and in return receives. If one goes out selfishly, one does not. I think that this is certainly true, I think that in this area one can be quite a lot of help if one is generous and broad. I find that I have fantastic friends. My friends span continents—

M.A. —and races, and sexes.

R.G. Yes. There are very few places I can go that I don't have a friend that I can't knock on the door and say, 'Look, I'm here, I'm out of money. What do I do?' And they'd say, 'What do you mean "what do you do?" You come in here.'

M.A. You come in first, and then we will think of what next to do.

R.G. And I find it's one of the most gratifying things. But then, too, my door is always open. Everything that I have belongs to my friends. I love my friends, male and female.

M.A. A number of young women I've met cannot conceive of having men friends, brother friends. And they don't realize how out-of-the-balance their lives are without a brother friend. And so I would like to encourage young women to reach out. In some cases, they have to do the instruction, because a number of men do not know anything about having a woman sister friend, because they're thinking, 'Are you expecting me to go to bed with you?'

R.G. Or marry you?

M.A. So that's why I think that a young woman must reach out and, knowing that if she liked somebody who she's not physically attracted to, but she is at one with them, and a generosity of spirit, and she can train him into becoming a brother friend . . . Everything worth having is going to cost the earth.

R.G. Yes, and on this level I say that you are certainly one of the people who can give better instructions in this because of your generosity and your understanding, and you do not mind the rejections, the primary rejection, the secondary rejection, and you will go again. And this, young women cannot stand. They cannot stand rejection. Because you say to a young man, 'I love you.' Right away, he thinks, she's trying to trap me, and he starts to run. His whole posture is the posture of someone who is very precious, who feels his preciousness, and is in demand, therefore vulnerable. That's something that young women find very, very hard. Young women band together. They say they'd rather be free. They have occasional affairs, and then it's over.

M.A. Yes, and they may be left with a child.

R.G. I think it's a tragedy. Here again, I'm a romantic. I love the relationship between man and woman. I like the idea of having a close male friend and of being able to be stroked.

M.A. I believe that Black women can find sex on any corner, and maybe romance in maybe every few blocks. But to find a brother friend who is not intimidated by the strength we have developed over these years of surviving and keeping the race alive, not intimidated by this, it's of such value that I would encourage every young woman to try to make a friend. I would encourage them because for a balanced life, if there is a husband or a lover who is also a friend, wonderful. But if the person is alone, maybe a single parent, or no parent at all, just alone struggling to make a living and struggling for her identity, I encourage the development of friendship, profound friendship between that particular woman and two, maybe three, other women and friendship with at least one man which does not include sex. And if you don't have that, I don't know how you can consider that you are safe in an unsafe world. I mean safe inside yourself. Nobody to give you advice and support and to thump you, and really tell you you are wrong. Somebody you appreciate and respect who will also tell you you are right when you are right. I think that for young women out there there is this mean and unsafe world, they are desperately in need.

R.G. And I think that there are many souls out there just struggling in the society for money and for position and power or something like that, hoping to get friends that way and feeling that's the only way to get friends. And some of them, because they're so busy struggling, they have nothing to give.

M.A. It is more convenient, more commodious, to fall in love and marry the boy next door, or people in your own culture, because you don't have the problem of having to translate or apologize to anybody. That is best. *But* if you find no one, no one comes

knocking at your door, I say again to Black women, widen, broaden
your views and realize that there are those people who would rather
see you martyred by loneliness, solitude and abandonment than to
see you happy. And I have only one life to live and be *present*, make
a contribution to life, not mope about, feeling *sorry* for oneself
because one is alone. If there is a chance for a balance in life, some
love, some laughter, some security, some growth—then take it.

R.G. The important thing is having someone on your corner when
you need them. The important thing is having someone who loves
you and whom you love. With all that we have to go through in work
and the struggle, the need for somebody to be there, is always
present. And I would never say to any young woman, 'Look, you're
a Black girl so you have to be with a Black guy.' No, just be with
somebody who is with you. I'm very upset by Black men being
unreasonably angry about Black women who will marry or make
deep friendships with white men, when they are not willing to give of
themselves at all. They stand on the sidelines and they criticize . . .

M.A. There is a terrible incident which devastated me for a long
time. This was in the early Seventies. *Caged Bird* had just come out. I
was living in New York. *The Post* had profiled me, I was the woman
of the week. There was also that day a release in *Newsweek*, with
Robert Gross's wonderful review of my book, there were like three
things in New York on that day. So I was so excited. I walked from
my apartment over to Terry's Pub. I ordered a Martini, knowing full
well that I am no able Martini-drinker. And there were five major
Black male journalists. And they sent me a drink. So I had the drink,
and I sent them a drink. Then the bartender gave me a third Martini
which I needed like one more hole in my head. Then this group sent
me another, a fourth Martini. I sent them a final drink. By this time I
was really looped, so I walked over. Five good-looking Black men of
my age group and each one was married to a white woman, and not
one had actually come over to say, 'Hello, Maya, congratulations.' So
I went over and I said, 'Let me tell you something. I have created
myself. I have taught myself so much. I have learned to speak a
number of languages, I'm a good cook and a good housekeeper. I
love to laugh, I enjoy sex, and I'm usually cheerful, and I'm
hardworking. I've done all this to attract you, and not one of you is
attracted by me or to me.' And my booze and the truth of it made me
weepy so I started to cry. I asked them, 'What more do I have to do?'

They all hung their heads. They were terribly embarrassed. I was too drunk to be embarrassed at the time. A Puerto Rican friend, married man friend, came by and asked me in Spanish how I was and did I want to go home. He said, 'You need a brother.' And I said, 'Yes, I do.' And he took me up. And I looked back at these five men who had bonded themselves together as if I had been an attacker, when in truth I was really almost literally begging for recognition, if not for love at the moment. That was in 1970. We are now in 1987. Not one of those men from that day to this has given me a friendly hello.

R.G. They're frightened. They feel somehow as though you wanted to trap them. You try so hard and you do everything that you know how . . . It's never enough . . .

M.A. Let's talk about hopeful expectations in 1987. Personal.

R.G. Well, I have three books under contract that I certainly should like finished. And I don't know exactly where I am going to sit down to write, whether I'm going to the West Indies or Europe, or the U.S., but wherever I am I would like very, very much to finish and promote them. I have a family that I'd like to get together. You know, I have grandchildren around that haven't been as close to me as I would like them or close to each other, and I would like to be useful in that sense as a grandmother. And being the continual romantic, I would like very much to consolidate a fantastic romance.

M.A. I think that just sounds the nit's tits to me. That sounds the best thing possible. I mean, to be able to get the work done, to have that adhesive and cohesive force in the family, and to have a love affair.

R.G. That's not asking for much, is it?

M.A. It seems not to me. When I think of my expectations or my desires of 1987, they are pretty much the same thing. I ask for health. I'd like to have health so that I can achieve the work that I have either contracted legally, or contracted inside my mind, and to be present as a family member, and to have some splendid love affair that will not ask too much . . . And yet, I want to make lots of money. I don't ever want to be without money. I think that's the most chicken shit thing in the world, to be without money.

R.G. I don't know that we can ever be really satisfied, but one hopes that in 1987 we do really come as near to achieving what we want. And I do hope that we can help influence the young . . .

M.A. That is the need, in fact. The desperate need. So many young Black women are not spoken to by white women. Are not spoken to by Black men. Are not spoken to by white men. And if we don't speak to them, there will be no voice reaching their ears or their hearts.

Index

241

Also by Maya Angelou

I KNOW WHY THE CAGED BIRD SINGS

'Verve, nerve and joy in her own talents effervesce throughout this book' – **Julia O'Faolain**

'Its humour, even in the face of appalling discrimination, is robust. Autobiographical writing at its very best' – **Philip Oakes**

In this first volume of her extraordinary autobiography, Maya Angelou beautifully evokes her childhood in the American South of the 1930s. She and her brother live with their grandmother, in Stamps, Arkansas, where Maya learns the power of the 'whitefolks' at the other end of town. A visit to her adored mother ends in tragedy when Maya is raped by her mother's lover. But her extraordinary sense of wholeness emerges; she discovers the pleasures of dance and drama and gives birth to a treasured son.

GATHER TOGETHER IN MY NAME

'She has warmth and humour and a sense of wholeness and content that glows through' – **Polly Toynbee, *Guardian***

'Remarkable, devoid of bitterness; pungent; funny . . . with that rare gift for hope in adversity' – **Fiona Maddocks, *New Statesman***

'Exceptional . . . should have been published here long ago' – **Paul Bailey, *Observer***

In this moving sequel to her bestselling *I Know Why The Caged Bird Sings*, the war is over and Maya has given birth to a son. Unemployed, isolated, she embarks on a series of brief lonely affairs and transient jobs – in shops, restaurants and nightclubs. Finally she turns to prostitution and the world of narcotics. But even in great adversity, Maya Angelou invests life with the remarkable sense of richness that has won her such an enormous following.

THE HEART OF A WOMAN

'The freshness of Maya Angelou's writing is something to marvel at' – **Philip Oakes**

'Loving the world, Maya Angelou also knows its cruelty and offers up her autobiography as an extraordinary mixture of innocence and depravity, of elegy and celebration' – **Nicci Gerrard, *New Statesman***

In the fourth volume of her enthralling autobiography, Maya Angelou leaves California for a new life in New York, where she becomes immersed in the world of Black writers and artists in Harlem. Increasingly active in the Black rights movement, she is appointed Northern Coordinator to Martin Luther King. Her personal life is as tempestuous as ever: swept off her feet by Vusumzi Make, South African freedom fighter, she marries him after a whirlwind courtship. They go to Egypt, where the marriage fails out her career blossoms. Holding the book together is Maya's absorbing account of her relationship with her son, as, with pain and joy, she watches him grow up to find his own identity.

ALL GOD'S CHILDREN NEED TRAVELLING SHOES

'Maya Angelou has an amazing ability to take her readers into her personal maze and lead them out again feeling refreshed and even jubilant' – **Clancy Sigal, *Guardian***

In the fifth volume of her brilliant autobiography Maya Angelou emigrates to Ghana, only to discover that 'you can't go home again'. Initially she experiences the joy of being Black in a Black country, certain that Africa must be her Promised Land. But Ghana leads its own paradoxical life: she finds official sexism but loving female friendships; Black solidarity but distrust of Black Americans. Through the circumstances of her new life – an affair with a seductive Malian, her son's near-tragic accident, politics, partying – her myth of 'Mother Africa' is dismantled. Encountering the country on its own terms, she comes to a new awareness of herself, of slavery and Black betrayal, of civil rights and mothering.

AND STILL I RISE

'Maya Angelou writes from the heart and her language rings clear and true . . . Whether joyful, sad or playful, her poems speak with delicacy and depth of feeling' – ***Publishers Weekly***

'It is true poetry she is writing . . . it has an innate purity about it, unquenchable dignity' – **M. F. K. Fisher**

Maya Angelou's poetry – lyrical and dramatic, exuberant and playful – speaks of love, longing, partings; of Saturday night partying, and the smells and sounds of Southern cities; of freedom and shattered dreams. 'The caged bird sings/with a fearful trill/of things unknown/but longed for still/and his tune is heard/on the distant hill/for the caged bird/sings of freedom.' Of her poetry, *Kirkus Reviews* has written, 'It is just as much a part of her autobiography as *I Know Why the Caged Bird Sings, Gather Together in My Name, Singing' and Swinging' and Gettin' Merry Like Christmas,* and *Heart of a Woman.*

Also by Maya Angelou

NOW SHEBA SINGS THE SONG
With art by Tom Feelings

Maya Angelou's poetry, familiar to readers of her highly acclaimed *And Still I Rise*, is complemented in this beautiful new book by the work of the Black American artist and illustrator, Tom Feelings. His eighty-five vibrant, sepia-toned portraits of Black women from America, Africa and South America, drawn from life over a period of twenty years, are the context for Maya Angelou's sensuous and lyrical verse which gives expression to the spirit of Black women everywhere. Maya Angelou first met Tom Feelings in Ghana in the mid-1960s. When, twenty years later, he gave her the drawings, 'without asking or suggesting what she might do', Maya kept them for six months, 'on the floor, on the walls, on chairs, and every ready surface'. During that time her poem, 'Now Sheba Sings the Song' emerged – 'to give these women their sound, their voices'.

JUST GIVE ME A COOL DRINK OF WATER 'FORE I DIIIE

'Black, bitter and beautiful, she speaks of our survival' – **James Baldwin**

'Maya Angelou liberates and exhilarates through her magical, lyrical, mystical medium – poetry' – **Mary Bryce, *Tribune***

From the best-selling author of *And Still I Rise* comes a marvellous new collection of poetry, published on her sixtieth birthday. Poems of love and regret, of racial strife and confrontation, songs of the people and songs of the heart – all are charged with Maya Angelou's zest for life and her rage at injustice. Lyrical, tender poems of longing, wry glances at betrayal and isolation combine with a fierce insight into 'hate and hateful wrath' in an unforgettable picture of the hopes and concerns of one of America's finest contemporary Black writers.

INVENTED LIVES
NARRATIVES OF BLACK WOMEN 1860–1960

Mary Helen Washington

'Ms Washington has created a most engaging dialogue between the great Black women writers and herself. This collection is, in fact, two fine books in one: at once an anthology and a critical study' — *New York Times*

In this marvellous companion volume to her anthology of stories by Black women writers, *Any Woman's Blues*, Mary Helen Washington explores the works, and the worlds, of Black American women writers between 1860 and 1960. Bringing together selected short stories and novel extracts from ten writers — Harriet Jacobs, Frances Ellen Watkins Harper, Pauline E. Hopkins, Fannie Barrier Williams, Marita Bonner, Nella Larsen, Zora Neale Hurston, Ann Petry, Dorothy West and Gwendolyn Brooks — she introduces a remarkable range of voices and draws out the hidden and overt challenges of a body of work rich in cultural, political and literary meaning. *Invented Lives* also includes an Introduction and six chapters in which Mary Helen Washington examines Black women writers' search for a narrative structure appropriate to their experiences in American society. The result is a stunning collection of prose and an eloquent affirmation of a neglected literary tradition.